SIMS REEVES

FIFTY YEARS OF MUSIC IN ENGLAND

BY

CHARLES E. PEARCE

AUTHOR OF "THE AMAZING DUCHESS," "POLLY PEACHUM,"
"MADAME VESTRIS," ETC.

WITH SIXTEEN ILLUSTRATIONS IN HALF-TONE

Travis & Emery

Charles E. Pearce

Sims Reeves

First published 1924.

Republished Travis & Emery 2009.

Published by
Travis & Emery Music Bookshop
17 Cecil Court, London, WC2N 4EZ, United Kingdom.
(+44) 20 7240 2129
neworders@travis-and-emery.com

ISBN Hardback: 978-1-906857-85-1   Paperback: 978-1-906857-86-8

SIMS REEVES

MADAME VESTRIS
AND HER TIMES

BY
CHARLES E. PEARCE

Author of "The Amazing Duchess" (Duchess of Kingston), "The Jolly Duchess" (Harriot Mellon), "Polly Peachum and the Beggar's Opera," etc. etc. Demy 8vo, fully illustrated, cloth, 16s. net.

LUCIA ELIZABETTA VESTRIS, grand-daughter of the celebrated engraver Bartolozzi, and one of the most fascinating figures that ever graced the English stage, has hitherto escaped the attention of biographers. Her history is a very remarkable one. She made her name in Italian opera, in the English ballad play, and as the originator of brilliant extravaganzas which drew all London. She was the first woman manager of a theatre, and her productions at the Olympia, the Lyceum and Covent Garden Theatres, were marked by an artistic completeness and an attention to detail which antici-pated the elaborations of the present day. No one was more sought after or more gossiped about than Madame Vestris. Her love affairs were numberless, and her associations with men of fashion an inexhaustible subject for scandal. Mr. Pearce has been fortunate enough to secure the original letters which passed between the famous actress and Montague Gore, and they are now put into print for the first time. "Madame Vestris and her Times" deals with a feverish period of life in London to which to-day there is no parallel. The book is packed with sprightly anecdotes illustra-tive of manners and tastes which have passed away.

LONDON: STANLEY PAUL & CO. LTD.
8 Endsleigh Gardens, Upper Woburn Place, W.C.1

SIMS REEVES IN 1850.
From a drawing by C. Baugniet.

[*Frontispiece.*

SIMS REEVES

FIFTY YEARS OF MUSIC IN ENGLAND

BY

CHARLES E. PEARCE

AUTHOR OF "THE AMAZING DUCHESS," "POLLY PEACHUM,"
"MADAME VESTRIS," ETC.

WITH SIXTEEN ILLUSTRATIONS IN HALF-TONE

LONDON
STANLEY PAUL & CO. LTD.
8 ENDSLEIGH GARDENS
UPPER WOBURN PLACE, W.C.1

First published 1924

INTRODUCTION

THE inception of this biography of England's greatest singer—John Sims Reeves—is due to his son, Mr. Herbert Reeves. I was glad to receive from Mr. Reeves the suggestion that I should undertake the task, and I commenced the collection of material in 1916. It was then hoped that the book would be completed in 1918—the centenary of Sims Reeves's birth—but the continuance of the War destroyed all prospect of this and further hindrances accrued to delay the production until the present year.

During Sims Reeves's lifetime innumerable biographical notices appeared in various forms. They were little more than bare summaries, and in many cases were inaccurate. Sims Reeves's autobiographical effort, *My Jubilee*, is fragmentary, and owing to the paucity of dates and for other reasons it cannot be accepted as authoritative. At best it is but a collection of memories, interesting enough, but falling far short of doing justice to the great services rendered by Sims Reeves towards the advancement of music in England. It may safely be said that Reeves in this respect, by his genius, by his conscientiousness, and by his glorious gift of voice, occupied a position which no other singer has ever approached. He was without a rival.

The career of Sims Reeves synchronises with the phases and development of musical art in England during the Victorian era. It is impossible to dissociate one from the other, and I have endeavoured—inadequately it may be—to give some idea of the music of a period which, though not very long ago, seems now quite remote.

It will be seen that I have made no attempt to go outside Reeves's musical life. His position as a singer and artist is all that matters, and I have endeavoured to follow that position from its beginning in 1838 to his farewell concert in 1891—roughly speaking, half a century. It is true that after this date circumstances compelled him to emerge from a well-earned retirement, but such re-appearances do not come within the scope of this book.

During the greater part of the fifty odd years that Reeves was before the public he was identified with Opera, with Oratorio, and with ballad singing in a way which made him a popular idol. Never was idol more worthy of worship. He was perfect in everything he undertook.

Singers and actors are at a disadvantage in comparison with painters and literary men. Their triumphs die with them. No amount of eulogy can reproduce their tones, their art, the spell they exercised over their audiences. To-day only those advanced in years, who listened to Reeves at his zenith, can form a just idea of his genius. It was not possible for anyone who, in the 'nineties, heard him for the first time, to realise his wondrous gifts. His artistic method, his mastery of vocalisation, his perfection of phrasing, remained to his last days, but the freshness, the force, and the resonance of his incomparable voice had departed.

I may perhaps be pardoned if I recall the inestimable privilege I had, when a boy, of hearing Sims Reeves many times in oratorio at Exeter Hall in the late 'fifties, and throughout the 'sixties at the Beaumont Institute, Mile End, where he always received a rapturous welcome. Memories such as these do not depart with advancing years. I regard my share in the production of this biography as a labour of love and as a humble tribute to a great artist whose name will never be forgotten as long as music exists in England.

I owe my grateful acknowledgments to Mr. Herbert Reeves for his cordial co-operation in the compilation of this biography and for the use of the letters from his father's contemporaries which he placed at my disposal. I have also to thank Mr. Clement K. Shorter for permitting me to reproduce Mr. Lance Calkin's drawing in *Black and White* (Feb. 27, 1892) of Reeves and his contemporaries, and the numerous correspondents from whom I received personal recollections of the great singer when his powers were in their prime.

CHARLES E. PEARCE.

CONTENTS

CHAPTER I

1818–1838

CHAPTER II

1838–1839

CHAPTER III

1840

CHAPTER IV

1841–1842

9

CHAPTER V
1842–1843

CHAPTER VI
1843–1845

CHAPTER VII
1845–1847

CHAPTER VIII
1847

CHAPTER IX
1848

CHAPTER X

1848 (*continued*)

CHAPTER XI

1848 (*continued*)

CHAPTER XII

1849

CHAPTER XIII

1850

CHAPTER XIV

1851–1852

CHAPTER XV

1853–1855

CHAPTER XVI

1856–1857

CHAPTER XVII

1858–1859

CHAPTER XVIII

1860

CHAPTER XIX
1861–1862

CHAPTER XX
1863–1864

CHAPTER XXI
1865–1868

CHAPTER XXII
1868–1869

CHAPTER XXIII
1870–1872

CHAPTER XXIV

1873–1877

CHAPTER XXV

1878–1882

CHAPTER XXVI

1883–1900

CHAPTER XXVII

LIST OF ILLUSTRATIONS

SIMS REEVES

FIFTY YEARS OF MUSIC IN ENGLAND

CHAPTER I

1818–1838

Birth of Sims Reeves—the date established. Parentage. Narrowly escapes becoming a Royal Artillery bandsman. Sings treble at the age of sixteen. First appearance of his name on a concert programme. The question of his voice breaking. His first musical lessons. Influence of the R.A. concerts. Engaged as treble singer and choirmaster at North Cray Church. The three tenor brothers. Sims Reeves's first London experience. Uncertain prospect for vocalists. Thinks of becoming a doctor. A grim practical joke. Abandons the idea of the medical profession and takes singing lessons. Is trained for a baritone. His first theatrical engagement.

JUST within the Woolwich Barracks, at the end of the New Road, and opposite the ugly, grimy structure known as the Royal Artillery Theatre, stands a block of buildings of a single story, as ugly and as grimy as the theatre. This block was formerly a portion of the married soldiers' quarters, and in the days of the Regency, in the house facing the stage-door of the theatre, resided Bombardier (afterwards Corporal) Reeves, and his wife Rosina. A century ago in an upper room, the window of which overlooks the theatre, was born to them a son destined to be the greatest English singer in the world—John Sims Reeves.

The date of Sims Reeves's birth (he was not christened "Sims," this name being added in after-years, but one cannot think of him as *John* Sims Reeves, although, I believe, his intimates addressed him indifferently as "John" or "Jack") was September 26th, 1818, figures which are at variance with those given by Sims Reeves himself, who put the date at October 21st, 1821. The

point was settled once and for all when the late Mr. W. T.
Vincent, an indefatigable historiographer of Woolwich,
searching the register of the parish church found a
baptismal entry, dated October 25th, 1818, which showed
that John, the son of John and Rosina Reeves, was
born September 26th, the "abode" being set down as
the New Road.

It is somewhat singular, in connection with Sims
Reeves's records of his early days, that he should make
no mention in either the *Life and Recollections* or in
My Jubilee of the fact that his father was in the Royal
Artillery Band. He simply styles his father a "musician,"
a statement which is, of course, correct, but incomplete.
The Royal Artillery Band has won for itself considerable
distinction. In its early days many of the officers were
excellent musicians, and both in its commanders, from
a musical point of view, and in its bandmasters the
regiment was exceedingly fortunate. Any man who
showed musical ability was encouraged, and in this way
it came about that Corporal Reeves made a reputation
as a singer.

The appearance of Corporal (then Bombardier) Reeves
at the Royal Artillery concerts held weekly during the
winter months at the officers' mess was primarily due
to Dr. Keening, of the R.H.A. Dr. Keening was an
accomplished violinist, and had interested himself in the
vocal class which Mr. George M'Kenzie, the bandmaster
who laid the foundation of the excellence which the
Royal Artillery Band afterwards attained, had established. Dr. Keening chanced to hear one of the Horse
Artillery recruits singing in the square, and struck by
his excellent bass voice, mentioned the fact to Mr.
M'Kenzie, who at once sent for the man and asked him
what he could sing. He replied that he had often sung
"The trumpet shall sound," "Why do the nations?"
and other famous bass solos, and having gone through
these test pieces to the satisfaction of the bandmaster,
he was transferred to the band and soon promoted to
the rank of Corporal.

Glee-singing was then at the height of its popularity,
and anyone who was at all musical was pressed into
service as a glee-singer. Glee-singing was a great leveller.

Even the " First Gentleman in Europe " did not disdain to take a part, and shortly after Mr. M'Kenzie formed his glee-party a concert was given by the band in honour of a visit the Prince paid to Sir William Congreve at the latter's house in Charlton. Being told that there were good singers among the band, his Royal Highness asked for Calcott's " The Derbyshire Ram," and accordingly this long-forgotten favourite of our great-grandfathers, which is not without touches of humour, was sung by Corporal Morris, Mr. M'Kenzie, and the Prince, H.R.H. taking the bass part.

Corporal John Reeves soon made himself useful as a singer in concerted music, and years later, at a concert at which Sir George Smart and Sir John Stevenson were present, the former invited Corporal Reeves and Mr. M'Kenzie to a musical party where glee-singing went on to the small hours. The Corporal's acquirements were not confined to glee-singing ; he played the violin and bassoon, and he sang the bass solos in the Artillery church, which building in 1863 became the present theatre. He also acted as church clerk, and by virtue of his office occupied the barrack house where his son was born.

The band in those piping times of peace had ample leisure for the study of music, and it was inevitable that this study should be accompanied by the discipline and severity which are inseparable from military life. The portrait of Mr. George M'Kenzie given in Mr. H. G. Farmer's *Memoirs of the Royal Artillery Band* suggests a precise, determined gentleman who was bound to have things done in the right way, and in his own way. There were severe musical critics on the military staff, and among them Lord Bloomfield, the commander. Lord Bloomfield was no theorist or mere dilettante, he helped practically to improve the band, and the story goes that on one occasion he was so displeased at certain piano passages being ignored that he came out of his quarters in a rage, took the conductor's place, and ordered the piece to be played over again with all the marks of expression observed. Lord Bloomfield was a 'cellist, and as he played duets with Lindley he must have been an executant of no mean powers.

Colonel Quist, the band commandant, was also a

musical enthusiast. It was he who instituted the " Royal Artillery Concerts " somewhere between 1800 and 1815, thus antedating the Philharmonic Society, and on Mr. M'Kenzie suggesting that boys should be introduced into the band, he warmly supported the idea. Thus when young John Reeves was nine or ten years old he was attached to the band as a treble singer, and his voice was so promising that application was made for him and another boy to be enlisted. Objection, however, was raised on account of the number of orphans whose fathers had been killed in the Peninsular War and whose mothers were anxious to have enrolled, and when permission came a year or so later Corporal Reeves informed Mr. M'Kenzie that a clergyman at North Cray had taken notice of the lad and that he thought he would be able to do better for him. It is unnecessary to say that the father's judgment was justified. But for the fortunate inter-position of the clergyman Sims Reeves might have remained an instrumentalist—an excellent one it is not to be doubted, but he would not have developed that marvellous voice of his, and the world of music would have been all the poorer in consequence.

I have in my possession a programme of a performance of *The Messiah* given in the Artillery Chapel on December 23rd, 1834. On this programme, among the treble singers, appears the name of " Master Reeves," a record which stimulates curiosity, as in 1834 " Master Reeves " would be sixteen—an exceptional age for a boy to be singing treble. The statement in the *Newcastle Chronicle* of October 4th, 1879, that " when he was about twelve years his voice ' broke ' and for a time he appears to have abandoned all hope of becoming eminent as a vocalist " is not to be accepted without question. Sims Reeves was in 1879 singing at Newcastle, and the writer of the notice would most likely have gathered biographical details from the singer himself. In pur-suance of his idiosyncrasy on the subject of his age, Mr. Reeves would give the date of his birth as 1821, when it would appear that in 1834 he was in his thirteenth year. But it is clearly established that he was three years older, and one is entitled to ask whether the fact of his voice breaking so late in life had any physiological bearing upon his phenomenal organ. If it were known precisely when the voices of the great tenors and basses passed from their boyish treble into the tones of manhood some theory might be deduced, but data on this interesting point are wanting.

A remarkable coincidence may, however, be mentioned. Sims Reeves's predecessor, John Braham, attained his seventeenth year before his voice broke. No memoir of Braham exists in book form so far as I know, and I derive my information from a lengthy biographical notice which appeared in the *Englishman*, a newspaper of the thirties. According to this authority, Braham was born in 1772,[1] and the writer says : " In 1789 Master Braham's voice broke, and as he had continued his vocal efforts too long after the certainty of his voice going he missed the opportunity of breaking it down to a bass and was in danger of losing his powers in this way altogether." The missing of such an " opportunity " was apparently regarded with regret by the biographer. Mr. Herbert Reeves tells me he has heard his father say that he could not remember his voice breaking, and if so, the transition must have been very gradual. At all events, he did not make Braham's mistake, and the critical period was passed over safely.

We get a glimpse of his early training in Mr. Sims Reeves's autobiography *My Jubilee*, and what is therein recorded suggests all the thoroughness, the strict attention to detail, and the constant repetition to achieve accuracy, typical of the military disciplinarian. Sims Reeves writes : " My father was a musician ; and he not only practised the divine art, but also taught it—in a manner which was anything but divine to me. I had learnt the musical notes almost with the notes of the alphabet, and when I was a child I had to rise, take my bath, dress, and be ready for my pianoforte lesson by five o'clock in the morning. I believe my father taught me well, but I am sure he taught me strictly and severely. A false note on the piano was speedily followed by a blow from his violin bow, which, directed at my knuckles, never missed its aim. Of course I had no business to make a mistake, but often the means adopted for setting

[1] *The Dictionary of National Biography* says 1774, but queries this date.

me right threw me into the greatest confusion, and sad indeed was my fate when blunders were followed by correction and correction again by blunders."

It is noticeable that Reeves, in referring to his father's instructions, only mentions instruments. He says nothing about his early singing lessons. Yet he must have had some, and from information supplied me by Mr. Messent, of Thomas Street, Woolwich, I am inclined to think that his father was not his sole music-master in his boyish days. Mr. Messent's house was at that time in the occupation of the bandmaster, Mr. George M'Kenzie, who carried on business there as a music-seller. Mr. Messent says he was told by the late Mr. James Lawson (for some years bandmaster of the Royal Artillery) that he had singing lessons from Mr. M'Kenzie at his house in Thomas Street, and that he had many times sang there with young Reeves. This may well have been so, but it would not have been for long ; Mr. Lawson having been born in 1826, he would be but eight when the future tenor was sixteen. Most likely Mr. M'Kenzie rehearsed the vocal class at his house, and it is quite probable that he also gave lessons separately to the most promising singers, John Reeves among the number.

Irksome and foreign to the spirit of youth as his father's severe régime must have been, it unquestionably bore fruit in later years. Sims Reeves had the soul of a great artist, but that soul could not have manifested itself with spontaneity and freedom without the most perfect mechanism as its foundation. The habit of doing his very best was indelibly fixed in his childhood, and to this rule Sims Reeves adhered rigidly to the end of his career. For this reason it may be claimed that his father's military training was to the son a distinct advantage. Other influences attaching to the barrack life at Woolwich were also at work. The Royal Artillery concerts both in the music selected and in its execution were of a high order. Nicholas Mori, Spagnoletti, Lindley, Howell, Drouet, and other London instrumentalists were occasionally engaged, and very early in life young Reeves was accustomed to hear the best of music admirably performed. Hence his tastes were judiciously directed and a standard of excellence fixed in his mind.

At North Cray he was also fortunate. The Vicar, the Rev. Wyatt Edgell, was a musical enthusiast, and must have appreciated the exceptional powers of the young treble singer, for although Sims Reeves was not that tiresome production a youthful prodigy, he could, when ten years old, play all Handel's organ accompaniments from the original figured bass. He had also learned the violin, 'cello, and bassoon. In most of Sims Reeves's biographies he is said to have been appointed organist of North Cray Church when he was fourteen, but this is not quite correct. The words in *My Jubilee* are that he " at least performed an organist's duties." He was really the leading treble singer and looked after the choir-boys, and it was only on certain occasions that he played the organ. His duties took him to North Cray three times a week, and the work was not a little arduous. From the *Worthing Gazette*, the representative of which interviewed him some time in October 1900, shortly before his death, I find that whilst he held this appointment, there used to be "Show Sundays," and large numbers of people, friends of the Vicar, were brought down from London to hear the young organist's choir. Two men from town on such occasions were engaged to help in the music—a counter-tenor and a bass—and one of these, it is interesting to learn, was the father of Edward Lloyd. Mr. Lloyd was the counter-tenor and Mr. J. Atkins the bass.

These performances were valuable in a material sense as they led to private engagements, not only for Sims Reeves, but for his brother Henry, and the money so earned enabled both to pay for lessons from good masters. Incidentally Mr. Reeves says that both his brothers had tenor voices, and that all sang " in the proper tenor register ; not the half counter-tenor voices of the present generation " (1889). Three tenor voices in one family are rarely met with, and when the brothers sang together, which must have occurred, it is fair to surmise that they may have joined in Bishop's round " When the wind blows," from *The Miller and his Men*— one of the few concerted pieces written for three tenors. If so, the effect of the haunting melody repeated and harmonised in tones so akin to each other must have been a musical treat altogether unique. Apropos of trios for three tenors, it is interesting to note that in 1857 Sims Reeves sang in *Evviva Bacco* by Curschmann (who had a fancy for writing trios for even voices) with Calzolari and Gardoni, and thirty-two years later introduced it at a concert at St. James's Hall with Mr. Edward Lloyd and Mr. Ben Davies.

John and Henry [1] seem to have been much attached to each other, and their visits to London for their music lessons were made pleasant ones owing to the notice taken of them by the Misses Edgell, who were then living in Lower Grosvenor Place. These ladies having a box at the King's Theatre, the young students frequently accompanied them thither, and heard all the great operatic singers of the day—Grisi, Persiani, Rubini, Lablache, Tamburini, and others, at that time in the full possession of their powers. Though precise details are wanting, Sims Reeves's life in London at this period can fairly well be determined. What with engagements at archery meetings, musical soirées (concerts at private houses were much in vogue), and other society functions, together with his appointment at North Cray where he maintained his tri-weekly visits, he no doubt was able to support himself. He speaks with evident sincerity of these times as " veritably happy days." He had plenty to do. There were lessons in harmony and counterpoint under Callcott, piano practice with John Cramer, and he added the oboe to his mastery of the violin, 'cello, and bassoon. Maybe he essayed others. Mr. John Coleman speaks of Sims Reeves, during his engagement at Edinburgh with Anderson, the " Wizard of the North," at rehearsals, taking up half a dozen instruments and playing difficult passages for the instruction of the bandsmen who were unable to execute them accurately. Interspersed with his musical studies was occupation of a different kind—he learned to engrave music-plates. This was in accordance with the advice of his father, who, with

[1] Mr. W. H. Reeves attained a provincial reputation as a tenor singer. Mr. J. C. Dibdin, in his *Annals of the Edinburgh Stage*, writing of the theatrical performances in October 1846— says : " A notable addition to the company was Mr. W. H. Reeves, brother of the great ' Sims ' himself, an excellent vocalist." He sustained the title-rôle in *Masaniello*.

Yorkshire caution (he was a native of one of the Ridings), thought his son ought to have a trade to fall back upon in case his voice should fail him. Accordingly, the lad, with characteristic energy and perseverance, worked away with the graver's tools and to some extent mastered the art.

It would appear that Sims Reeves himself had at this time misgivings as to his future. He certainly had not made up his mind to adopt music as a profession. At that time an English singer, no matter how good, had very little chance of distinguishing himself. There were few concerts for music lovers among London's middle class, and a wide gap existed between the sing-songs of the taverns, the al-fresco entertainments of the tea-gardens, and the Italian opera at the King's Theatre (afterwards " Her Majesty's "), which was the preserve of the rich. Indeed the future prince of tenors must have deemed success as a vocalist impossible, for he seriously thought of turning his attention to medicine and surgery. The *Illustrated News* for 1847 mentions this, and *The Dictionary of National Biography*, in repeating the statement, adds that he forsook music for a year, but that " a gruesome practical joke played upon him by one of his fellow-students turned him from further anatomical pursuits."

In explanation of this, Mr. Herbert Reeves says he remembers his father telling him how in some of the rooms set aside for anatomical purposes was kept a complete skeleton fitted with springs, by which the limbs were made to move, and how on one occasion a fellow-student contrived that it should fall upon him and clasp him round the body. The shock not only destroyed Reeves's fancy for becoming a doctor, but had, he always believed, something to do with the nervousness and sensitiveness from which during the whole of his life he was never wholly free. Whether this was so or not, one can be but thankful for this early distaste for doctoring, as his thoughts were once more forced to revert to music and the stage ; and in the reaction which followed, he found relief in private theatricals. During this period he was an assiduous theatre-goer.

While gaining experience in this agreeable way, Reeves

was being trained as a baritone. What master it was who
advised him to cultivate the lower rather than the higher
register of his voice he does not tell us. The unequalled
richness of his upper tones would not, of course, have
been developed, in spite of his twenty-one years, but
that they were round and full is tolerably certain, and their
unusually robust quality may have misled his teacher.
I have had the privilege of hearing Sims Reeves in his
prime many times (dating from 1856), and it has always
seemed to me that his voice in declamatory music demanding manliness, vigour, and passion, appertained in
its resonance to that of a fine baritone. What a blending
of tones was that when he joined with Santley in that
old-world duet " All's well! " The timbre of the two
voices seemed the same. So also in the phrase " Paradisi
Gloria " for tenor and bass in the quartet " Quando
Corpus " from Rossini's *Stabat Mater*. Mr. Herbert
Reeves cites a still more striking instance of the "baritony"
character of the middle register from the reminiscences
of his mother, who told him that in a duet for tenor and
baritone in Benedict's *Crusaders*, where both have the
same notes to sing, his voice so nearly approached his
companion's that only those who knew could distinguish
which was which.

When singing music that demanded the full range of
his powers, his voice was unlike that of any other tenor.
In an interview given to the representative of *Musical
Opinion* in 1892, shortly after his appointment as one of
the professors at the Guildhall School of Music, we find
Mr. Reeves saying, " The modern voice has a wide range,
but no middle. It has been written up till the middle
register has grown weak and thin. If a tenor has a good
strong middle voice, he is now called a baritone. I think
I may claim to be called a tenor, yet I used to be called
a baritone at first because I had preserved this part of my
voice fresh and strong." It may be hazarded that the
master who thought he was a baritone and trained him as
such did him a positive service. His pupil even at twenty-
one may have had the high notes which were afterwards
developed with such wondrous effect, but of this
the master was probably unaware, or he might have
been led to exercise them prematurely and possibly would

have sacrificed some of the magnificent resonance and purity of tone which were their dominant characteristics.

Sims Reeves points out that there are instances of a singer making his appearance as a tenor and finding afterwards that he was a baritone. Lablache is said to have played the light tenor part of Count Almaviva in his youth and of subsequently discovering his *métier* in the sonorous bass with which he is identified. But save in the case of Jean de Reszke, Mr. Reeves says he never knew any instance of a singer beginning as a baritone and ending as a tenor. However this may be, Sims Reeves in his endeavours in 1838–9 to obtain a stage engagement would, no doubt, describe himself as a baritone, and as such he would be put down in the books of Mr. Turnour of Little Russell Street, Covent Garden, a well-known theatrical agent of the day, when " without much delay he (Mr. Turnour) procured me an opening at the Theatre Royal, Newcastle-on-Tyne, and here in the month of December 1839 (?) I made my first appearance on any stage " (*My Jubilee*).

CHAPTER II

1838-1839

In determining the date of Sims Reeves's " first appearance on any stage " one is faced with one of the puzzles which seem inseparable from theatrical chronology. Mr. Reeves says it was " in the month of December 1839." He further states that the performance was for the benefit of Mr. George Barker (more or less reminiscent as the composer of the once popular " Irish Emigrant " and " White Squall "), given during a starring engagement of Mr. and Mrs. Woods, hard-working and popular artistes of that day. This seems definite enough, but how is it to be reconciled with an advertisement in the *Newcastle Chronicle* of December 15th, 1838, running thus ?—" For the benefit of Mr. Barker and last night of his engagement, this evening, December 14th, 1838, will be presented the operatic play of *Guy Mannering*, after which the successful interlude of *Personation* and a variety of other entertainments, and to conclude with the farce of *The Wandering Minstrel*." The *Chronicle*, in the last week of December 1838, says : " Mr. Reeve [sic] also made his appearance as a singer, but from his extreme trepidation it was difficult to judge of his powers of song or ability as an actor." A second visit seems to have modified the critic's opinion. On January 5th, 1839, he wrote : " On Wednesday night Mr. Reeves introduced the song of ' The Pride of Kildare,' which he sang with great taste. His voice is of excellent quality, and when he becomes more accustomed to the business of the stage, we have no doubt he will very much eclipse his present efforts."

The writer of a biographical notice of Reeves in the *Newcastle Chronicle* of October 4th, 1879, in pointing out this discrepancy, wrote : " From a reference to the files of the *Newcastle Chronicle* we learn that in the last week of December 1838 a Mr. Reeve made his first appearance here, but whether it was Sims Reeves or another vocalist of similar name, does not appear." In the issue for the following week (October 11th, 1879) came the following, signed " W. A." : " In consequence of the difference of opinion as to the exact date of Sims Reeves's first appearance in Newcastle, whether 1840–1 or 1838–9, I took the liberty of applying at the fountain-head—the great tenor himself—to decide the dispute. With gentlemanly courtesy he replied, ' I am not quite certain as to its being 1840 or the last month of 1839. I think the latter. I could tell if I were at home. I recollect that Mr. Penley was leaving, and that Mr. Ternan was taking possession of the theatre. I am certain that it was not 1838–9.' "

Whatever may be the facts, there is no record in the Newcastle papers of December 1839, either of Mr. George Barker's benefit or of a performance of *Guy Mannering*. The Ternans at this time were producing musical plays, and in November and December we have Mr. Barker advertising a " benefit concert on a grand scale " if he could get enough support, but this was to take place at the Assembly Rooms, not at the theatre. It would seem that this support was not forthcoming, as beyond the advertisement there is no reference to the matter. Neither do the names of Mr. and Mrs. Woods appear in any capacity. There is, however, an announcement ten months earlier in the year—February 2nd, to be precise —in which we are told that Mr. and Mrs. Woods are playing in *Guy Mannering*, but there is no mention of Mr. Reeves or of George Barker. This adds to the confusion, and whether Mr. Sims Reeves made his first appearance on the stage in December 1838, when, undoubtedly, Mr. Barker *did* have a benefit and when *Guy Mannering* certainly was produced, or in February 1839, when Mr. and Mrs. Woods were " starring," or in

December 1839, when Mr. Penley was leaving, it is impossible to say. The weight of evidence inclines towards December 1838, and if so, the only explanation is that in fixing 1839–40 Mr. Reeves's memory played him false.

To the question of Mr. Reeves's age there can be but one answer. In *My Jubilee* it is stated that he had just entered upon his eighteenth year when he went to Newcastle; but he was really twenty—that is, if the year of his first appearance was 1838. The matter is of some interest as it touches upon the register of his voice. He had been, as we know, trained as a baritone, but the only thing Franco, the gipsy boy (the part in *Guy Mannering* assigned to him), had to sing was the first solo in " The Chough and Crow." This solo was written for a treble, but, of course, it could be sung by a tenor—hardly by a baritone. However, the absence of any song in the text for Franco proves nothing. The musical plays which did duty for English opera in the days of Bishop were very elastic. Songs were introduced or cut out according to the requirements of the singer. When Braham appeared in a musical play, all he cared for were the songs which he had made popular. Mr. John Coleman tells amusingly how Braham pitchforked his interpolations into *Guy Mannering*. " In the last scene (the cave in which Meg Merrilies confronts and confounds Dirk Hatteraick and Gilbert Glossin) a grand piano was discovered, at sight whereof Braham blandly remarked, ' A piano! That reminds me of the delightful aria I heard at " La Scala " the other night. Let me see if I remember it.' Sitting down, he accompanied himself in a delightful Italian ditty; then an encore was vociferously demanded—he responded with ' Waft her, angels.' The audience accepted these incongruities as a matter of course. But neither good taste nor the unities were considered much in those days; everything was governed by fashion. Braham's version of ' Be mine, dear maid,' was frilled and flounced by Bishop to suit the vulgar style which this great singer too often affected. Sinclair, the Scottish tenor, had *his* favourite ditties, and Madame Vestris and Miss Stephens theirs. ' Mr. Reeve ' at Newcastle, whoever he may have been, was within his rights in dragging in ' The Pride of Kildare.' "

SIR HENRY R. BISHOP.
From an engraving by Woolroth.

It does not matter very much whether Sims Reeves was engaged at Newcastle as a singer or an actor. In provincial companies the two capacities overlapped each other. A correspondent of the *Newcastle Chronicle* of November 4th, 1879, has some very pertinent remarks on this point, evidently written from personal knowledge.

" At this period " (1840–1), he writes, " professional singers occupied a different position from what they do at the present day [1879]. Concerts were comparatively few, and the programmes of these were made up in a fashion that would not be considered *en règle* now, whilst vocalists found scope for their talents principally in connection with opera, the lyric drama, and the rendition of the great oratorios. At all the leading temples of Thespis in the provinces it was customary to retain at least a tenor and a soprano on the season staff of the company. In towns boasting of a specially exacting musical constituency a bass or baritone joined, or a lady with a contralto voice might be added to the company, and thus with the aid of ' useful people ' always to be found among the actors and actresses, operas and musical dramas could be regularly produced in a style of finished completeness, not now to be hoped for.

" To the legitimate business the vocalists attached to the company introduced songs, duets, and concerted pieces between the play and the farce, and no week passed without some performance being given in which the musical element considerably predominated, and *Guy Mannering, Rob Roy, The Vampire, Love in a Village, The Waterman*, and *The Miller and his Men* were favourite vehicles for this sort of display. . . .

" It was under Mr. Ternan that Sims Reeves made his first appearance on any stage, and it should be mentioned that whilst published biographies of the great vocalist state that at the time his voice was regarded as a baritone one, and that he sang parts written for that range, yet the old playgoers of Newcastle insist that he was the ordinary season tenor, and that he sang in the same line of business as was always taken on those boards by Mr. Williams, Donald King, W. H. Reeves (brother to Sims Reeves), Arden, Romer, Rolfe, Cotte, etc."

But in those days the line between the two registers was

evidently not very strictly drawn where English singers in the provinces were concerned. George Barker at one of his benefit concerts at Worcester sang " Adelaida " (" as introduced and sung by him in *Fidelio* at Liverpool and Manchester," so ran the advertisement. What would be thought of such an " introduction " nowadays ?), and followed on with the baritone air from *Sonnambula*, " As I view those scenes so charming."

Mr. F. Belton, who was playing under Mr. Ternan at this time, is silent on the question of dates. He says (*Random Recollections of an Old Actor*) : " Sims Reeves, the great tenor, was playing ' little business ' and occasionally ' singing walking gentleman ' at a salary of 35/- per week." According to Mr. Belton, Reeves first met Macready at Newcastle and played Cleremont in *Richelieu*. Mr. Belton makes several references to his acquaintance-ship with Reeves, but most of these references are so full of inaccuracies that they are not worth quoting. He may, however, be correct in saying that while in Newcastle Reeves sang professionally at the Catholic chapel there. According to the old actor, " the head priest had a brother who was chapel-master at the Vatican. He had sent over a choice *morceau* which was much approved of by the Pope, and the priest much wished that Reeves should sing it on the following Sunday. He glanced it over and said, ' I'll sing it this morning if you like.' ' Oh, impossible to do it full justice ! ' ' Try me ; if Watson will play the accompaniment, after looking it well over.' It was agreed upon, and I don't think he looked at it again until a portion of the service admitted it to be sung. *He did sing it*, and with that holy calmness of effect which rendered him so great in sacred singing."

Between the termination of the season at Newcastle and his debut at Drury Lane Theatre, Reeves's movements are difficult to trace. In *My Jubilee* he speaks only of two engagements during this period, one at Worcester and one at the Grecian Saloon in London. At Worcester he says he played " walking gentleman, small parts in tragedies, and tenor, not baritone, parts in operettas, and even a part in a pantomime." This would go to show that he was a considerable time at Worcester, bringing him up to the winter of 1839.

Nothing of this, however, can be traced in the Worcester journals.

Of his experience at Worcester he gave an interesting reminiscence to the representative of the *Birmingham Daily Mail* on the occasion of his farewell concert in that city in 1879. " I can tell you," said he, " I have had to serve my apprenticeship in theatrical training, and I can recall with amusement an experience at Worcester, where I was engaged, singing in a modest sort of operatic venture. The lessee was a Mr. Bennett—I believe that was his name —and it was what we call a summer theatre. After the conclusion of the short season, and to keep the wolf from the door until the opening of the regular season, we, that is, the company, formed ourselves into a sort of common-wealth, sharing, you know, after expenses. The business was not at all times rosy, and occasionally my share amounted to the magnificent sum of one shilling per night. However, the training did me good and, I think, the rough schools I have worked in knocked the corners out of me. Art, you know, naturally engenders conceit, and there is nothing like a severe school to take the nonsense out of one. During this Worcester engagement, I had not only to do double, but sometimes triple parts, and, in addition, used occasionally to slip on a long black cloak and take my seat on the conducting-stool to direct our meagre orchestra, which consisted of a few strings, minus a viola plus just a taste of bass." It was at Worcester when, irritated by the inefficiency of the musical director, he in the exuberance of youthful spirits threw a black cloak over the incompetent man's head and conducted the band himself.

Whether he came direct from Worcester to London cannot be decided. He mentions incidentally that he was offered " the important parts—baritone parts, be it observed—of Count Rodolpho in the *Sonnambula* and of Dandini in *La Cenerentola*," and that his " impersona-tions were much admired," but when or where he does not state. Anyhow, we find him back in the metropolis, where at first he must have had a hard time. Possibly he had engagements at humble places of entertainment, but he had nothing regular until we hear of him at the Grecian Saloon, whose proprietor, Mr. Thomas Rouse,

better known as " Brayvo " Rouse, was one of the pioneers
of good music in combination with low prices. The
Grecian with the other " saloons " was not looked upon
as being on the same plane as the regular theatres. The
" saloons " were attached to taverns, and were really
expansions of " sing-songs " and " free-and-easies." The
" Grecian " was an adjunct of the " Eagle Tavern," the
" Albert Saloon," not far distant in Shepherdess Walk,
of the " Albert Tavern," while the " Britannia Saloon "
was an annexe of the Hoxton tavern of that name.
The lowest in the list was the ",Bower Saloon," Lambeth,
the home of a species of melodrama more lurid even than
that afterwards associated with the " Vic."

The attractions of the " Grecian " comprised a theatre,
a ball- and a concert-room, and an open-air spacious
dancing-platform. The prices of admission were sixpence
for " ladies and juveniles " and a shilling for " gentlemen,"
including a refreshment ticket which might mean a glass
of hot punch or a syrupy beverage known as " capillaire,"
very popular with Mr. Rouse's patrons. The " Grecian "
with its well-appointed theatre, almost as large as Drury
Lane, and its excellent concerts, was in its palmy days
one of the most popular places of amusement in London.
Here " Brayvo " Rouse (who commenced life as a brick-
layer, but was a born showman of the type of the late
William Holland) used nightly to sit in a private box with
one eye on his company and the other on the audience,
whose thunderous applause he received with a sort of
regal graciousness. Undoubtedly he was a remarkable
personage, popular, though autocratic.

Sims Reeves, who was present on the occasion, gives in
My Jubilee an account of a droll incident characteristic
of Rouse. " There had been," he says, " a great crush
at the doors, and he (Rouse) was attempting to get the
people into the theatre, when, in the confusion, someone
picked his pocket. As soon as the audience was seated, he
went to the stage and delivered himself of the following
pretty speech : ' Gentlemen, I've lost my purse.' This
announcement was received with loud and prolonged
laughter and cheers, at which he was rather disconcerted.
At this moment, however, someone came on the stage
and put something into his hand, which he carefully

examined. When he had done so, he recommenced,
' Gentlemen, I've found my purse.' This caused a second
outburst of cheers and laughter, which culminated in
an uproar on his saying, ' I've found my purse, but there's
no money in it.' The scene was almost indescribable,
and continued for several minutes. The farce of *The
Lottery Ticket* followed this episode, but its fun was
completely spoilt by the farcical performance which had
preceded it.''

Mr. Reeves says nothing about his performances at the
" Grecian," and we are left in doubt as to whether he
figured on the stage or on the concert platform. In all
probability, he had no special function, but whatever it
was, we may be sure he was worth the small salary that
he was paid, " Brayvo " Rouse being a remarkably good
judge of the abilities of his actors and singers. It would
appear that the young vocalist was not particularly proud
of his connection with the " Grecian," as he judged it
prudent to sink his personality under the modest *nom
de théâtre* of " Johnson." How long he stayed at the
" Grecian " is not known. He writes : " I found the entertainments so mixed up with smoking and drinking that I
very soon took my leave." From another source, however,
comes the information that it was a question of a rise in
his salary from one pound to five-and-twenty shillings,
which Mr. Rouse refused to give.

CHAPTER III

1840

THE exact period when Reeves took lessons of Hobbs, a very pleasing light tenor (whose pretty ballad " Phyllis is my only joy " is not yet forgotten), and T. Cooke is difficult to fix. The inference to be drawn from the mention of these lessons in *My Jubilee* is that it was soon after his engagement at the " Grecian " terminated. After recounting his experiences with Rouse, Mr. Reeves writes : " Having now found through personal experience the true register of my voice, I placed myself in the hands of Mr. Hobbs and Mr. T. Cooke for training as a tenor, and before long I was offered an appearance at Drury Lane." The evidence of Mr. Herbert Reeves on this point is interesting. He says that his father always thought he was a tenor, the upper notes coming so readily to him, " but he did not care to take any risks and from G upwards he went cautiously, never forcing his voice up to A, but, to use his own expression, ' sailing on to the note fluently and easily,' and using a beautiful *misto voce* capable of increasing from half power to full power or the reverse rarely brought to such perfection as by my father."

My Jubilee would have been valuable had it thrown light on this and kindred matters more or less obscure, but unfortunately, owing to its want of order and precision, its absence of dates, and for various other reasons, not so much reliance can be placed on the autobiography as could be wished. Indeed, many of the statements are somewhat misleading. In regard to Cooke, an article

appeared in the *Manchester Guardian* during November
1890 in which the writer says : " It is now more than fifty
years since Mr. Reeves first made his bow to a Manchester
audience at the old Theatre Royal in Fountain Street,
and there are playgoers still living who remember how
much his voice was admired even then. The late Mr.
H. B. Peacock[1] had a pleasant recollection of going one
afternoon to dine with Mr. T. Cooke, then renowned as a
teacher, who was lodging in a house near the site of the
present Queen's Hotel, and being detained for some time
by his host, who explained that he had been giving a
lesson " to a pupil who had a splendid voice if he only
knew how to use it—a young man of the name of Reeves."
In Mr. Herbert Reeves's opinion, it is questionable
whether his father was much indebted to Cooke. I
have been unable to obtain any confirmation of Mr.
Peacock's recollections. The *Manchester Guardian* of
1840–1 reveals nothing relative to Mr. Reeves in any
capacity, nor can it be established that Cooke at this time
was living in Manchester.

The important question is, however, did Hobbs and
Cooke train Reeves as a tenor ? Mr. Reeves says so, and
one feels bound to accept his authority, but it does not
agree with the assertion of M. Fétis that it was Bordogni
who made the discovery. M. Fétis's words are : " *Ce fut
alors que ce professeur lui découvrit l'erreur de son premier
maître et lui démontra qu'il possédait un ténor de plus
grande puissance et de la plus rare étendue dans les sons de
l'octave aiguë* " (" Sims Reeves," *Biographie Universelle
des Musiciens*). The point cannot be settled, but it may
be urged in support of M. Fétis's contention that none of
the music in which Reeves was called upon to sing prior
to his going to Bordogni was of a character likely to give
him an opportunity of displaying the true quality of the
upper register. The ballads which fell to his lot could be
sung by anybody and in any key. They were not written
specially for tenors. The nearest approach is " Come if
you dare," but its highest note is G, which, owing to the

---

[1] In Willert Beale's *The Enterprising Impresario* is a reference to Mr.
Peacock. He was art critic on the *Manchester Guardian* and " one of the
most active workers in Manchester in the cause of social reform through
the medium of the sister arts, and especially music."

low pitch then in use, was nearer the present F. In
" Britons, strike home," there is an A, but the passage in
which it occurs is not one for effect. On the whole,
it is hard to avoid coming to the conclusion that neither
Hobbs nor Cooke was aware of the exceptional powers of
their pupil. He probably gained from them grace and
style, after the artificial fashion of the day, but nothing
of the dramatic force which enabled him in after-years
to rival and eclipse Braham.

How Reeves in the autumn of 1841 came to be engaged
by Macready cannot be said. It is scarcely to be supposed
that an untried singer would be accepted by so fastidious
a manager without some guarantee of his ability. If,
however, he was known to Cooke, Macready's musical
director, an explanation is at hand. It is pretty certain
that after leaving the " Grecian " he found all paths
leading to vocal success closed save the one by way of
the stage. Music, and especially vocal music, in 1841
was governed by fashion. Italian opera held the sway,
though there were signs of a reaction. The absurd
Tamburini riot at Her Majesty's in May 1840 had
disgusted sensible people, and the newspapers other than
the organs of the " fashionables " were beginning to be
restive. It is hard in these days to realise how in the
first years of the Victorian era the world of West End
frivolity went mad over its favourite operatic singers.
The despotism exercised by the subscribers to the opera
would not now be tolerated for a moment. They
dictated to the manager what operas he should put on,
what singers he should engage, and whom leave out.
The ballet was even a matter of greater importance, and
the jealousies of the partisans of prominent ballerinas
must have given the goaded impresario many a sleepless
night. But without his subscribers he was helpless and
he had to submit. So long as subscribers and managers
kept their quarrels out of sight, the general public were
indifferent. Italian opera was not in their world. It was
an exotic for which they had neither taste nor money.
But when the young bloods of the omnibus box outraged decency and openly flaunted the manager and those
of the audience who did not agree with them simply
because a certain singer was not engaged, Italian opera

became a burning question. The conduct of the malcontents excited strong censure from the press, the *Era* denouncing them as "a few notorious young noblemen who, because they passed the holidays with Tamburini at Strathfieldsaye, determined to thrust him down Laporte's throat to the disarrangement of the whole season." Mr. Lumley suggests that the riot was instigated by the "Old Guard" of singers, Grisi, Persiani, Rubini, Mario, Lablache, and Tamburini, but there is no direct evidence of this. I question if Mario took part in such a plot; he was far too refined. Tamburini, who was a master of execution and embellishment, was the subject during his prime of the most extravagant laudation, and no doubt he was a most accomplished vocalist. Sims Reeves, however, writes: "I never liked Tamburini; his style was affected and meretricious. He looked and carried himself well on the stage, but Giorgio Ronconi, to use a slang expression, knocked him into a cocked hat both as an actor and singer."

Concerts in those days were given principally by prominent singers, who made sure of meeting their expenses by the sale of tickets beforehand. Wealthy people then had a craze for concerts at their own houses, when Italian operatic artists were engaged at enormous fees. The fashion was set in the thirties, Sir George Warrender and the opulent lady who began life as Harriot Mellon and ended it as the Duchess of St. Albans rivalling each other in the costly pastime. The *Era* in July 1840 found a peg on which to hang a further remonstrance against alien musicians, apropos of a concert given by Miss Burdett-Coutts, and its remarks are noticeable because of their reference to an Italian musician with whom Sims Reeves afterwards became closely associated. "Will English people," it cried, "never open their eyes to the folly of that patronage which supports foreign artists at the expense of our native composers and singers? Could people of fashion but get behind the scenes as we do, and see the ridicule with which they are treated by those insolent and upstart foreigners whom they pay so lavishly to conduct their concerts, from the conductor who is paid a large sum merely for the purpose of mainly accompanying the

singers up to the highest and down to the lowest of the
clique, they would shrink within themselves for shame."
The *Era*, however, excepted Miss Burdett-Coutts. She
is complimented on having preferred as a conductor an
Englishman, Mr. Potter (Cipriani Potter, the Principal
of the Royal Academy of Music), the writer remarking
that his engagement " must have been a bitter pill to
the foreigners and must convince those who have hitherto
patronised Signor Costa [1] and clique that there are other
directors quite equal to, if not better than, those who have
hitherto arrogated to themselves a superiority which
has been accorded to them rather by the false taste of a
certain set of fashionable amateurs than by their own
merit."

In the early forties everything was ridiculously ornamented, from Thalberg's preposterous trills, scale passages,
and arpeggios downwards. The public were *Norma*
and *Sonnambula* mad. Fancy names were invented for
the simplest programmes. The pretentious harpist,
Bochsa, toured the provinces with a " Voyage Musical."
There were " Musical Mélanges," " Musical Homages "

---

[1] The circumstances under which Costa was introduced to the British
public are somewhat curious. Zingarelli had accepted a commission to
write a cantata for the Birmingham Festival of 1829, but when the time
came for him to journey to England to conduct his work, he had an attack
of stage-fright and sent as his deputy his favourite pupil, Michael Costa.
Costa was so young that the Festival Committee refused to allow him to
conduct, but—could he sing ? " Yes," was Costa's reply, but conducting
was his business. The committee had its own views on the matter, and
vowed that unless he sang, not one shilling of his expenses would be paid,
and the young musician accepted the huckstering terms. Twenty-six
years later the Festival Committee was glad to have the honour of producing Costa's oratorio *Eli*. Alluding to Costa's first appearance, Mr. J.
E. Cox says (*Musical Recollections*) that through extreme nervousness the
young Italian failed as a singer. He adds : " At the morning performance
Costa heard Braham for the first time and in his *chef-d'œuvre*, . . .
' Deeper and deeper still.' . . . He sat . . . just behind Malibran on
the front of the orchestra, and with open mouth indicative of most
earnest attention lost not a note of that incomparable performance.
When Braham concluded with that burst of agony on the words ' I can
no more,' . . . Costa, not understanding a word of the text, asked
Malibran in a whisper and in Italian, ' What does the man say ? ' To
which that versatile creature replied in the same language on the instant,
' Poor devil ! it's all up with him.' Not till long afterwards did he
understand the information he had asked for."

(the dishings of Italian operatic scraps), " Bardic Tours " (ordinary English ballads and ordinary English singers), " Souvenirs " of this opera or that, " Musical Effusions," and in fact anything that struck the imagination as likely to impress an ignorant public. Taste in music at this time was as bald and barren as the furniture.

But despite the artificiality and insipidity with which the art was then clogged, it was striving to make its way to better things, and maybe some conviction of this kind led Macready, wedded though he was to the legitimate drama, and more particularly to tragedy, to determine to make music, of which he was very ignorant and for which he had not much taste, the attraction when he entered upon his campaign at Drury Lane in 1841.

The *Musical World* had for some time previous been persistent in its demands for English opera, by which it meant operas by English composers. The success in 1834 of John Barnett's *Mountain Sylph*—a work which, says Professor G. A. Macfarren, " was the first English opera constructed in the acknowledged form of its age since Arne's time-honoured *Artaxerxes*, and opened a new period for music in this country from which is to be dated the establishment of an English dramatic school "—raised hopes which were not destined to be realised. Barnett signally failed a few years later in his attempt at the St. James's Theatre to found an English Opera House, and up to the beginning of 1841 an " English Operatic School " was as far off as ever. In the early months of this year, however, Balfe opened the Lyceum to embody an idea which struck the *Musical World* as excellent, since he interdicted " all tragedy, comedy, farce, and pantomime—he will have nothing but music. By this he saves the expense of three or four distinct companies, and rids his theatre of that riotous kind of audience which impatiently endures an opera in anticipation of an hour's practical nonsense at its conclusion." But when Balfe brought out his opera *Keolanthe*, the *Musical World* hinted that he spent his subscribers' money in the production of his own compositions and in the attempt to establish his *cara sposa* as a " first singer on the English stage." At the outset of his enterprise he had crowded houses, but misfortunes soon followed.

Mr. H. Phillips seceded, and when the treasury dwindled Mr. Wilson, known as the Scottish tenor, followed suit. Mr. John Barnett withdrew his support, and in three months the house was closed. On the other hand, at the Surrey Theatre, operas in English combined with Bishop's musical plays were well patronised and proved highly remunerative. It may, therefore, be assumed that Macready came to the conclusion that for the moment the " legitimate " drama could not hold its own unsupported by music.

In the *Musical World* of August 12th, 1841, appeared the following reference to the great tragedian's enterprise under the heading " Operas at Drury Lane " : " We have great pleasure in communicating to our readers that Mr. Macready has expressed his wish and intention to produce genuine English operas, and that music by native composers will have preference of all others. . . . We trust our musicians will be on the alert now that there is a door open for their welcome and a prospect of their labours receiving due appreciation—and we recommend them to choose warily the dramas to which they wed their music in order that they may fairly compete with the other classical works that are likely to form the staple of Mr. Macready's enterprise."

This prediction, if Macready read it, must have bewildered him not a little. His notion of English opera at that moment was embodied in *Acis and Galatea* (which is not an opera) by Handel (who was not an Englishman). In his diary under September 25th is the entry : " Read the *Acis and Galatea* to Serle, which he thought would succeed if Stanfield painted the scenery." Apparently neither Macready nor his adviser had much faith in music alone, but music had to be prominent, and in his preliminary scheme Macready announced that " music will be associated with those aids of the picturesque in scenery and action that peculiarly belong to it in its dramatic form, and the utmost attention and encourage-ment given to improve in genuine English opera a school of art."

This vague and high-sounding programme could hardly have been accepted by Tom Cooke, Macready's musical director, without a quiet chuckle. Cooke, an Irishman with a strong sense of humour, was nothing if not a practical musician, and had no flights of imagination concerning either " genuine English opera " or " a school of art." His business was to get together a company of useful singers who should be able to do justice to *Acis and Galatea* or any other " English opera " which the management elected to produce, and thus it came about that with Miss Romer, Miss Poole, Henry Phillips, Allen (composer of a popular setting of " Maid of Athens "), an accomplished tenor singer, if of limited powers, Sims Reeves obtained his engagement at Drury Lane as second tenor.

CHAPTER IV

1841–1842

MACREADY opened his season on December 27th, 1841, not with English opera, as he had promised, but with *The Merchant of Venice*. It was preceded by " God save the Queen," which the playbill tells us was sung by " H. Phillips, Giubilei, Allen, J. Reeves, Miss Romer, and Miss Poole, etc." The date is memorable, as it marks the first appearance of Reeves on the Drury Lane boards. The services of the young second tenor were soon utilised, and until the production of *Acis and Galatea*, " J. Reeves," as he was termed, took the part of one of the minstrels in *The Two Gentlemen of Verona*.

On January 20th, 1842, *Acis and Galatea* was announced in the following grandiloquent fashion : " The first of a series of operas adapted and arranged for stage representation from the *Serenata* of Handel, in aid of the endeavour to establish upon the English stage the works of the greatest composers of the English school. Mr. Stanfield has been engaged to furnish the scenic illustrations for the representation of the first of a series of operas proposed to be revived at this theatre." " Proposed to be revived ! " If any English musician had taken the *Musical World's* advice to be on the " alert " and was looking out for the " open door," his hopes must have been thoroughly dashed.

Acis and Galatea was produced on February 5th, 1842, and Mr. " J. Reeves " figures in the bill as one of the

Sicilian shepherds. The " opera " was a veritable *tour de force* so far as scenic effect went, but musically speaking it invited severe criticism, especially on one point. To Miss P. Horton was assigned the part of Acis—proof of Macready's ignorance of music. Cooke, of course, would know better, but he was probably far too diplomatic to raise a protest against anything which that " harbitrary gent " Macready had decided upon. Macready was always very partial to Miss Priscilla Horton, and may have had her in view when he determined upon producing the *Serenata*, as there is an entry in his Diary during the preceding September which records : " Spoke to Miss P. Horton about taking lessons in singing." The absurdity of a lady attempting the part of a tenor must have been patent to everyone in the theatre save Macready, and especially so to the tenors Allen and Reeves. Anyone now living who has heard Sims Reeves in those delightful amatory songs of contrast, " Love in her eyes " and " Love sounds the alarm," will wonder what *his* thoughts were when poor Miss Horton was struggling with her difficulties.

The criticism was very mixed. The *Athenæum* could find praise alone for Allen's Damon. Miss P. Horton's Acis was pronounced " ineffective." Miss Romer's Galatea was " mouthing, heavy and ungraceful." [1] The Polyphemus of Mr. Phillips was " fairly sung. . . . But when we say that while listening to Damon . . . he all but laid his thumb to his nose after the polite fashion of the New Cut, we have indicated the amount of classicality in his conception of the part." The *Examiner* wrote in much the same strain. The *Times*, suavely complimentary, slurred over the Acis incongruity. The *Morning Post* was equally non-committal save in the case of Mr. H. Phillips, at whom it launched some jocosities. Phillips had to sing through a hideous

[1] Henry Phillips does not endorse this verdict. " Miss Romer," he says, " had a charming liquid voice and figure light as air, and the smallest foot ever possessed by a European lady." Sir Charles Santley also speaks highly of her singing. Mr. Herbert Reeves adds : " If not *de trop*, may I add that Miss Lucombe, who became Mrs. Sims Reeves (my mother), also was pronounced to have the smallest foot ever known, so much so that her shoe was exhibited at an exhibition in Paris. I still retain the little pair of shoes."

pantomimic mask, and to add to his height wore shoes with soles several inches thick, and was "otherwise encased from top to toe in cotton wool in order that a corresponding bulk might be produced. . . . Encumbered with this ludicrous gear, Mr. Phillips had great difficulty in forcing his notes through his mask, and when he commenced 'I rage, I melt, I burn,' there were many who thought he had abundant reason for the complaint. Very funny, too, was the comparison suggested by the words, 'Thou trusty pine, prop of my godlike steps, I lay thee by.' The 'godlike steps' were made by a pair of legs each as thick as a nine gallon cask and the 'trusty pine' was a washerwoman's clothes-prop." The *Weekly Despatch* indulged in low abuse which forced Macready into taking legal action, out of which he got little satisfaction and less damages.

For the production generally the critics had unanimous approval. The chorus singing they considered superb, and the stage management a marvel of mechanism, especially the realistic sea. Macready, however, belonged to the unregenerates. He was not a believer in nothing but music, and when *Acis and Galatea* was produced he interdicted neither comedy nor farce. There was always an after-piece in which the Keeleys were generally the attraction, and what probably outraged the feelings of the musical purist still more, the actor manager descended to the level of " that riotous kind of audience," denounced by the *Musical World*, by permitting " second price at end of opera."

Sims Reeves had his first chance in what, had he been only an actor, would have been called a "speaking part." He appeared on March 2nd as Lubin in *The Quaker*, Henry Phillips being Farmer Steady. Lubin has the lion's share of the music—duets with Fioretta, four songs, including the once well-known " I locked up all my treasure," and a part in a quartette. Of his singing in *The Quaker* I find the *Era* of March 20th saying: " Mr. Reeves made a successful debut as Lubin. This gentleman has a tenor voice of great compass with much sweetness and facility."

On March 28th was produced *The Students of Bonn*, an operetta by G. H. Rodwell, in which Reeves took the part of Hernstein, one of the students, singing " a troubadour lay which had the right stamp of the true Menestral," remarked the *Era* of April 3rd. Mrs. Keeley's charming personality helped to make the operetta a success. It was played for twenty-three nights. At the end of April *Macbeth* was revived. Phillips was Hecate, and Giubilei, Allen, and Reeves were the witches ; Miss Romer, Miss Horton, Mrs. Keeley, and Mrs. Serle also joined in the music. Macready on May 10th showed signs of surrendering his claims to be considered the high-priest of English opera. He produced *La Sonnambula* with Miss Romer as Amina and Allen as Elvino, returning at the end of the month to the legitimate with Gerald Griffin's *Gisippus*, Sheridan's comic opera *The Duenna* being played as an after-piece. In this Reeves was Antonio, Miss Romer, Miss P. Horton, and Allen filling the other parts. The season ended on May 20th, when Macready took his benefit.

Between the seasons Reeves obtained some provincial engagements and in the course of his tour visited Edinburgh. Mr. J. C. Dibdin, in his *Annals of the Edinburgh Stage*, says that on August 8th, 1842, he made his first appearance in that city, billed as " John Reeves, from Drury Lane." This was at the Adelphi Theatre. He appeared chiefly in a number of Scottish plays which were got up during Queen Victoria's visit to Edinburgh, playing Francis Osbaldistone in *Rob Roy*, Henry Bertram in *Guy Mannering*, and singing the interpolated songs " Maiden, I will ne'er deceive thee," " The Flower of Ellerslie," and " Let the toast be ' Dear woman.' " He also played such parts as Lorenzo in *The Merchant of Venice*, Frederick in *No Song, no Supper*, Blue Peter in *Black-eyed Susan*, besides singing " Macgregor's Gathering " and other songs between the pieces. In Mr. Baynham's *The Glasgow Stage* is a reference to Sims Reeves's early appearance in *Rob Roy* at Miller's Theatre, Glasgow. Mr. Baynham does not give the date, but in all probability it was during this Scottish tour in 1842. Mr. Baynham quotes a local critic of the day recording that " he [Reeves] seems to have something of the same antipathy to steel as that described of James VI. When he ought to have drawn his sword, he had none to draw, and when he dared Rashleigh to combat, he coolly walked off the stage to provide himself with a claymore." The dilemma was awkward, but with all his nervousness, Reeves had the requisite *sang-froid* when it was wanted.

On October 1st Drury Lane Theatre reopened with *As You Like it*, Reeves being one of the foresters. *Acis and Galatea* was still an attraction, and was played alternately with Shakespeare until November 9th. Meanwhile Madame Vestris had joined the company, and on November 5th, presumably for her sake, *The Duenna* was revived. On November 7th the *Times* wrote : " As sure as a sterling comedy is put on, with the exception of *The School for Scandal*, or perhaps *The Rivals*, so sure will the number of spectators be more or less scanty. The *Duenna* was respectably played ; . . . the very pretty music, though nicely sung by Miss Romer, Miss P. Horton, Allen, and J. Reeves, was heard listlessly ; and the only exception was Madame Vestris, who played Don Carlos, and sang her beautiful songs charmingly." Hazlitt calls *The Duenna* " a perfect work of art," but it would seem that its attraction was its music, hodge-podge though this was, after the style of *The Beggar's Opera*, the songs being fitted to popular melodies. " Had I a heart for falsehood framed," for instance, was adapted to " The harp that once through Tara's halls."

By this time Macready had decided upon his second plunge into English opera and elected to produce Dryden's dramatic opera *King Arthur*, known to playgoers of John Kemble's day as *Arthur and Emmeline*. Cooke was entrusted with the task of tacking as many additions to Purcell's music as the text would bear ; and accordingly he laid the same composer's *Libertine*, *The Indian Queen*, *Dido and Æneas*, and *Bonduca* under contribution, and made up the tale with the compositions of Arne. These additions were in a way necessary, for but a fragment of the music which Purcell wrote for the opera existed. Purcell, careless about his manuscripts, was indifferent to his fame. *King Arthur* was never published during his life, and when the time came to collect the various " numbers," it was found that he had made but a single copy of the opera, and that after his death this copy was in the hands of persons (most probably the managers of the theatre) who did not choose to part with it for the purposes of publication. Gradually the parts were collected, but much is still wanting.[1]

A curious reference to "Come if you dare" is to be found in Henry Phillips's *Recollections*. Phillips says he once had in his possession a letter from Arne to Garrick, who had requested him to arrange the music to *King Arthur*. Arne wrote that it was a most thankless task to arrange " and endeavour to improve such trashy and unmeaning stuff as Purcell's music, particularly that noisy and blustering song ' Come if you dare.' I have set it to music. Hear mine."[2] Against this we have Dibdin's statement that " Arne, though according to Garrick's plan obliged to introduce music of his own, was so far from mutilating Purcell that he rescued those beauties from oblivion that time and ignorance had obscured. Arne idolised Purcell, and it was his pride to place him in that conspicuous situation the brilliancy of his reputation demanded."

Madame Vestris was to be the bright particular star of *King Arthur*, but between two such autocratic spirits as Madame and Macready there was sure to be trouble, and on November 5th is an entry in the tragedian's Diary which shows that strained relations had set in, arising from that constant source of theatrical turmoil— money. The entry runs : " About to begin rehearsal . . . when Mr. C. Mathews wished to speak to me. Madame Vestris followed him into my room and began a *scene* which lasted two or three hours—on the lady's part much ' Billingsgate ' and false assertion ; on his, much weakness and equivocation. . . . I would not relinquish their engagement, but offered to defer the pecuniary point. She threw down her part in *King Arthur* and left the room, stating that she would not act after next week if the full salary were not paid." The lady was as good as her word and the cast was completed without her. The true version of this difference shows

---

[1] The music of *King Arthur*, edited by Professor Taylor, was printed for the first time in 1843, for the " Musical Antiquarian Society."

[2] I have an impression that since the above was written a copy of the letter in question was sold at Sotheby's.—C. E. P.

4

that Madame had right on her side. Macready's entry is both disingenuous and misleading.

While awaiting the production of *King Arthur*, Reeves appears to have been at liberty to accept concert engagements, and from a notice in the *Musical World* of November 3rd, 1842, we get a glimpse of the fare provided at musical entertainments in the distant suburbs of the forties. The notice is worth quoting, as it affords a quaint and interesting contrast between those days and these, and in more ways than one. The *World* wrote thus : " It is quite delightful to perceive how music is spreading her charmed meshes over the semi-rural portions of the metropolitan villages—scarcely a nestling hamlet of the great maternal city but has its periodical music-meetings, and many of them furnish a store of superior entertainments which may well bring a blush upon grander civic affairs. We attended a very pleasant concert on Monday evening, the first of a series intended to resolve the discords of the coming winter, in the locality of Peckham, and we trudged our way home with a lighter heart and a more elastic step from the sociable and musical enjoyment we had experienced. Miss Rainforth (our special favourite), Miss Betts (who always pleases us), Miss Russell (whom we should like to hear more frequently), and Miss Lyons (with whom we desire better acquaintance), sang a variety of captivating songs and were co-minstrelled by Mr. Reeves, a very promising tenor of Drury Lane Theatre." Peckham residents of to-day will read with some amusement the conclusion of the notice. "The ancient Mr. Ashley," writes the critic sympathisingly, " was to have interspersed the vocal treat with a strain or two on his well-remembered violoncello, but the uncertainties of the journey into such remote regions— the dangers of flood and field—were fain to be considered by the company, for the ancient came not." This concert was given in the Hill Street Concert Room, and Reeves sang his Hernstein song in *The Students of Bonn*, and joined in a duet from one of Donizetti's operas.

Though Reeves had achieved nothing great, his singing had attracted the notice of musicians who appreciated his budding qualities, and his name is found among the tenors engaged to sing in a series of six " subscription classical evening concerts," three at the Hanover Square Rooms and three at the London Tavern during October, November, and December.

In *King Arthur* Reeves had his first opportunity of showing the magnificent quality of his voice and the possession of true dramatic instinct. He appeared as the First Warrior, and created a sensation by his impassioned and fiery delivery of the battle-songs " Come if you dare " and " Britons, strike home " (the latter from *Bonduca*). Some time in the sixties I had the advantage of hearing Sims Reeves sing " Come if you dare " at the Beaumont Institution, Mile End. The colour he could infuse into his voice was marvellous, and though there was neither scenic adjunct nor orchestra, one could realise perfectly the effect he wanted to produce. But Sims Reeves was always great in martial music, as those who may remember him in " Sound an alarm," " Call forth thy powers," and " Philistines, hark ! " will admit. Perhaps there was something in the melodies of war which roused his own combative spirit.

Whatever criticism was evoked by the principals or by the production of *King Arthur* as a whole, the critics were unanimous in praising the excellence of the chorus and of the singing of Sims Reeves, at that time a quite unknown man. Even the *Sunday Times*, which had its private reasons for denouncing Macready and all his works, had nothing adverse to say of this portion of the opera, beyond asserting that " Come if you dare," which it terms the " crack song " of the opera, " was commonplace and vulgar." If the critic could have sneered at the singer most assuredly he would have done so. He fell foul of the favourite English baritone of the day, remarking that " the less popular but better pieces assigned to Mr. H. Phillips were barbarously murdered by that unrelenting vocalist, . . . and sung intolerably out of tune." For the production in general and for Macready in particular the *Sunday Times* reserved the vials of its wrath. " *King Arthur*," it proclaimed, " was a dull, stupid effort made by a stupid man. . . . The claqueurs did their duty manfully, but nothing could contend against the combined dullness of Macready and Dryden. . . . On the principle laid down by Muller, the audience abstained from hissing for that they could not hiss and yawn at the same time." On this piece of savage criticism Macready had this comment in his Diary : " Read the above of myself from the *Sunday Times* —quantity of low ribald falsehood which did not anger me at all. I believe it was written to provoke a prosecution."

The *Times* was exceedingly laudatory. " The manly, massive music of Purcell," it wrote, " was in perfect keeping with the massive character of the spectacle and . . . it was interesting to observe the genuine enthusiasm with which the audience seized on such invigorating strains as ' Come if you dare ' and ' Britons, strike home.' If one were to ask, Was not this enthusiasm due to Reeves's singing ? the answer, I believe, would be in the affirmative."

The *Athenæum*, on the other hand, was not impressed. It found " the music absolutely overlaid by scenic splendours ; for instance, the fine chorus ' Come if you dare ' was not to be trusted alone to produce its effect, but after it is sung the orchestra plays the air half a dozen times, while a mimic battle of plank and canvas warriors is manœuvred in the background." It thought " the finest stage effect was that where the crowd of armed men rushed upon the stage with ' Britons, strike home.' Here we ought to say that the execution of the chorus throughout was of the highest order." Lastly, the *Era*. It was highly pleased with the entire production. " Mr. Reeves gave the soli portions of ' Come if you dare ' and ' Britons, strike home ' with considerable animation. To a tenor voice of extensive register and always in perfect tune, he adds feeling and taste and must become a popular tenor singer." Henry Phillips wrote with the enthusiasm of a brother artiste that " Sims Reeves sang ' Come if you dare ' with all that splendid tone and energy now so universally admired all over Europe."

In connection with Reeves being selected to play the part of the First Warrior, a choice which undoubtedly laid the foundation-stone of his future success, Mr. J. Anderson (who was the King Arthur) has a story in his *Recollections* which baffles comprehension, notwithstanding its circumstantiality and air of truth. Mr. Anderson writes :

" The celebrated Sims Reeves was this season a simple member of the chorus in Drury Lane Theatre. I believe I was the humble cause of his early promotion, although he was never aware of it, I am sure.

" During the last rehearsal of Dryden's *King Arthur* . . . Tom Cooke, the musical director, entered the manager's room, where I happened to be at the time ; he was in a state of great agitation because he could find no one to whom he could entrust the solos of ' Come if you dare,' etc. He proposed the postponement of the piece until he could procure an adequate singer for the purpose.

" The proposal was annoying to the manager, as he had always kept faith with the public at any sacrifice. He looked at Tom Serle and myself, and asked ' what was to be done ? '

" I ventured to suggest that if Cooke would only try once more he might yet find a gentleman who could do ample justice to the music. Cooke was not a little angry that I should presume to meddle in musical matters. ' Absurd,' said he. ' You know Sims Reeves in the chorus?' Whether Cooke was prejudiced against Reeves or whether he had never heard him sing, I do not know, but he laughed at the bare idea. ' Never mind,' I went on persistently, ' only give him a trial, and if *he* is not the man you want, I'm a Dutchman.' I had often listened to his fine voice in the choruses and felt certain he was all there.

" The manager laughed and requested Cooke to take Mr. Reeves into the music-room *alone* and find out what he was made of. In less than twenty minutes Cooke returned in raptures of delight. Rushing up to me, he embraced me again and again, swearing in his odd and humorous way that we must change places—I must conduct the orchestra and *he* take my place on the stage. The result was delightful ; Mr. Reeves made a great hit, and was nightly encored in his magnificent solos."

If this story is to be accepted, we must be prepared to swallow any number of improbabilities. We shall have to suppose that Cooke engaged Reeves without knowing

what his voice was and without remembering that Reeves
had been his pupil. Though leader of the orchestra, we
must imagine him deaf when Reeves was singing his songs
in *The Quaker* and *The Duenna* and as Hernstein in *The
Students of Bonn*, while his presence on the stage in *Acis
and Galatea*, also in *Macbeth* and *The Two Gentlemen
of Verona*, must have gone unnoticed.

Equally apocryphal must be pronounced Mr. Belton's
version as to how Reeves came into prominence under
Macready. Mr. Belton writes : " He [Reeves] wrote
to say he had achieved a signal triumph. It seems that
Acis and Galatea was to be produced and Allen (first tenor)
possessed a sweet voice but with little power. He failed
in giving due effect in ' Sound the Alarm ' [a slip for
" Love sounds the Alarm "]. The manager ordered it
to be cut out. This the leader protested against, when
Reeves stepped forward and said he was up in the music
and would sing it if they would allow him. They did,
and he perfectly electrified them ; he sang it nightly,
and from that moment his star was in the ascendant."
Apart from the inherent improbability of this story, it is
hardly necessary to point out that the air in question was
sung by Miss P. Horton and not by Allen, who took the
part of Damon.

CHAPTER V

1842–1843

King Arthur was produced on November 16th, 1842. Anderson was King Arthur ; John Ryder (" Blasphemous Jack," not yet forgotten by old playgoers), Malcolm ; Mrs. Nisbet, Emmeline ; Miss P. Horton, Philidel ; and Miss Fairbrother (afterwards the wife of the Duke of Cambridge), Venus.   Apart from the scurrilous nonsense of the *Sunday Times*, the production itself was not received without criticism.   The *Musical World* called it a " Purcell Pasticcic " of which " the execution was perfect —the performance was triumphantly successful."   The editor, however, in his capacity as the champion of English opera, felt it his duty to suggest to Macready that the " expense attending this revival would have produced at least three original operas, would have given him three chances of profit, and would have thrice better served the cause of art in this country."

It was in *King Arthur* that Sims Reeves exhibited his independence of thought and determination to uphold what he deemed to be right.   It required no little courage to stand up to a martinet like Macready, but Reeves, young as he was, did it.   The story, which he tells himself in *My Jubilee*, is well known, but it cannot be omitted here, as it marks a phase in Reeves's character which showed itself many times during his career.

The incident is best described in Mr. Reeves's own words.   " The famous war-song being entrusted to me, I could not but seek to do justice to it, and having in the character of a British warrior to address a host of enemies

55

threatening me from the rear, I, of course, knew that in singing defiance to them, I must not shun their gaze. It was equally necessary, however, that I should not turn my back upon the audience. . . . In my difficulty . . . I stood sideways, so that I could at the same time menace the advancing foe and allow my menaces to be heard by the attentive audience. Why, I wonder, did not the intelligent manager arrange for my enemies to enter from one of the side-wings? This, however, did not suit the stage picture as conceived by him [Macready], and nothing would satisfy him but that I should sing my war-song in such a position that, though my daring adversaries would hear it, the audience would not.

"At the end of the performances Mr. Macready fell into one of his customary rages and gave me my dismissal. I had not, however, been absent long from the theatre when he sent for me and asked me to resume my engagement. . . . Delighting in the exercise of arbitrary power, the stern director informed me that for disobeying his orders I was sentenced to pay a fine of five pounds."

In this account Reeves softened down what really happened and did himself an injustice. Mr. Herbert Reeves says that on one occasion, when referring to the incident, his father told him that resenting Macready's overbearing manner and feeling that he was right, his natural impetuosity asserted itself and, flinging the music he had in his hand at the time in the autocratic tragedian's face, he walked out of the theatre. The dismissal came from him and not from Macready, who, as he states, had to send for him to come back. As manager Macready was within his right in fining the recalcitrant tenor £5— "just one week's salary," said Reeves, with a shrug of his shoulders. This tells us what his Drury Lane engagement was worth. In the course of the altercation Reeves remarked that perhaps the day might come when he [Macready] would ask for his services. That day *did* come. On the occasion of Macready's farewell to the stage the tragedian begged Reeves to sing for him. The answer was in the negative.

Macready, it would seem, looked upon singers, no matter what were their talents and standing, as persons "meet to be sent on errands." Henry Phillips, to his mortification, found that he was expected to sing in a couple of glees in *As You Like It*. He went through his task reluctantly and " eventually left the establishment in disgust ; for it was not likely that a person bearing any rank in his profession would submit longer than possible to a degradation which placed him almost on a level with a chorus singer." Phillips adds : " I have misgivings that my friend Sims Reeves had equal cause of complaint in the same establishment."

King Arthur, alternately with *Acis and Galatea*, ran to the end of the year. In January, Macready yielded once more to the temptations of Italian opera and put on Rossini's *La Gazza Ladra* with Miss Sabilla Novello. On February 6th the manager again strayed from the path of English opera pure and undefiled, and produced *Der Freischütz*, and on the same night—a strange mixture—*Macbeth*. In Weber's opera Reeves was Otto-car ; H. Phillips, Kaspar ; Miss Romer, Linda ; Miss P. Horton, Rose ; Mr. Howell, Zamiel. Save in the *finale*, where he has some scraps of solo singing, Ottocar has little to do and Reeves had no chance of distinguishing himself.

During February the programme was wholly un-English. *La Gazza*, *Sonnambula*, and *Der Freischütz* filled the bill, but for his benefit Macready went back to his original pretensions, selecting *Comus*, which was played in conjunction with *Much Ado About Nothing*, Reeves singing in the first as one of the Bacchanals and in the second as a minstrel. During the whole of March the changes were rung on *Comus*, *Der Freischütz*, and *Sonnambula*, and then came the debut on the English stage of a singer destined to be associated with Sims Reeves in many of his triumphs in oratorio—Miss Clara Novello.

Like Madame Vestris, Clara Novello had her own ideas and stuck to them—much to the disgust of Macready. On March 20th he wrote in his Diary : " She is handsome, but not winning—much assertion, some affectation, and evidently a *great* opinion of herself. She did not prepossess me. She gave me a shock and a fright in wishing to be announced ' Clara Novello ' with all her *titles* from the various foreign academies." Macready, however, had to submit, and on the playbill of March 25th was the announcement: " Miss Clara Novello, from the principal theatres in Italy, is engaged for a limited period and will shortly make her first appearance."

The opera chosen was Pacini's *Sappho*. It was the tragedian's first experience of operatic " stars," and Miss Novello proved herself no exception to the rule which governs prima donnas—*aut Cæsar aut nihil*. " Miss Novello," he notes on the 21st, " conspicuously ridiculous —it was painful to see her. On being told that the first cornet was in the Queen's band, and, therefore, could not come, she answered, ' Oh, then, I suppose either the Queen must wait or I.' " On another point the lady had more justice for her displeasure. On the 24th appears the entry : " Clara Novello was much distressed at the incorrectness of the orchestra, and the inefficiency of Mr. T. Cooke, who was with his back to the stage fiddling out the passage as if to learn the music from the score."

It was characteristic of Macready that on this purely musical matter he should consult three non-musical authorities, Serle, Anderson, and Willmott, " who all seemed to feel the same way. . . . I took their opinion, all agreeing in the propriety of calling in Benedict. . . . Planche thought that Cooke was not equal to Italian opera. . . . Serle took the score to Benedict to look over." No further mention of the squabble is to be found in the Diary, and Cooke retained his position. It is interesting to note that the adaptation of the music to the English stage was by Mr. J. L. Hatton, to whose talents as a composer of the purely English school sufficient recognition of late years has hardly been paid.

Reeves had a small part—Hippias—in *Sappho*. It was of no consequence to him as a singer, but it probably made him known to Clara Novello. It may be surmised, however, neither suspected that within a few years the second tenor of Drury Lane, who had to be contented with anything that fell to his lot, would rival and out-distance the prima donna. *Sappho* (produced on April 3rd, 1843) had but a " *succès d'estime*." The critics praised Clara Novello's voice, but did not rate her histrionic powers very highly. The *Times* considered

" her action as short, abrupt, deficient in dignity, and she does not stride the stage with that ease and elasticity to make her movements graceful and winning." The public remained cold, and Macready let off the steam in this fashion : " House was below even my calculation ; in spirit it was an assemblage of brutes."

It is possible that Macready was not much inclined to give the tenor who had defied his authority a helping hand. When *Acis* was performed on May 5th, as Handel intended it to be sung, Clara Novello taking the part of Galatea, Allen that of Acis, and with Staudigl as Polyphemus, Reeves resumed his humble rôle of a Sicilian shepherd. On May 29th, on the occasion of a concert the proceeds of which went to the fund for erecting a memorial to Mrs. Siddons, the two principal acts of *Der Freischütz* were given, Staudigl being Kaspar, and Reeves, Ottocar ; but after this, when *Der Freischütz* was repeated on three dates (June 1st, 3rd, and 6th), Ottocar was omitted. Whether this was part of Reeves's punishment cannot be said, but it seems probable. His name appears for the last time on the bill when Macready took his benefit, and on this night ended his management with his favourite play *Macbeth*, Reeves, as before, being one of the witches.

According to Mr. Sutherland Edwards, " a strange and interesting incident happened to the young tenor while he was playing the part of First Warrior. . . . A gentleman who was an enthusiastic lover of music had heard the performance, and speaking of it to some ladies whom he wished to take to Drury Lane Theatre, said to them, ' Come and hear a new singer who will be the first tenor in the world.' A party was formed and one of the members of it was Miss Lucombe—at that time a student of singing, afterwards a very brilliant singer—who subsequently became the wife of the admired tenor at whose early performances she had been invited to assist."

The incident may be true, but Mr. Edwards is mistaken in saying that Miss Lucombe was at the time a student of singing. In 1843 she had attained a deserved reputation, and was well known to the public. She was singing with much success at the Sacred Harmonic Society's concerts in the spring and winter of 1842, and at many other concerts, including a series at St. James's Theatre. She was a member of Thalberg's party when in the same year he toured the provinces, and at the end of Macready's season she was engaged by Henry Phillips to assist in the vocal illustrations of a musical lecture on Hebrew Melodies from which Phillips hoped great things, but which failed to attract.

"I knew quite enough about singing to be sure that I was in need of further instruction, and in 1843 I went to Paris, in order to take lessons of a very distinguished master, Signor Bordogni." Reeves thus sums up his four and a half years' experience of musical plays and "English opera." His time had not been wasted if it led him to only this conclusion. He had amassed a considerable amount of practical knowledge. He had acquired a familiarity with stage-craft without which he could not have entered upon his operatic career with confidence. He did not, three years later, come before the critical, instinctively dramatic Italians as a novice, and this was an immense stride towards success. His English admirers of the sixties and seventies, who had only heard him in oratorio and in the concert-room, must have found it difficult to associate the fervent singer who could move them to tears in the *Messiah* Passion music, in "Deeper and deeper still," or in "Total eclipse," with the stage ; and certainly not the prim audiences which regarded the Sacred Harmonic Society's functions as a sort of religious observance. These respectable Victorians who looked askance at Haydn's *Seasons* because of the sprightly chorus "A wealthy lord" and its allusion to a kiss, and with their prejudices against the theatres, might not have regarded Sims Reeves with such favour had they known of his early life, as what they would probably call a strolling player.

Reeves's association with Drury Lane was valuable in more senses than one. Besides gaining ground in the estimation of the public, he made good his footing in the profession. It is noteworthy that at the outset of his career many of the artists whom he subsequently distanced were already established singers sought after by impresarios. Clara Novello was one of these. Miss Dolby was well on the way to fame. Miss Poole had

MISS EMMA LUCOMBE (MRS. SIMS REEVES).
From a Water-colour Drawing.

substantiated her claims to be considered as among the most artistic and sympathetic ballad singers of her time. Miss Rainforth (destined years after to play Lucia to Sims Reeves's Edgardo and Polly to his Macheath) was in constant request, and Madame Dorus Gras, who shared with Reeves his success in his first appearance in *Lucia di Lammermoor* in England, was a recognised Italian operatic "star." Henry Phillips was easily at the head of popular baritones; Weiss (two years older than Reeves) was even in 1842 acknowledged as a bass of the first rank. Beletti, who had not then come to London, where he became identified with oratorio, had long been known on the Continent as one of the greatest baritones. Sontag, Grisi, Persiani, Tamburini, Mario, with all of whom Reeves subsequently sang, had attained a world-wide reputation. Of English tenor contemporaries whose fame had lasted to that time there was but one left—John Braham. But in the early forties Braham had out-sung his day; he had lost his fortune in ruinous specula-tions, and was reduced to touring the provinces in concert enterprises with his sons Charles and Hamilton.

When Macready's operatic experiments came to an end, Reeves must have found himself somewhat puzzled what to do. There was no chance for fame in the so-called English opera as it then was, and little hope for the realisation of the high artistic aims which he had ever before him. The period, in truth, presented a very blank prospect for English operatic singers, even for those who had made their name. The monologue interspersed with songs had been introduced by Henry Russell, and its success tempted well-known singers to try their fortunes in the same path. Wilson, the "Scotch tenor," had his "Nichts wi' Burns"; Henry Phillips followed suit with lectures musically illustrated; Templeton, "Malibran's tenor," ran a similar entertainment. But such ventures could only be undertaken by singers sure of an audience.

The conviction must then have been forced upon Reeves that, fashion or no fashion, Italian opera was the goal to aim at. It had the advantage of being certain. Without Italian opera the "fashionables" would find the season insupportable. English opera, on the other hand, was spasmodic. Enterprise after enterprise had failed. Whatever may have been the merits of the works produced, they could not be compared with the masterpieces of Mozart, Weber, and Rossini, not even with the prolific outpourings of Bellini and Donizetti. Moreover, the group of Italian singers then before the public was unapproachable. As a body these singers represented a trade-union of which the motive power was jealousy, accompanied by a supreme contempt for English vocal art and acting. This attitude was strongly supported by their aristocratic patrons. For an English tenor to think of enrolling himself in the ranks of these exclusives must have seemed like the dream of a madman. That Sims Reeves should have resolved upon this daring feat and that he should have succeeded argues the possession of a dauntless spirit altogether exceptional. But he did not deceive himself. He knew very well that unless he could hold his own against the first singers of the day he would but court disaster and ridicule.

CHAPTER VI

1843–1845

Reeves's lessons under Bordogni. The exact date uncertain. Engagement at Aberdeen in September 1843. An unexpected episode. His first appearance in Manchester. Enthusiastic reception. His rivalry with Donald King. Musical partisans. His hard work at Manchester in 1843-4. Engaged by Mr. Robert Roxby in June and July at Manchester. Is a member of Madame Céleste's company at the Theatre Royal, Williamson Square, Liverpool, in the autumn of 1844. A compliment from Charles Kean. Sings in *The Messiah* at Glasgow in December. A curious criticism of " Thou shalt break them." Probable influence of Bordogni's teaching. Sings at Liverpool concerts. His connection with Liverpool. Is engaged as leading tenor by Anderson, the " Wizard of the North," at the New City Theatre, Glasgow. Mr. John Coleman's narrative of a " disturbance " on Reeves's benefit, September 1845. Reeves at Dublin. His accident while singing in *Fra Diavolo*.

WHEN did Reeves determine to take lessons of Bordogni and at what period were these lessons given ? He himself says positively that it was in 1843, but the autobiography contains so many ¦positive statements which upon investigation turn out to be erroneous that this one must not be accepted offhand. Macready's " season " terminated at the end of June 1843 ; in September Reeves was playing in Aberdeen. July and August are always barren months, professionally speaking, and it may be assumed that he availed himself of the opportunity of visiting Paris and placing himself under Bordogni. A couple of months' tuition is not much, but in the case of such a pupil as Reeves it would suffice to correct any faults—they were not many, one may be sure—if not long enough to mature his style.

The Aberdeen engagement has its points of interest. The date was September 25th, 1843, and the printed bill made the following announcement : " Aberdeen Theatre Royal. Mr. Lloyd, of the Theatre Royal, Edinburgh, begs most respectfully to inform the nobility, gentry, and the public of Aberdeen and vicinity that having entered into an arrangement with the proprietor of the above theatre he will have the honour of opening it for two nights only, on which occasion the following ladies and gentlemen will appear : Mr. John Reeves of the Theatre Royal, Drury Lane, and the Nobilities' Concerts, London, and Theatre Royal, Edinburgh. His first appearance here. Mr. Sam Cowell, Mr. Leigh, Miss Clara Lee, and Mrs. Leigh, all of the Theatre Royal, Edinburgh, and first appearance here."

The performance was to commence with *The Two Gregories*, in which Reeves was to play the part of John Bull, with the song of " The Thorn," after which was to follow a concert, Reeves to sing " My pretty Jane " and " The White Squall," to conclude with the farce *The Young Widow*. The events of the evening were totally unexpected, and may be best described in the words of the *Aberdeen Journal*, which recalled the occasion in an article recording Mr. Reeves's farewell visit to the city on September 25th, 1881.

" A goodly audience," says the writer, " assembled in the Old House in Marischal Street, eager for the entertainment. . . . When, however, a quarter to eight arrived, and nothing in the shape or sound of an orchestra put in an appearance, a whisper began to pass along that something or somebody was out of joint. Then at eight o'clock, with no response to the sharp call for ' Fiddlers, fiddlers,' the doubtful whisper grew into an ominous gallery growl ; and this again some ten minutes after into bad humour with significant noises. Suddenly the prompter's bell was heard. . . . Mr. Lloyd . . . explained that through an order of the magistrates . . . by a clause in the recently passed Act for the regulation of public entertainments it was impossible for the company to enter upon the dramatic portion of the entertainment, . . . ' but,' continued in effect Mr. Lloyd, ' it so happens that we are pretty strong in vocal talent, and if you will kindly stay and accept our services in that line we shall do our very best to make you happy here, and send you home satisfied.' Warm applause followed the well-put words, . . . up went the curtain, a piano was drawn down to the footlights, and with a bow a keen-faced, dark-haired, handsome young man took his place thereat. This was Mr. John Reeves. And what a night of mirth and music followed ! . . . In the year of Mr. Reeves's first visit to Aberdeen he had just reached manhood[1] and his voice was of singular beauty, fine compass, and great power. He had not, of course, acquired the intensity, the touching expression, the finished artistic management of tone with that perfect method of phrasing that time and study brought in such rich measure, but as already said, there was a charm, a feeling of freshness about his singing in now distant 1843 which no after-efforts have effaced.

" Mr. Reeves did a right good night's work on that 25th of September. Over and above contributing five or six songs, he presided throughout at the piano, accompanying Lloyd and Sam Cowell in all their comic ditties and Mr. and Mrs. Leigh in the ballads. Perhaps one of the most amusing incidents of the evening was the rendering of Dr. Calcott's glee ' The Red Cross Knight,' in which Cowell apparently took the bass, the left hand, however, of the pianist providing the profounder notes, Reeves's voice meanwhile ringing out clarion clear in the highest leading melody."

A notable occasion was his first appearance on October 14th, 1843, at the Theatre Royal, Manchester, in Fountain Street. The play was *The Tempest*, and on the opening night the whole of the company before the performance sang the National Anthem. " In front," wrote a correspondent of the *Manchester Guardian*, " stood a very swarthy-looking young man . . . who sang a verse or two of the anthem in a style which astonished the audience. This was Mr. John Reeves, the new ' singing man ' (in succession to Donald King). . . . Of this first appearance, two of our most discriminating critics took quite diverse views. One said : ' His voice is pure and his compass very considerable ; we think we are correct in saying that it reaches B in alt without falsetto.' The other remarked : ' The new tenor made some rather astonishing variations, more creditable to the boldness of his fancy than to the purity of his taste, in the verses allotted to him.' "

He was then twenty-five.

It would seem that in 1843 Lancashire folk took music very seriously (as indeed they are inclined to do at the present day), and the *Guardian's* correspondent goes on to inform us that " each critic had his followers and during the entire season these are wont to frequent two well-known ' houses of call ' and there fight their battles over until closing time."   The subject of discussion was, of course, the respective merits of Reeves and Donald King—the latter a great favourite in the Midlands and in the North.   Mr. Reeves, in *My Jubilee*, referring to this rivalry, speaks of the favour with which he was received by the Manchester public and also of the " very bitter treatment at the hands of a Mr. Sever, who held the post of critic to the *Manchester Guardian.* He was at the time a great friend of Mr. Donald King,[1] whom I succeeded."

A search through the *Manchester Guardian* for 1843 yielded two criticisms, presumably written by Mr. Sever.   One is the notice of the opening night already quoted, and the other (November 1st) has reference to Reeves's Lorenzo in *The Merchant of Venice*.   It runs : " Mr. J. Reeves sang two songs with great power.   Indeed he sang with so much force as even to weaken the effect by marring the natural sweetness of his voice. With careful cultivation we may expect much from him, but he appears to have had no good example on which to form his style."   It is not extraordinary that Reeves should have been irritated by this " damning with faint praise."   The sting was in the tail.   If he had already been under Bordogni, the assumption that he had no " good example " for style must have been extremely galling— a feeling which could not have been lessened by the superfluous advice of " careful cultivation." Whatever may have been the motive, it is certain that not a word of praise during this season came from the critic of the *Guardian*.

[1] I met Donald King on one occasion in the seventies.   He was nearing three score and ten, but sang " Goodbye, sweetheart," extremely well and with considerable power.   He told me that he had been a choirboy at one of the Chapels Royal and had sung at the Coronation of George IV. His memory, so far as the words of his song were concerned, was failing, and for fear of accidents he carried with him cards on which they were written.—C. E. P.

The reference in the *Guardian* of 1890 to bygone times moved another correspondent to write thus : " I have a vivid recollection of that night, as I accompanied my uncle, who had formerly been conductor of a local band of more than average reputation. He was a thorough musician and a worshipper of Braham. He had been on the lookout for years for a tenor singer worthy to fill Braham's place, and I had the pleasure of going with him in his search on many occasions. We heard Allen, Donald W. King, and others, but they did not satisfy my uncle, whose invariable verdict was ' Good singer, but not a Braham.' . . . Mr. Reeves had not sung two lines before I felt my arm firmly gripped, and when he had finished his verse I felt a heavy smack between the shoulders, . . . and my uncle jumped up exclaiming, ' That's the only lad to step into Braham's shoes.' "

The desire of the Manchester public to hear the new tenor drew crowds to the theatre. His singing was a revelation and his audiences fully appreciated it. " Mr. Reeves appeared one night," says the *Guardian* correspondent quoted above, " as Francis Osbaldistone, Major Galbraith being represented by Mr. Bass—a good comedian, and a general favourite. In the drinking scene at Lucky M'Call's the two agreed to sing ' Auld Lang Syne,' each a verse alternately. Reeves sang the first verse most superbly ; I never heard anything so grand. Bass looked up in wonder and admiration, forgetting for the moment his character, and when his turn came, he could no more sing than he could fly. So he acted as being too drunk to sing and stammered a request that his young friend would finish the song. This his young friend did, in a style which no living man could equal."

It is worthy of remark that even in the early days of 1843 Reeves identified himself with many of the English ballads, " My pretty Jane,"[1] " The Pilgrim of Love,"

---

[1] Edward Fitzball, who wrote the words, says that " My pretty Jane " was composed for and sung by Robinson, a favourite vocalist of the thirties at Vauxhall Gardens, and was encored every night of the season. Fitzball adds : " Sims Reeves has taken up the air lately and charmingly he sings it, but it ought to be sung in the open air under the moonlit summer trees as at Vauxhall. . . . Bishop thought nothing of the melody. . . . I don't believe he would have consented to its being sung,

etc., which afterwards became his own, and which no other tenor ever attempted to wrest from him. Braham was still singing his stock successes, " The Death of Nelson," " The Bay of Biscay," etc., and at this period the coming tenor let these alone, only adding them to his list after Braham's death.

Reeves's work at Manchester in 1843 was of the most arduous character. Four nights after the opening on October 17th he played Tom Tug in *The Waterman*, singing " The Jolly Young Waterman," " Farewell, my trim-built wherry," and " The White Squall." Then followed the musical farce of *'Twas I*, in which he sang for the first time in Manchester " My pretty Jane." During the season he was Leander in *The Padlock*, Frederick in *No*, Hecate in *Macbeth*, Sir Harry Bumper in *The School for Scandal*, Ganem in *The Forty Thieves*, Lorenzo in *The Merchant of Venice*, Paul in *Paul and Virginia*, David Dulcat in *Amateurs and Actors*, Henry Bertram in *Guy Mannering*, Macheath in *The Beggar's Opera*, Osbaldistone in *Rob Roy*, Captain Malcolm in *The Slave*, Edwy in Sheridan Knowles's *Alfred the Great*, Jocoso in *Clair*, Fenton in *Merry Wives*, Balthazar in *Much Ado*, Elvino in *Sonnambula*, Amiens in *As You Like It*, Rodolpho in *Der Freischütz*, Oswy in *One o'Clock*, Belville in *Rosina*, Hawthorn in *Love in a Village*, Max in *Why Don't She Marry?* Arbaces in *Artaxerxes*, and Blue Peter in *Black-eyed Susan*. This ample list implies not only a prodigious amount of hard work, but also a ver- satility with which Reeves has hardly been credited, great as his varied powers proved to be in after-years. It should also be remembered that Reeves was thorough in everything he undertook. The word " slovenly " was not in his vocabulary. The season extended to the end of January 1844, when the *Guardian* (otherwise Mr. Sever,

but in the moment of necessity no new song could be supplied for Robin- son." Mr. J. A. Fitzgerald, in his *Stories of Famous Songs*, says that the song was based on a love episode in which Fitzball himself figured. Robin- son was in a hurry for a song and called on Fitzball, who said, " If ' Pretty Jane ' won't do, I shall write no more." Fitzball went off to Bishop for the music, but the composer was out. On searching the room, however, Fitzball found the MS. in a waste-paper basket, and Robinson sang the song the same night with ample success. A few years later the copyright was sold for £500.

it may be presumed) of January 31st, in noticing the second night of *La Sonnambula*, said frigidly that " it was played much better than on its first production, and Miss Rafter and Mr. Reeves were called for at the close and applauded." On this night the theatre was burnt down, and for some time Manchester was without its regular home of the drama.

During May and June Cooke's Circus was under the management of Mr. Robert Roxby, who engaged Reeves as his leading tenor for operatic productions. The *Manchester Courier* in noticing the final performance said : " In taking leave of this fine company we cannot refrain from bestowing some notice upon the musical entertainment, at the head of which stands Mr. J. Reeves. Now, Mr. Reeves has never from the first had any efficient support this season. Undoubtedly a vocalist of the highest order, he, for the reasons just indicated, has never appeared to due advantage. . . . Mr. Reeves . . . is destined, if we are not egregiously mistaken, to occupy, and that ere long, the very highest rank in his profession. He possesses a noble voice, a refined taste, and a facility and power of execution that need only a few of those nice finishing touches to be obtained only in the schools of Italy to make them perfect."

Reeves appears to have visited Glasgow more than once during 1844. Mr. Baynham says that in that year (the month is not given) Miller, the proprietor of the Adelphi Theatre, contemplated producing opera, " but could not come to terms with Sims Reeves." He sang at a performance of *The Messiah* on April 2nd, given by the Glasgow Musical Association, with Henry Phillips, Miss Whitnall, and Mrs. Bushe, and an advertisement in the *Glasgow Herald* of the same week runs as follows : " Mr. J. Reeve [sic], late of Drury Lane Theatre, of the Nobilities' Concerts, and primo tenore of the late grand oratorio, respectfully announces that he intends giving a grand concert of miscellaneous music in the City Hall on the evening of Tuesday, April 5th. He will be assisted by several artists of the first talent." No notice of this concert is to be found in the pages of the *Herald*.

During the summer months of 1844 Reeves probably continued to sing in the provinces, visiting Dublin in

July, where on August 19th he appeared as Tom Tug, on September 2nd as Francis Osbaldistone, and on September 24th as Henry Bertram. In the autumn he was engaged at the Theatre Royal, Williamson Square, Liverpool, then under the management of Madame Céleste and Benjamin Webster. The season commenced on October 14th with *Rob Roy*, Reeves playing Francis Osbaldistone. During November, Mr. and Mrs. Charles Kean were the attractions, when *Don Cæsar de Bazan* and *As You Like It* were produced. It was probably at this time that he was complimented by Charles Kean upon his rendering of the songs " Under the greenwood tree " and " Blow, blow, thou winter wind." He (Charles Kean), says Reeves, " strongly urged me at the time to go to London, promising to procure me an engagement with one of the principal theatres ; but I felt that I had so much more to learn before I made such a venture that I firmly refused his kind offer." The uninterrupted success of Reeves's subsequent career shows that he was right in not yielding to a temptation to which most men at the foot of the ladder would have succumbed. The season at Liverpool ended on December 11th with his benefit. He played Rodolpho in *Der Freischütz*, the advertisement also announcing " copious selections from Balfe's last three operas, *The Bohemian Girl*, *The Castle of Aymon*, and *The Daughter of St. Mark*. Tickets to be had of Mr. J. Reeves, 14, Russell Street."

Within five days he was at Glasgow fulfilling an engagement with the Glasgow Musical Association to sing once more in *The Messiah*. Of his performance, the *Glasgow Herald* has a notice which calls for passing mention. " Mr. Reeves," remarks the critic, " sustained his reputation as an excellent tenor, and the execution of the air ' Thou shalt break them with a rod of iron ' was remarkable for its grace and sweetness." Those who remember Reeves's fire and energy in this solo—regarded, indeed, as one of his supreme efforts—will be inclined to smile at the critic's description. But might there not be justification for it ? In Bordogni,[1] Reeves

---

[1] Bordogni, who held a high position at " Les Italiens," visited London in 1829 and sung in *La Gazza Ladra*. He was admitted to be an elegant singer and master of his art, but through his modesty of demeanour, his

found a master who believed in purity of tone and simplicity of style. Larousse writes of him : " *A l'époque où florissait Bordogni il y avait encore un public connaisseur ayant horreur des excentricités vocales, et ce public adoptait vite Bordogni.*" From this remark may be gathered the nature of the studies imposed upon Reeves. The statement by M. Fétis as to Bordogni's discovery of Reeves's tenor voice has already been discussed, and must be left as it stands ; but the interesting question remains whether the Paris master did not influence his pupil overmuch in the way of smoothness and absence of dramatic effect. If so, the " grace and smoothness " which so impressed the *Herald* critic can be understood. The musical qualifications of the average provincial reporter are, as a rule, not very high, but he would hardly have committed himself to so definite a statement without foundation. When singing in the fullness of his powers " Thou shalt dash them," Reeves was regarded by some musical purists as aiming at a theatrical effect. But this was in the narrow days when people drew a distinction between what they absurdly called " sacred " and " secular " music. They would hardly admit that the first could be, or ought to be, dramatic.

In the early part of 1845 we find him back at Liverpool. On January 25th he sang at a concert at the Music Hall, Bold Street, at which Miss Dolby and Miss Birch, the Sacred Harmonic Society " stars," assisted. In addition to Thalberg (the lion of the day), the universally popular John Parry and a Liverpool favourite lady vocalist, Miss Whitnall, took part. Referring to Miss Whitnall and to Reeves, the *Mercury* spoke of them as " two of our most accomplished local professionals," showing that in 1844–5 Reeves had established himself at Liverpool. Besides singing at concerts, he also had an engagement at the theatre. Mr. John Coleman speaks of him as taking the part of Edward the page in *Don Cæsar de Bazan,*

unaffected delivery, and possibly a certain lack of power, he failed to make any impression on a public who had been accustomed by Catalini and other Italian singers to believe in volume of tone. " Take him for all in all," wrote Mr. J. E. Cox (*Musical Recollections*), " I very much doubt whether I have heard a more finished or accomplished artist."

remarking that " the purity and beauty of his style were even at that time phenomenal. To this moment I recall with the delight of a revelation his singing of ' The Pilgrim of Love.' "

Once again he is at Glasgow. Mr. J. H. Anderson, better known as " The Wizard of the North," had built on Glasgow Green a magnificent structure which he called the City Theatre, and opened it on August 25th, 1845, with an operatic company in which Reeves (announced as Mr. J. S. Reeves) was the leading tenor. He also engaged a dramatic company with Mr. James Bennett and Barry Sullivan. Nothing but dissension followed the dual undertaking, caused by the rivalry between the leading actors and actresses, two ladies and two gentlemen having been enrolled for every line of business, and also, says Mr. John Coleman, who was a member of the company, " by the unprecedented coercion of nearly every member of the dramatic company into the chorus for the various operas." Music took the lead, and Reeves created a perfect furore in *The Bohemian Girl.*

Coleman, in his flamboyant style, says : " The termination of our opera season was signalised by a scene between Anderson and Sims Reeves of a somewhat grotesque character. During the last week *Lucia di Lammermoor* was announced, but the performance came to grief during the second act. Who was to blame I don't know. . . . Reeves placed the blame upon the band and the chorus ; Anderson placed it upon Reeves and his colleagues. One thing is quite certain, . . . Reeves refused to go on with the third act, and the audience resented it. . . . There was a row and measureless confusion.

" Saturday was the last night of the engagement, and when it came to a settlement, Anderson, by way of penalty for breach of agreement, mulcted Reeves & Co. their share of the receipts of the night on which the breakdown occurred. It was growing late (nearly twelve o'clock) ; Anderson was on the stage. Down came Reeves with ' his martial cloak around him ' and wrath upon his brow." Reeves, according to Coleman, demanded the money due to him. Anderson refused to pay, upon which the singer declined to quit the theatre until he had his share of the

receipts. Anderson, still obdurate, ordered every door
to be locked, which meant that Reeves and his company
would not be able to leave the building until Monday
morning.

"Without another word," continues Coleman, " off
went the Wizard. . . . I waited to see the end. Reeves,
Morley, Mr. and Mrs. Alban Croft held an eager and
excited conference, amidst which locks, bolts, etc., were
heard being shot, bolted, and barred in all parts of the
theatre. Then came the big bell of St. Mungo . . .
then the great tenor and his colleagues gave it up as a bad
job, and made their exit."

The above story must be received with caution—so
far, at least, as regards the manner in which it is told.
Mr. Coleman's book—a most irritating compilation,
full of irrelevancies and with not a date from beginning
to end—abounds in similar flourishes. Baynham is
silent on the subject of any disturbance, so also is the
Glasgow Herald. Reeves's engagement with Anderson
lasted from September 8th to September 19th, during
which time *Fra Diavolo*, *The Beggar's Opera*, and *Lucia
di Lammermoor* were produced. The night of the
alleged "disturbance" was his benefit, and on this
occasion, in addition to *Lucia*, he sang in *Rob Roy*.

In October Reeves was fulfilling an engagement at the
Theatre Royal, Dublin, under Calcraft's management.
An advertisement in the *Dublin Freeman's Journal* told
the Dublin playgoers that " Mr. and Mrs. Alban Croft and
Mr. Reeves, who are engaged for a few nights, will make
their first appearance," and on October 17th Reeves,
announced as " Mr. J. Reeves," started with *Lucia di
Lammermoor*. Concerning the opera, the *Freeman's
Journal* remarks that " with all its popularity and with all
our love for music, last Saturday was the first time on which
it was presented as a whole in Dublin." The *Journal*
adds : " Mr. Reeves is likely to become a great acquisition
if he becomes a fixture on our boards ; he has a strong
tenor voice and acts and sings well. He was much
applauded, especially in the magnificent finale of the last
act."

Other operas produced were *Sonnambula* and *Fra
Diavolo*, and his benefit was advertised for October 29th,

when he was to appear in *The Bohemian Girl* and in *The Beggar's Opera* compressed into two acts; but this benefit was destined not to come off, not at least on the night for which it had been fixed. On October 31st it was announced: " It is confidently hoped that Mr. J. S. Reeves will be sufficiently recovered from his severe accident to appear." But this hope was not realised, and not until November 17th was he able to complete his engagement. There is nothing in the *Journal* to indicate the nature of this accident, but in *My Jubilee* we get an account of it, the scene, with that perversity of inaccuracy which marks the autobiography, being placed in Cork. While playing in *Fra Diavolo* he narrowly escaped being fired into point blank by the soldiers. As it was, he was near enough to receive several wads, which went through his cloak, pierced his jacket, and inflicted severe contusions.

On November 18th he made his reappearance in *No Song, No Supper*, into which he introduced " The Death of Nelson." Why he chose the last suggests matter for speculation. Braham's concert party was then in Dublin, and on the same night Braham was singing at the Music Hall. The interesting question arises, did Reeves give " The Death of Nelson " as a sort of challenge, or was it an acknowledgment of the presence of the composer and veteran singer in the Irish capital? I am disposed to think the latter supposition is the true one. Throughout Reeves's career there is an entire absence of the braggadocio spirit; and as his star was rising while that of Braham had long been on the wane, he could afford to be generous. Years after they met and sang together, as will be recorded in the proper place, and there does not appear to be evidence of rivalry at any time on Reeves's part. Reeves took his benefit at Dublin on November 20th in *Rosina* and *The Waterman*, when he sang " The Thorn " and " Norah, the Pride of Kildare," and on this very night Braham at his concert gave " The Death of Nelson." This could hardly have been mere coincidence; it may be regarded rather as returning Reeves's compliment. Whether the two forgathered at this time there is no means of knowing. One can only hope that they did.

CHAPTER VII

1845–1847

Reeves again takes lessons of Bordogni in Paris and of Mazzucato in Milan. Is engaged to sing in *Lucia di Lammermoor* at La Scala. His association with Catherine Hayes. The critical Milanese audience. Great success of both singers. Reeves is congratulated by Rubini. Rubini's exquisite singing and his mannerisms. Reeves's opinion of Rubini. Reeves compared with Rubini and Braham. Reeves sings at the principal Italian theatres and in Vienna. He returns to London.

TOWARDS the end of 1845 Reeves had arrived at the turning-point of his career. He was now in a position to defray the expenses of his studies under Continental masters. In referring in *My Jubilee* to his visit to Bordogni in 1843 his words are : " After a time I went by Signor Bordogni's advice to Milan, where I placed myself under Signor Mazzucato, Director of the Milan Conservatorio," the inference being that no considerable interval elapsed between the two courses of study. But as a matter of fact quite two years passed over before he went to Italy, and it is reasonable to assume that Bordogni gave him this advice not in 1843, but on the occasion of his second visit to Paris. This was either at the end of 1845 or the beginning of 1846, as he speaks of travelling from Paris to Milan by diligence " in the depth of an almost Siberian winter." At Paris, he says, he made " a long stay, occupying myself with my singing lessons." These lessons could have been given by no one save Bordogni. This is not expressly stated, but there can hardly be any doubt, as Bordogni gave him a letter of introduction to Mazzucato, which, as Reeves tells us, he delivered to the Milan master five days after his arrival. It is to be noted that Reeves speaks of 1845 (*My Jubilee*, p. 173) as the year in which he made his appearance in opera at Milan. But it was in 1846.

Mazzucato had attained a considerable reputation as a

composer, as a teacher, and as a writer of musical treatises, and subsequently was Principal of the Milan Conservatorio. His opera *Luigi V, re di Francia*, produced in 1843, was well received, and so also was his *Esmeralda*; but the star of Verdi was rising and the coming composer's genius was asserting itself with irresistible force. Mazzucato had the temerity to enter into direct competition with the new-comer. He reset *Ernani*, which was produced in 1844, immediately after Verdi's version, and as Larousse puts it, "*une chute éclatante fut le résultat de cette tentative audacieuse.*" After this defeat Mazzucato let composition severely alone and devoted himself to teaching and writing. That he was an excellent master is universally admitted, and his experience in producing dramatic effects could not have been otherwise than of the greatest possible service to his English pupil.

Reeves's naturalness and sociability soon made him hosts of friends in Milan, and the contrast between life in the musical sunny Italian city and that in the commercial towns in the Midlands, with their murky skies and their unlovely streets, must have made his sojourn in Milan a perpetual delight. Indeed, he says as much. It was not long before Mazzucato, struck by his exceptional voice and talent, introduced him to Merelli, the impresario of La Scala, who was equally impressed, and the result was an engagement to sing in *Lucia di Lammermoor*, then all the rage in every musical city on the Continent.[1]

It was a daring venture on the part of both. No one could know better than Merelli the jealousy with which Italian singers regarded the intrusion of a foreigner—especially an Englishman—into their ranks. The operatic artists of Italy came from all classes; as a rule they were not well educated; they believed in their voices and nothing else, and the fact that they had been the pets of the well-to-do since the days of Farinelli and Tenducci gave them a very exalted idea of their

---

[1] "Under the Maestro Bajetti, Mr. Reeves's schooling may be regarded to have terminated for finish of expression and refinement of method, and then he made his debut at the Scala" (*Illustrated London News*, December 11th, 1847). I can find no confirmation of this statement.—C. E. P.

SIMS REEVES AND CATHERINE HAYES IN "LUCIA DI LAMMERMOOR."
From a photograph by the Fotografia Americana, Genoa (1846).

importance. Reeves was well aware of the stupendous obstacles which he had to encounter, but he never lost heart, though he must have wondered at his audacity in jumping at one bound from an English provincial theatre, with a scratch company and a ragged orchestra, to the very hub of the operatic world, where every note, every gesture, the pronunciation of every word—for it must not be forgotten that Reeves was singing in a strange tongue—would be subjected to the keenest criticism.

Merelli was a man of great experience. He had faith in his audience and the audience believed in him. He knew they would appreciate what was good and he had confidence in his protégé. Any disaffection in his company he could control, for, like most impresarios, he was a despot. But there may have been another reason why he was hopeful of success. A brilliant Irishwoman had taken the susceptible Italians by storm, and had won their hearts as much by her personal beauty as by the sweetness of her vocalisation and the charm of her acting. Catherine Hayes made her debut at Marseilles in 1844 and had won victory after victory in Italy, and in no city was she more appreciated than in Milan. Catherine Hayes was to play Lucia to Reeves's Edgardo, and thus Merelli was doubly armed.

The curious thing is that in all the English records of Sims Reeves's first appearance in *Lucia* not a word is said about Catherine Hayes. Reeves himself in his reference to his debut is silent in regard to Miss Hayes—a most unaccountable omission, for elsewhere he is most enthusiastic in his praise of her singing. He speaks of her as the beau ideal of Lucia, and declares that of all the Lucias he had ever sung with Catherine Hayes was the sweetest of them all. He puts her before Jenny Lind.

The non-mention of Miss Hayes is all the more inexplicable because, without desiring to take from Reeves the smallest atom of the triumph which is justly his, one is at liberty to doubt whether that triumph would have been so complete had he not been stimulated by so perfect a Lucia. There is another point worthy of consideration. Throughout his career, Reeves was subject to a nervousness which his audiences never suspected. Only his indomitable will, his love for his art, and his belief in himself enabled him to contend against this temperamental weakness.

While studying with Mazzucato, Reeves would without a doubt be a constant attendant at La Scala and would know the trial that awaited him. " A first night at the Scala," writes Willert Beale in *The Enterprising Impresario*, " is proverbial for being the most severe ordeal that either singers or composers can encounter. . . . The Milanese pride themselves upon the rigour of their criticism. . . . They applaud and laugh at the artists during the performance of a solo, approving one phrase, and condemning the next. Their applause is the most boisterous and enthusiastic it is possible to imagine ; they hiss, hoot, laugh, and whistle with still greater zeal, if the unfortunate singer happens to displease them."

It is only reasonable to conceive that when the English tenor faced the critically expectant audience which crowded the huge La Scala on that memorable night of October 29th, 1846, and in an opera in which Duprez and Rubini were thought to be unsurpassable, that he must have felt a trepidation which in one less powerfully equipped might have led to disaster. But in Catherine Hayes he had a friendly and sympathetic associate. She was English-speaking. She, too, was a stranger, and one may be sure that she was as anxious as he himself that he should succeed. It is but natural that there should have been mutual encouragement. At any rate, there was mutual triumph, and what an eminent critic, Lampertini, a Professor of the Conservatorio, thought of that triumph he has set down in the *Gazzetta Privilegiata di Milano* of October 28th, 1846. Of his notice the following is an English equivalent :

" To alternate the operas performed in the present season at the T. R. Teatro alla Scala we had last night a revival of that very charming opera *Lucia di Lammermoor*, a genial work which makes one regret all the more the lamentable physical condition of its distinguished composer. The desire to listen once more to those delicate harmonic thoughts, as well as the debut of representatives of the principal parts, accounted for the large audience which attended the performance in spite of the continual

bad weather. Of the new singers the palm must be
awarded to Miss Hayes, with her sweet voice, her
clearness of diction, her training in a school of pure
vocalisation, her accurate execution, and her perfect
intonation. Ashton was represented by Signor Bozzani
and the Edgardo was Mr. Reeves, an Englishman. We
have not space to particularise the fine gifts and faults of
these new singers, but it is only fair to say that if Miss
Hayes won continuous plaudits as hearty as they were
spontaneous, those won by Signor Bozzani were not less
so and augured well for his future.

" A flattering reception was given to Mr. Reeves,
whose principal gifts are an extraordinarily powerful voice
and an energy which in large theatres will stand him in
good stead. But apart from his pronunciation we should
like to see him when he is more used to opera-houses in
order to appreciate better his acting. It would be well
to consider him in moments when he is not called upon
for so much energy, and we should like to decide whether
that energy was the result of the natural excitement of
a first performance and in consequence somewhat
exaggerated. It would be interesting to discover if the
great resisting power of his voice can make us forget the
sweet and graceful singing and the melodic agility which
we have admired in a few other singers. These points
can only be settled on some future occasion. . . . He
has now with him Miss Hayes, who has only need to envy
his power."

To conquer a Milanese audience and to win the warm
praise of a Milanese musical critic was a superb victory,
but the crowning success arrived when, coming off the
stage flushed with success, he was visited in his dressing-
room by Rubini, and heartily congratulated. It was a
generous act, for Rubini was the most illustrious tenor
of his time, though if the description given by J. E.
Cox (*Musical Recollections*, 1872) of his singing be
correct, it is doubtful whether the musical critic of
to-day would confirm the opinion which was held in the
thirties and forties. " Rubini's voice," Mr. Cox tells
us, " was of the richest quality of a compass of eleven or
twelve notes from about E flat or F to B or C. His
intonation was of the purest, and his delivery free from all

impediment, but he may be said to have introduced that system of tremolo of which there has been so much reason to complain in hosts of modern singers. . . . His shake was excellent, and he was never weary of introducing it, accompanied with an overwhelming multitude of roulades. . . . He had also a habit of forcing out his voice, as it were, in gusts and so suddenly withdrawing it as to be nearly inaudible. This was done on no fixed principle, but simply to produce a succession of contrasts. . . . His roulades were destitute of variety. . . . Whoever heard him once might be said to have heard him always ; for he poured out the whole store of his embellishments in a single air, employing them indiscriminately—according to the Italian fashion— which is now (1872) altogether lost and gone."

Mr. Cox, who had strong opinions which he had no hesitation in expressing, may have been thinking of Rubini in his decadence, when his voice was " a wreck, and his peculiarities had become mannerisms " (F. A. M. in Grove's *Dictionary of Music*), but even in his prime the great tenor must at times have been exceedingly irritating. Mr. H. F. Chorley says : " He would walk through a good third of any given opera languidly, giving the notes correctly and little more—in a duet blending his voice intimately with that of his partner (in this he was un- surpassed) ; but when his own moment arrived there was no longer coldness or hesitation, but a passion, a fervour, a putting forth to the utmost of every resource of con- summate vocal art and emotion which converted the most incredulous, and satisfied those till then disposed to treat him as one whose reputation had been overrated." Rubini had mean features pitted with smallpox, and his figure was awkward, and he dressed in any costume which was given him without reference to the character he was to portray. But in spite of his defects, he ruled the stage by the geniality of his expression and " by the mere act of singing more completely than anyone, woman or man, has been able to do in my time," is Mr. Chorley's final judgment.[1]

[1] The writer of Rubini's biography in Grove's *Dictionary of Music* speaks of him as " the foundation and *raison d'être* of the whole phase of Italian opera that succeeded the Rossinian period "—that is to say, the

Sims Reeves does not agree with Mr. Cox so far as the compass of Rubini's voice was concerned, and in the other points is more in accord with Mr. Chorley. He says : " I knew the *Lucia* (*My Jubilee*, p. 102) before going to Italy, and had heard Rubini sing the part of Edgardo at Her Majesty's Theatre. Rubini had an extraordinary tenor voice of the finest quality, but his high notes, extending to E flat and even F, were quite beyond the tenor register. He struck the high F in the tenor part of the *finale* to *I Puritani*." Bellini is known to have composed this opera as well as *La Sonnambula* with Rubini by his side, and often Rubini sang his part as Bellini wrote it. In the final piece he had written the note D flat in the tenor part, and Rubini, looking over his shoulder, misread it, singing F natural instead. " If you can sing it, you shall have it," said Bellini, and he at once altered the passage so as to give Rubini this exceptionally high note, which at first performance is said to have had a thrilling effect. Reeves adds that " though Rubini was no actor, he was truly a dramatic singer ; the dramatic effect being produced by the tone, the accent, the intense feeling with which he sang."

Rubini had one great defect—his peculiar egotism. He only cared for the songs he had to sing, nothing for the general effect, nothing for the character he was personating. It was a musical display at which he aimed— the perfection of vocal excellence. The reputation of many Italian tenors rests upon this mechanical perfection. Giuglini, who, like Rubini, was an indifferent actor, may be cited as an example within living memory. To hear Giuglini was like listening to some beautiful instrument exquisitely played, but there admiration ended. Sims Reeves, admirer as he was of Rubini, never copied him.

Donizetti and Bellini school. No wonder, it was said, that he and Bellini were born for each other. Both had their day of success, but Rubini, unfortunately, has left two legacies not yet forgotten. One is the detestable vibrato and the other " that species of musical sob produced by the reper- cussion of a prolonged note before the final cadence, which, electrifying at first as a new effect, has become one of the commonest of vocal vulgarisms." *Pagliacci*, where libretto and vocal phrase justify its use, possibly furnishes an exception. Caruso by the same method has produced a prodigious effect.—HERBERT REEVES.

6

He had no straining after the cultivation of the refinement
of mechanism. He was purely natural. He had ever
the human note. His tone was unlike that of any
musical instrument ever devised. The Italian critics must
have been conscious of this, and it probably came upon
them as a revelation, so different was his style and volume
of sound from those of their own singers, with their
prettinesses engrafted on the eternal *bel canto*.

Yet to Rubini, Reeves may have owed something.
Reeves excelled in contrast, but, unlike Rubini, he did not
exaggerate it, nor was it ever introduced simply to
astonish. He always had a dramatic purpose in view.
A better instance can hardly be cited than his rendering
of " Deeper and deeper still " ; but how much of the
impassioned emotion he infused into this famous recitative
was due to Rubini's influence and how much to Braham's
reading it would be hard to say. In " The Recollections
of Mr. Joseph Heywood " (*Cornhill Magazine*, December
1865) we have a discriminating criticism of Braham's
method. Mr. Heywood writes that he " was doubtless
among the greatest singers of any age or country ; but
although the stamp of genius was on everything that he did,
strangely mixed up with it was a love of gallery popularity
which led him continually into faults of taste. What could
exceed the profound pathos of his ' Deeper and deeper
still ' ? His ' Lash me into madness ' still rings through
all my fibres ; but then, again, just at the end of ' Waft
her, angels,' with which he had seemed to lift one into
paradise, he must needs roar out an interminable cadence,
hideous and vulgar, for which the gods cheered him, but
for which in sober truth he deserved to be hissed." [1]

---

[1] In the same article Mr. Heywood draws a vivid picture of Braham's
singing in *Israel in Egypt*. " A little, thick-set man," he says, " with a
light brown wig all over his eyes, a generally common appearance and a
most unmistakably Jewish aspect, got up to sing one single line of recitative.
He stood with his head well on one side, held his music also on one side,
and far out before him gave a funny little stamp with his foot, and then
proceeded to lay in his provision of breath with such a tremendous shrug
of his shoulders and swelling of his chest that I very nearly burst out
laughing. He said ' But the children of Israel went on dry land ' and then
paused ; and every sound was hushed throughout that great space ; and
then, as if carved out upon the solid stillness came those three little
words ' *through the sea.*' Our breath failed and our pulses ceased to beat

Barring the cadenza, this description fits Reeves's rendering of " Deeper and deeper still " and " Waft her, angels," exactly. Mr. Heywood's period was anterior to that of Reeves's in oratorio, or we might have had from him an instructive comparison between these two great English tenors. Reeves, no doubt, had many opportunities of studying Braham's singing, but he could not have heard him in his prime, as between 1831 and 1839 Braham was wholly engaged in dissipating his huge fortune in ruinous speculation, and when he returned to the stage and concert-room his voice was showing the ravages of time.

While in Milan Reeves had an experience of the " fatherly " way singers in those days were regarded by the authorities. He was suffering from a sore throat and was quite unable to sing. The doctor attached to La Scala was, however, of a contrary opinion, and after examining the larynx declared that he could sing if he liked. But Reeves, with characteristic spirit, refused to make the attempt and the authorities resolved to use force. A squad of gendarmes called at his lodgings with a carriage, put the obstinate singer into it, and drove to the theatre. Force, however, had no avail. " I was firm," writes Reeves, " in my resolve neither to injure my voice nor to pain the ears of a public which had hitherto applauded me." He won the day and the resolve which he then made he adhered to with very few exceptions throughout his long career—a resolve which cost him many thousands of pounds, to say nothing of the utterly unfounded reputation for caprice, and worse, which he had to endure.

Merelli, the impresario of La Scala, was also director of opera-houses in various parts of Italy, and also of the Imperial Opera House at Vienna. As under his contracts he could order his singers to appear at any of the theatres under his control, Reeves had the advantage of singing at the principal Italian opera-houses. Then followed Vienna, and by this time five months' salary had accumulated. The contract had been cunningly

and we bent our heads as all the wonder of the miracle seemed to pass over us with those accents—awful, radiant, resonant, triumphant. He sat down while the whole house thundered its applause."

drawn up so that, writes Reeves, " although I had the right to recover, if I could, any money that might be due to me, I could not by reason of nonpayment at once terminate my engagement." I was determined not, if I could avoid it, to go on singing for nothing. But I could not leave Vienna without getting my passport properly *viséd* and it was doubtful whether . . . permission to quit Vienna would be given to me without the consent of my director." In his dilemma he applied to Lord Burghesh, who was then Ambassador at Vienna, a man of musical attainments and connected with the Royal Academy of Music, where Reeves had made his acquaintance. The Ambassador's influence was all-powerful; Reeves obtained his passport, but whether he also obtained his money cannot be said.

The date of Reeves's return to London is difficult to fix. He was in Italy quite six months after his first appearance in Milan and probably longer, and there was also the Vienna engagement. He had fluttered his wings successfully, his fame had spread, and the time had now come for higher flights in the land of his birth.

CHAPTER VIII

1847

ALL the biographers of Sims Reeves are contented with repeating the statement that his first appearance in London after his return from Italy was at Drury Lane in *Lucia*, with which Jullien opened his campaign of " English opera." But this is not the fact. Mr. W. Kuhe, in *My Musical Recollections*, speaks of being present in 1847 at a " miscellaneous performance " at Drury Lane, " when Sims Reeves, an unknown tenor, came, without any preliminary flourish of trumpets, and, consequently, little or no curiosity was manifested in his appearance. He sang ' Fra Poco ' from *Lucia*, and hardly had he concluded the opening recitative when it became clear to the whole audience that the future king of English tenors stood before them."

Mr. Kuhe is not quite correct here. Reeves did not sing " Fra Poco," but an air from Verdi's *Ernani*. The date was April 17th, 1847, and the occasion the benefit of Vincent Wallace. The *Musical World*, in its notice, speaks of the " first appearance of a new English tenor, Mr. J. S. Reeves. Mr. Reeves produced a great impression. His voice is powerful and full-toned, and his singing is characterised by sweet expression and taste." The *Times* was also eulogistic, but in a more restrained tone.

On June 21st Reeves sang at a function where it would hardly be expected he would be found—at one of

the Antient Concerts. The performances of the Antient
Concerts, in spite of the patronage of Royalty, of the
nobility, and of the Church, were more often than not
the sport of critics. Each concert was presided over by
a director who had the fixing of the programme, and as
few of the lords and bishops had much musical knowledge
this may account for the odd mixtures sometimes placed
before the audience. George III, who was a regular
attendant, had, however, no doubt as to his capacity.
" Watch my finger," he said one day to young Cramer
the organist, " and take the time from me." The advent
of Prince Albert, who really had some musical proficiency,
improved matters somewhat, but in 1847 the Antient
Concerts had outlived their day.

The chief soloists of the institution in its early days had
permanent posts. Bartleman, without doubt a great
artist, was for years the principal bass, and Henry Phillips
succeeded him. Vaughan, the tenor, was another fixture.
The chorus was rarely allowed to travel outside Handel's
oratorios, and then only isolated selections were given.
The sopranos were specially imported from Lancashire,
presumably because the voices in this county were
supposed to be better than those in any other. Lancashire ladies notwithstanding, the chorus at times sang
villainously. Here is the *Morning Post* criticism of a
concert in 1828 under the presidency of Earl Fortescue.
Two selections were given from Mozart's *Requiem*, the
" Rex tremendae " and the " Benedictus." " Both,"
says the *Post*, " were inefficiently executed. The chorus
singers bellow loud enough in the middle of an old
chorus, but as for attacking a ' point ' with vigour, it is
out of the question ; it really gave us pain to hear the
drowsy drones begin ' Rex ' as if they had just recovered
from a swoon."

The extraordinary liberties taken by soloists, both
vocal and instrumental, which were permissible at other
concerts were sternly prohibited at the Antient Concerts
—an interdiction, however, rather to their credit. As an
example of ornamentation run mad, Henry Phillips
instances a freak of Lindley, the distinguished 'cellist of
the twenties and thirties, who was given to extravagant
roulades. At a certain musical festival he accompanied

Braham in " O Liberty, thou choicest treasure," at a morning performance in the Cathedral, and when he came to the concluding symphony he played, to the astonishment of the whole orchestra, in harmonics " Over the hills and far away." This was bad enough, but what was equally extraordinary was that the audience were in no way outraged. Phillips adds gravely : " The bishop and nobility present were delighted and a repetition was immediately demanded. Lindley laughed to such a degree and took too much snuff, in both of which feasts Dragonetti joined, that he said he could not play it again, and he would not, and did not." Such frivolity would have shocked the patrons of the Antient Concerts beyond measure. Mrs. Salmon once essayed an elaborate cadenza at the end of " From mighty kings," upon which Greatorex, the director, started the full organ upon her. For an instant all was confusion, the lady sat down and became fearfully red, and a noble lord inquired what was the matter. " A cadenza, my lord," said Greatorex. " Oh," said his lordship, who probably had not the least idea what a cadenza was, and the concert proceeded with its usual solemnity.

Braham was never asked to sing at the Antient Concerts, so Phillips says, to his intense disappointment, and this disappointment, no doubt, was the foundation of his sarcasm at the expense of Vaughan, the tenor. At a dinner party at which Braham was present the matter was discussed, and someone remarked that Vaughan was a most chaste singer. " Do you know," said Braham, " what a chaste singer is ?   I'll tell you : a chaste singer is one who never ravishes the ears of his audience."

The directors prided themselves on giving no music which had not stood the test of time, and on engaging no singers who had not received the *cachet* of public approbation.   One wonders how it came about that a tenor who was not known—for his solitary contribution to Vincent Wallace's concert could not count for much—was engaged.   It may have been due to the musical Earl of Westmorland, who, when Lord Burghesh, had befriended Reeves in Vienna and knew his powers ; or it may have been due to Tom Cooke, who was nominally the first violin.

But to sing at the Antient Concerts was no particular advancement, and Reeves owed little to the privilege. His choice of songs was narrowed by a sort of censorship and he would not be allowed to sing what he liked, but what the committee approved. They probably had a regard for the feelings of the Archbishop of York, who presided in the place of the King of Hanover. Reeves chose the air " A te fra tante " from Mozart's *Davide Penitente*, which, said the *Times*, " was rendered with much expression by Mr. Reeves, the English tenor, who has passed a considerable time in Italy, not without advantage."

The *Athenæum* was guarded, and it was apparently conscious that the new tenor was likely to be a dangerous rival to Mr. Lockey, who it had pronounced a month previous to be " our best tenor." It was of opinion that Reeves sang Mozart's air " impressively rather than delicately," and added, " the vocal studies of Mr. Reeves appear to have been conducted on the modern Italian fashion—which is to develop the voice to its utmost volume without reference to those finer executive powers which the less *ex*-clamatory works of the older school demand. . . . He has striking, rich, full tones. We have no opportunity to speak of his mezzoforte or piano, and as little of his facility." The notice cannot be called enthusiastic ; perhaps it was influenced by the depressing nature of the concert generally, despite the attraction of Madame Dorus Gras, who some months later was to share the honours with Reeves at Drury Lane. Pischek, the Bohemian baritone, who just then was all the rage, also took part, but his contribution, " Deeper and deeper still," transposed to suit his voice, could hardly have added to the cheerfulness of the evening.

Eighteen hundred and forty-seven was the year of the Jenny Lind fever, and in the autumn she toured the provinces, appearing in Edinburgh in September. Howard Glover was the conductor of her concerts, and amongst the artists he engaged was Sims Reeves. Already Reeves was a notability, and soon after his singing at the Antient Concerts Jullien secured his services for his forthcoming operatic venture at Drury Lane Theatre,

the *Athenæum* of July 24th announcing that " a contemporary informs us that Miss Birch, Mr. Reeves, and
Mr. Whitworth have been already engaged by Jullien for
his Drury Lane Operas." Between this date and
September Reeves's movements are difficult to trace.
It was the summer season, and his engagements were
probably few and those most likely in the provinces. At
any rate, the Jenny Lind tour seems to provide the first
definite announcement.

Jenny Lind was advertised at Edinburgh to appear on
September 13th, but she was indisposed and the date was
postponed to the 16th, a second concert being given on the
20th. At the latter Reeves sang " Una furtiva lagrima,"
and at the former he and Madame F. Lablache between
them sang songs by Howard Glover, of which the critic
of the *Edinburgh Evening Courant* remarked : " One
piece would have been a reasonable allowance, and
would have given Mr. J. Reeves and Madame Lablache
better scope for the display of their talents in something
more classical and refined. . . . The songs allotted him
did not give him an opportunity for display as would
have been desirable." Reeves probably had no choice
in the matter. It was not likely Howard Glover would
lose the chance of exploiting his own wares—and there
were the music publishers to be thought of. After
Reeves's tremendous success at Drury Lane, Glover's
" Love wakes and weeps " and " Voices from home "
were extensively advertised " as sung by Mr. Sims Reeves
at Jenny Lind's concerts at Edinburgh." When Reeves
subsequently sang these ballads in London, Mr. Chorley
reproved him and denounced them—and no doubt
justly—as " namby-pamby."

It must be confessed that during his career Sims
Reeves was responsible for the introduction and popularity
of hosts of songs now buried and without the slightest
chance of exhumation. It is fair to urge, however,
that a very large proportion of the public found pleasure
in vocal sentimentality of this kind. Critics are not the
only people in the world, and if classical and operatic
music is above the heads of the " crowds," this is no
reason why they should not have that which appeals to
them. Moreover, the fact is undeniable that whatever

Sims Reeves sang he invested with a charm which dwelt
in the memory of the listener, quite apart from the
music, " namby-pamby " though the latter might be.
The tempestuous Kitty Clive, angry with herself for
being moved to tears by Garrick's acting, exclaimed,
" Damn him !   I believe he could act a gridiron " ;
and so in the same sense could Sims Reeves sing one.

Meanwhile, Jullien was energetically making preparations for his operatic campaign, and in pursuit of " stars "
had even journeyed to Italy, hoping to secure Catherine
Hayes (known on the Continent as La Hayez), a hope
which was not realised.   In 1847 Louis Antonio Jullien
was at the height of his popularity, and it is no exaggeration to say that the lovers of classical music owe much
to the musician whom some prim critics of his day described as appertaining to a mountebank.   The charge
was utterly groundless.   Jullien believed, it is true, in
advertisement and was a genius in the art, but he never
promised anything that he did not endeavour to perform
faithfully, and he was only contented when he had
secured the best material available.   With a faith in the
British public's love for good music—a faith that was
justified—Jullien gave his shilling " promenaders "
Mozart and Beethoven, performed in a style which
equalled that of the exclusive Philharmonic Society, and
went far beyond that of the prosy and pretentious Antient
Concerts.   It was a bold experiment, for the overdressed,
boisterous, and pleasure-loving promenader of 1847 was
a very different individual from the decorous, slightly
dowdy, Queen's Hall area patron.   Jullien's " Beethoven
nights " were successes, and while his eccentricities and
affectations pleased the eyes of the groundlings, the
judicious were not so grieved as to be unconscious of the
inherent merit of his productions.

Jullien had an instinct for " effect."   So long as he was
talked about, he did not care whether he was criticised
favourably or unfavourably.   I have a vivid recollection
of his conducting his promenade concerts in the fifties.
Whether it was due to the tailor's art or to his overpowering personality, I do not know, but the impression
produced upon my boyish mind was that of a colossal
figure, a grand torso, wildly waving arms, and, especially,

of snow-white kid gloves. The shortness of his legs was not apparent. The crash of the final chord over, he sank, to all appearance exhausted, into a magnificent throne-like arm-chair, superbly upholstered. Mopping his forehead with a delicate pocket-handkerchief, taking care to show the blazing diamond ring on his little finger, he was seemingly deaf to the applause thundering round him. But in due time he rose with majesty, and one saw nothing but a vast area of shirt-front (ornamented, it was said, by representations of landscapes in embroidery) in the centre of which sparkled another diamond. His sweeping bow was graciousness itself. Anon a page-boy with three rows of gilt buttons sprouting from neck to waist appeared, bearing a salver on which was a second pair of white kid gloves, and these the great conductor put on in full sight of the audience before entering upon the next piece. When he conducted Beethoven, he used a specially jewelled baton. It was all very harmless vanity, and suggested a childish love of display rather than an offensive conceit. Moreover, in conducting his " madness " had considerable method. " I have had the honour," says one of his orchestra, writing in the *British Bandsman*, " of playing under his baton. . . . I unhesitatingly assert that with all his peculiarities and study of the picturesque, he was the best conductor I ever played under. . . . One felt it was impossible to go wrong."

Jullien had a great scheme of founding a school of English Opera, and he set out with ideas which were not less vague than those of his predecessors who had essayed to settle this vexed question. He appears to have had some dream of a possible connection between the Royal Academy of Music and English Opera, but it was all speculation, for most certainly he would have had no encouragement from the solemn Doctors of Music and Professors of the Academy. When he issued his advertisement of his opera season, however, he had abandoned this notion, and had formulated a definition of an English School of Opera which, no doubt, he thought meant something, but which really signified very little.

Everybody wanted English opera of some sort. The *Athenæum* approved of Jullien's enterprise, pointing out that the English taste for opera must be strong to have held out when " so inadequately met—nay, more, to have so far vindicated itself as to encourage the attempt towards something better in every point of view." However this may be, one thing at least was certain—the musical play of Shield, Storace, Dibdin, and Bishop was dying. Bishop's English travesties of Italian opera were in no better case. The thoughts and energies of English musicians were in the direction of opera of a much higher standard than heretofore. Balfe had already written sixteen operas, and his *Bohemian Girl* had achieved a success which marked the beginning of a new epoch in English musical history. Vincent Wallace had produced *Maritana,* and his *Matilda of Hungary,* if not so popular as its predecessor, had a long run. Benedict had written *The Crusaders,* Macfarren *Don Quixote,* and J. L. Hatton was giving promise with distinctly clever and melodious operettas—a promise which somehow he failed to fulfil. The time chosen by Jullien for his venture was clearly propitious.

It was the brilliant Frenchman's weakness to be too much under the spell of his sanguine temperament and his vivid imagination. Berlioz remarks dryly that "Jullien in his incontestable, uncontested character of madman had engaged a splendid orchestra, a first-rate chorus, and a very fair set of singers ; he had forgotten nothing but the repertoire." With the all-absorbing idea that English opera must be the object in view, Jullien considered that *Lucia* was only subsidiary to Balfe's *Maid of Honour.* Jullien was at that time not nearly so mad as Berlioz would have one believe. He had promised the British public English opera, and he meant to give it them—if he could. He had unbounded audacity, he believed in his good luck, and good luck he certainly had in the advent of Sims Reeves. Berlioz admits as much. Yet even Jullien did not know the tower of strength he had in the great English tenor, and but for his feverish desire to keep faith with the public and his determination to carry out his contract with Balfe the end of his experiment might have been different.

What he failed to realise was the stupendous financial obstacles in the way of success. Italian opera in England would have been impossible but for the guarantee of a subscription list, which was the first thought of an impresario, as the records of Ebers, Lumley, and Gye amply prove. Jullien made no attempt to invite subscriptions. He trusted entirely to the quality and completeness of his productions and to his own popularity. It was a leap in the dark. He forgot that the ordinary paying public outside the aristocracy had to be educated up to his standard, and that this would take time. His system of lavish expenditure meant an outlay for which no adequate return could be expected immediately. However, he started with undaunted courage.

His advertisements show that he did not intend to hide his light under a bushel. The advertisements were of an unusual length for those days. Besides his soloists, among whom Madame Dorus Gras and Sims Reeves (advertised thus for the first time—it is said that he took the name of " Sims " at the suggestion of Madame Puzzi) occupied the most prominent positions, the others including Miss Birch, W. H. Weiss, and H. Whitworth, he engaged an orchestra every member of which was a distinguished instrumentalist, while the chorus was " selected from the two Italian operas, neither of which (by itself) was so effective as could be desired, one possessing the best sopranos and contraltos, and the other the best basses and tenors." The name of every member of the company was given—orchestra, chorus, the *corps de ballet*, even down to the supernumerary ladies and the children for the pantomime ; Sir Henry Bishop and Messrs. Planché, Grieve, and Telbin were " attached to the establishment " in various capacities ; the " comic pantomime " was to be written by Alfred Crowquil and Albert Smith ; and lastly, as his *chef d'orchestre* he engaged the most prominent French musician at that time, Hector Berlioz.[1] Nothing that was worth mentioning was left out, and with this brave array he opened Drury Lane Theatre on December 6th with *Lucia*,

---

[1] " As a vigorous conductor, Hector Berlioz was conspicuous. On one occasion at rehearsal the harps with their cases were put together to enclose a small space wherein he could change his shirt, the operation being necessary in consequence of his intense exertions."—T. C. Croger, *Notes on Conductors and Conducting.*

reverting to Scott's original title of *The Bride of Lammermoor*, and dressing the company in costumes suitable to the story instead of the incongruous Italian garb which had formerly prevailed.

The success of the first night was stupendous. Sims Reeves electrified the house and his triumph was complete. He had found himself, and that night he established a hold upon the British public which was never weakened for nearly fifty years, even when his glorious voice was but an echo of what it was in his prime.

The critics were unanimous. Never was so loud a pæan of praise sounded over any singer as that which was heard in every quarter. It would be wearisome to quote from all the eulogiums which appeared in the newspapers of the day, but a few may be noticed as representing different sections of the public. That of the *Times* has appeared in several biographies of Reeves, and it is only necessary to reproduce its salient portions. " So rare a success," wrote the critic, " has seldom been achieved by an English vocalist. . . . The duet in the first act showed the complete management of the voice, and the ability of the artist to adapt it to the softest expressions of tenderness ; but it left an impression that he would scarcely be equal to the terrible passion of the second act. But this act was his triumph. The malediction delivered with the greatest force took the audience greatly by surprise ; and the zeal with which he abandoned himself to the strong emotion of the scene produced an electrical effect. . . . At the fall of the curtain the first impulse of the audience was an universal cry of Reeves."

The *Sunday Times*, catering for the pit and amphitheatre, considered that " the public owe to the taste and discrimination of the management the introduction of Mr. J. S. Reeves, the best tenor unquestionably on the English stage. . . . He received the gratifying verdict of the audience of unanimous and unqualified approval. What renders this triumph more extraordinary was that Mr. Reeves was labouring under an attack of influenza so severe that it was doubtful until the last moment whether he could attempt to sing. His reluctance to disappoint the public, and feeling perhaps that a disappointment might be considered unfavourably, determined him at all hazards to make a trial, and the result has been as we have seen."

In the concluding words the *Sunday Times* touches upon a point which must have been uppermost in the minds of many. "We have now at Drury Lane," it remarks, "a genuine National Opera which only requires support to render it immediately successful. Will the aristocratic patronage hitherto bestowed upon the Italian lyric drama now condescend to support its own artists? We shall see. At all events, they can no longer plead the superiority of the foreign, for their neglect of English art." There is evidence that the aristocracy was won over. A few nights after the first performance it was found that there was not enough seats in the better parts of the house, and an extra number of stalls were provided, and also an additional row in the dress circle. Paragraphs also appeared noting the presence of noble personages.

The *Athenæum*, the organ of the cultured intellectuals, was roused out of its habitual calm. "The success of Mr. Reeves amounted to a furore—and deservedly so," it began. "His voice is neither a forced-up baritone nor an oily and unnatural counter-tenor; he is a legitimate tenor of rich and sweet quality, sufficient in compass and so adequate in power that we have but to beg its owner not to over-exert it in passages of passion, however tempted by the eagerness of the moment, the applause of his audience, or the canons of the school in which he has studied. Mr. Reeves seems to have cultivated his *piano* and *mezzo-piano* sedulously, and his voice appears to be carefully graduated rather than worked into flexibility. But his great merit . . . is the dramatic and musical earnestness with which he throws himself into his part. The character was throughout sung and played with passion, yet without a shade of coarseness. . . . Our theatre has now a tenor as excellent as any of his contemporaries on the European stage."

The *Morning Post*, the champion of the Italian opera, was not less warm in its praise. It proclaimed Sims Reeves to be "one of the greatest, if not the greatest, tenor in Europe. . . . At the end of the final act with its 'Fra Poco' the enthusiasm of the public here reached its height, and Mr. Reeves was summoned before the curtain amidst cheers, waving of hats, handkerchiefs, and every sort of demonstration of delight."

Keen as was this appreciation, Reeves's singing was regarded even more highly by musicians who could better estimate the difficulties he had surmounted. The *Musical World* wrote : " The new tenor, Mr. Sims Reeves, achieved, and most deservedly achieved, the most unqualified success we have witnessed on the English stage for a quarter of a century. . . . Mr. Reeves's voice is a pure high tenor of delicious quality, his tone velvety and equal throughout. His management of this exquisite organ displays considerable skill and proves the artist must have studied deeply and laboured hard in his early youth. We have heard no voice out of Italy so decidedly Italian as Mr. S. Reeves's. . . . He is now an accomplished, nay, we may add, a great singer, and it will be his own fault if he is not one of the very greatest artists on the modern stage."

It is but fair to add that the critics were unanimous in declaring that Reeves was most adequately supported. Madame Dorus Gras, though past her best days, sang with exceptional brilliancy and grappled with the English language, of which previous to her appearance on the Drury Lane stage she knew but little, with great success. Mr. W. H. Weiss and Mr. Henry Whitworth were warmly praised, and Berlioz was greeted in a cordial fashion which must for the time being have chased away the melancholy which always, more or less, overshadowed him. As the *Musical World* pointed out, however, it was hard to discover why Beethoven's *Leonora* overture should have been played to introduce the opera. Possibly Berlioz wanted to show the quality of his orchestra, to which Donizetti's music gave scant chance, and the splendid performance of the overture may be said to have justified the innovation. Hardly as much can be said for Jullien's introduction of a minuet, but Jullien did not care a button for the " critics," and he would probably argue that the gloomy passion of the opera needed a contrast. It is interesting to note that Berlioz had his own ideas as to the arrangement of his orchestra. Near him he had his three principal double basses and 'cellos. His first violins were on his right, and his seconds on his left. The wind instruments were placed at the extremities and the brass in close proximity, not separated, the *Morning Post* remarks, as under Costa and others. " The superiority of the arrangement," said the *Post*, " was triumphantly proved."

CHAPTER IX

1848

The Bride of Lammermoor ran from December 6th to December 18th. The house was packed at every performance, and the venture should have more than paid its expenses, but it did not. Berlioz says the outlay was £400 a night, but that the receipts never reached that amount. The truth was that Jullien's lavish expenditure was on a scale quite regardless of a balance-sheet. Still, had the " run " continued, he might with economy have pulled through with the assistance of a man of business to check extravagance. He stopped the opera in order to keep faith with Balfe.

The public received with great surprise the announcement that *The Bride* in the full tide of success was to be withdrawn in favour of Balfe's new opera, *The Maid of Honour*. The contract laid it down that Donizetti's opera was only to be performed until Balfe's was ready, and a definite date was fixed for its production, failing which Jullien was under a penalty of £200. No doubt Balfe was anxious enough for his own reputation to see *The Maid of Honour* in the bill, but underlying this was another and perhaps more important reason—the commercial instincts of the music publishers. They cared nothing for musical art. It was little to them that the " first tenor in Europe " should continue to delight thousands in the opera with which practically he had identified himself. All that had been written about the creation of an English School of Opera, the representatives of which should rival the best Italian artists, was in their eyes so much waste paper. The one thought in their minds was to get hold of Mr. Balfe's songs so that they might be on sale before Christmas for young lady and gentleman amateur vocalists to torture their friends with at evening parties.

It was due to the *Sunday Times* (December 26th, 1847) that this fact was made public. "The composer, or his publishers," it wrote, "refused to forgo this advantage, so that M. Jullien had only the alternative of paying the penalty or bringing out the opera according to agreement. We wish for Mr. Balfe's own sake that he had shown a little more consideration and liberality in not pressing the withdrawal of *The Bride of Lammermoor* at the height of its popularity, and we are sorry for M. Jullien's sake that he did not pay the £200 penalty and keep *The Maid of Honour* until wanted." But the die was cast, and on December 20th, 1847, Balfe's opera was produced, very nearly escaping a fiasco on the first night, for Alfred Crowquil had omitted to get the licence from the Lord Chamberlain, and the indispensable document only arrived a few minutes before the opening of the doors.

There is no need to say much about *The Maid of Honour*; it is one of the least interesting of Balfe's efforts, and its weakness was evident when contrasted with the fervour and dramatic spirit of *Lucia*. The libretto, written by the industrious Edward Fitzball, hardly reached the standard of the mediocre material to which Balfe was accustomed to wed his haunting melodies —often with a complete disregard for rhythm. The plot of *The Maid of Honour* is founded on the ballet of *Henriette, ou le Marché de Richmond*, produced some years before at Drury Lane by Alfred Bunn under the title of *Lady Henrietta, or the Statute Fair*, and later was made use of by Flotow for his opera of *Martha*. The papers gave lengthy notices, but the work was disappointing and fell flat, despite the magnificent singing of Reeves. He made a hit with the ballad "In this old chair," and as this became highly popular, no doubt the music publishers were satisfied.

In this song Reeves showed the magic of his style, evinced scores of times afterwards in innumerable inane ballads, varying according to the fashion of the day. Like Goldsmith, he touched nothing that he did not adorn. He asks in *My Jubilee*, " Why . . . was I made to sing a song about a chair in no way connected with the opera ? " and he gives the answer, " Presumably introduced with the view of finding favour in the eyes of the music publishers." The air, melodious enough, is thoroughly Balfeian, the words are utterly bald, but the charm of the voice was irresistible. From personal experience (it was one of Reeves's stock concert songs in after-years) I can quite believe how Thackeray was so much affected by Reeves's singing of " In this old chair " that it " drew tears from his heart, as well as his eyes " (W. A. Barrett's *Life of Balfe*).

Interest in the opera began to wane. There was nothing in the personality of Miss Birch, who took the principal soprano part, to attract. She was of the Clara Novello school, an admirable oratorio singer, but as an actress cold and mechanical. Moreover, the inter-position of a pantomime, in deference, as Jullien con-ceived, to the British taste, did not assist the success of the opera, though it gave a rest to the singers. Like his répertoire, Jullien's company was insufficient. On January 10th, 1848, *Linda di Chamouni* was put on with Santiago, a new tenor, of whose singing, remarked the *Athenæum*, " the most partial friend would do best to say nothing." Santiago replaced Reeves once in *The Maid of Honour* (Reeves's understudy having retired), and met with the hostile reception which the audience of those days were never slow to give when they were displeased, and, in default of anything else in readiness, *The Bride* was revived, with crowded houses.

By this time nothing was talked about in musical circles but the singing of Sims Reeves, and the hall-mark of success was seen when paragraphs other than criticisms began to appear in the papers. Thus we have the *Athenæum* of February 5th, 1848, writing : " It is with regret that we copy from one of our contemporaries the rumour that it is the intention of Mr. Reeves to return to Italy at the close of this season. If this be true, we are sorry for two reasons, because the loss to the English operatic stage is a serious one, . . . and because, as the opera in Italy now stands, we believe that Mr. Reeves has derived thence all the advantage it is capable of yielding. It may tell upon his voice. In England the artist who aspires to a first-class occupation cannot sustain himself upon trash. He must be able to sing Handel, Mozart, Rossini, and this range implies almost every possible vocal and musical accomplishment." By "trash" in the connection in which the word is used the *Athenæum* presumably meant the music of the Bellini school; and by the reference to Handel and Mozart it may have had in view the possibility of Sims Reeves assuming the mantle of Braham in oratorio. The "rumour" as to the return to Italy was but a *canard*, but it is not unlikely that the *Athenæum's* advice in the last part of the comment had its effect on Reeves's mind.

By the beginning of February it must have been pretty clear to all connected with Drury Lane Theatre that Jullien was drawing near the end of his tether, and the future must have given the "first tenor in Europe" cause for anxiety. Reeves, like the loyal, staunch man he always showed himself to be, would not desert the sinking ship, but others did not follow his example. On February 5th the opera announced was *The Maid of Honour,* but medical certificates on behalf of Miss Birch and Mr. Whitworth were put in, whereupon the management thought to substitute *The Bride,* but Madame Dorus Gras declined on the plea that she had sung the night before, and the management was left to get on as best it could. The mysterious "illness" which affects theatrical artists at convenient times also struck down the principal danseuse Madame Giubelei, and altogether there were signs of the coming storm.

But outwardly all seemed well. There was a "command" performance of *The Maid of Honour* on February 16th, when Queen Victoria came in state. *The Marriage of Figaro* (in which Reeves had no part), after being postponed several times, was produced, and received very flattering notices, but there was nothing in reserve to back up *The Bride of Lammermoor*. Gluck's *Iphigénie en Tauride* had been announced when the season commenced, but it had not been put into rehearsal (in spite of advertisements to the contrary), and for a very good reason. Jullien knew nothing whatever about the opera. A conference of experts was determined upon, and Sir George Smart, Planché, Gye, Marrizeack the chorusmaster, and Berlioz were summoned. Berlioz in his Autobiography gives a very amusing account of the proceedings. Various suggestions were made, among them the production of *Robert the Devil*; and when it was found that the opera would have to be ready in six days, that there was no translation available, and that the singers did not know a note of the music, the idea was abandoned in favour of *Iphigénie en Tauride*. But here again was an obstacle. The English committee was as ignorant as Jullien concerning Gluck's opera. " But *you* must know it," exclaimed the entrepreneur, turning to Berlioz. Berlioz assented, and having explained the requirements of the opera as to the singers, went on to describe the dresses, remarking that Pylades, the tenor, made his entry in the fourth act wearing a gold helmet. Jullien's fervid imagination instantly was on fire. " We're saved," he cried ; " I shall order a gilt helmet from Paris with a coronet of pearls, and a tuft of ostrich feathers as long as my arm." This finished the discussion and put an end to the project, " the divine tenor, Reeves," Berlioz adds, laughing heartily at picturing himself thus decked.

The ill-luck which dogged Sims Reeves's benefits at Glasgow and Dublin followed him to London. His benefit was announced for February 8th, with *The Bride of Lammermoor* and the last act of *Sonnambula*. The audience, after waiting for three-quarters of an hour for the performance to begin, raised a disturbance, in the midst of which Berlioz took his seat in the orchestra and started the overture. " The house was satisfied, but," says one of the daily journals, " just as the curtain should have gone up, out stole from the side-wings a gentleman in mourning, portentously clad and immensely affected as to his aspect, and announced that Madame Dorus Gras refused to appear, whereupon there ensued such an uproar as would be difficult to describe. Everyone has

JULLIEN.
From a photograph by Mayall.

witnessed a mob hurricane ; it is, therefore, useless to say a word about it. The storm of dissension had somewhat appeased itself and the portentously clad and solemnly visaged gentleman, who had been for a long time essaying to edge in a word through the furious noise of the tempest, was heard to declare that Miss Miran would kindly undertake the part of Lucy, not on the shortest notice, but on no notice at all, and claimed the special indulgence of the audience on the twofold grounds of innocence of the music and incapacity to sing it, if she *did* know it, seeing Miss Miran rejoices in a contralto voice, whereas Lucy of Lammermoor never descends lower than a soprano. This declaration of our ebon friend was received with as much vociferant delight by the audience as the announcement of Madame Gras's refusal was with vehement demonstrations of feeling."

Miss Miran bravely went through the first act, book in hand, and meanwhile Miss Messent, who was a soprano and who knew the music, had been sent for, and appeared in the second and third acts. Despite the drawback, " Reeves," the *Times* tells us, " the hero of the night, was in fine voice and sang superbly. . . . *Sonnambula* was the occasion of a second triumph for Reeves, whose singing was alike remarkable for grace, correctness, and intensity. Only the final act was given, as, owing to the attitude taken up by Madame Dorus Gras, there was no possibility of a rehearsal."

A letter from M. Dorus Gras, the husband of Madame Dorus Gras, followed, in which he asserted that upwards of £1,200 was due to his wife, and that he had in consequence " determined not to allow Madame Dorus Gras to perform at Drury Lane unless her fair share of the receipts of each future evening's performance were secured to be paid to her. . . . Although the performance of this evening (February 9th) was advertised for the benefit of Mr. Reeves, such was not at all probable, as that gentleman has, according to M. Jullien and his solicitor's own statements, been paid nearly the whole amount due to him under his engagement to the present time, but I am informed, and I believe correctly, that the receipts of this evening are intended to be applied towards the liquidation of other debts of M. Jullien."

Jullien's rejoinder put quite a different complexion on this story. He admitted that he had not been able to pay Madame Dorus Gras with that regularity which until he entered this speculation had characterised his money transactions in this country, " but," he went on to say, " that lady is blameable for much of the difficulty in which the establishment has been thrown by her own conduct. Soon after Christmas Madame Dorus Gras, being announced to sing once only in eight days, refused to perform a second time on the plea that to play two nights in succession was not in her engagement. This request was made to her in consequence of the severe illness of Miss Birch and Whitworth, but the lady remained unmoved, and the opera was changed, to the great injury of the theatre. Madame Dorus Gras also absolutely refused to perform the characters allotted to her, viz. that of Amina in *Sonnambula* and Susanna in *The Marriage of Figaro*; she had consequently during the whole season performed only thirteen times, and for that had already received the sum of £433. . . . It is not true that the whole of Mr. Reeves's salary was paid, but I offered to him as a mode of liquidating it that he should have a night set aside for his benefit, the expenses and *risk* being mine, he receiving the sum due to him out of the receipts. I offered the same advantage to Madame Dorus Gras, but she refused it, and she therefore ought not to complain of my not promising to appropriate the proceeds of Mr. Reeves's night to the payment of her salary. . . . "

The conclusion of this letter is a fine tribute to Reeves's sterling character. " In justice to Mr. Reeves, I cannot omit publicly acknowledging my gratitude towards him for his kind and considerate conduct during the many difficulties which have arisen in the course of the season. He has at all times used his utmost exertions to serve the theatre, and has on several occasions waived privileges for the general good which, as an artist of his standing, he might well have exacted."

On the whole, the lady did not come out of the transaction well, and her conduct in regard to Sims Reeves showed, as Jullien put it, " anything but a kindly feeling towards a fellow-artist."

Jullien's experiment with English opera, which had begun so brilliantly, ended thus in failure. His bankruptcy was announced in April, and he hastened to retrieve his fortunes by resuming the *métier* which suited him best—the conducting of promenade concerts. His venture, however, had brought Sims Reeves to the front. *The* English tenor had arrived, and the whole world of music—Italian opera, oratorio, the concert room—lay before him.

Before the Drury Lane season terminated, Reeves had come into great request. He sang for Berlioz at the latter's benefit concert on February 7th, when the entire programme was made up of the *bénéficiaire's* music, including a portion of his *Damnation of Faust*, in which Reeves took|a part. Shortly afterwards he joined Jullien's concert party, and visited the chief towns in the provinces and Ireland, when he was advertised as " the greatest tenor that has appeared in England since the retirement of Rubini." In the Irish tour Koenig (cornet) and Richardson (flute) were of the party.

It was in connection with Jullien's second provincial tour that Mr. George Haddock, well known in Yorkshire as a violinist of exceptional talent, tells (*Musical Recollections*) the story of Sims Reeves being hissed the first time he sang in Yorkshire. It was on the occasion of his singing " In this old chair," and, writes Mr. Haddock, " it was his method then, as it was throughout his career, to begin quietly and in almost a whisper, reserving his magnificent voice for a specially grand passage or for a gradually worked-up climax, when he would let go his voice, which was as clear and thrilling then as a silver trumpet. This he did on his first appearance before his first Yorkshire audience, and they, thinking they were being treated in an offhand style by the new young tenor, refused to have it, and a hiss being started, it was taken up throughout the house. Reeves looked up in amazement, threw his music to the floor and stalked off the platform.

" Jullien sank back in his gilded chair as though he had been shot, and it was some time before the great man could be brought to understand what had happened. In the end, however, he started another orchestral piece, but as

the audience would not have it and were calling out for
Reeves, he stopped the band and, turning to the audience,
said in his broken English that he did not know why they
wished to insult the great English tenor, but that he
would do his best to induce him to appear again, after
which he walked off the platform. Then followed an
interval of waiting, relieved by loud applause and cries
for Reeves, and after some time Jullien was seen walking
backwards on the platform, dragging Sims Reeves by the
tails of his coat. After getting him firmly planted, he
picked up the music, put it into his hands, mounted his
rostrum, and again started the symphony of the song.
This time, as if Reeves had felt what his audience desired,
he sang in all the matchless glory of his grand fresh
silvery tenor voice. At the conclusion there was a roar
of tumultuous applause, which would not be appeased
until the tenor had been brought back again and again,
after which he was compelled to grant an encore."

Reeves's most important engagement in the early part
of the year was in connection with a performance of
Judas Maccabæus, given under the direction of Mr.
John Hullah, whose efforts to improve and extend English
choral singing were beginning to show magnificent
results. The date first announced was altered, the
Times announcing that "the engagements of Mr. Sims
Reeves requiring him to leave London earlier than was
anticipated, Handel's oratorio *Judas Maccabæus* will be
performed on Thursday, February 10th, instead of the
24th, when Mr. Sims Reeves will sing for the first time in
Exeter Hall." Reeves's words in *My Jubilee* are: " I
had not attempted sacred music until at the beginning of
1849 I resolved to appear in oratorio." This statement
has been repeated many times, but it is not correct.
Reeves forgot that he sang twice at Glasgow in 1844 in
The Messiah. It was, however, as the *Times* announced,
his first appearance at Exeter Hall.

It is a remarkable and noteworthy fact that the connection of Sims Reeves with oratorio should synchronise
with the newly awakened love for choral singing, which
at that time was making extraordinary strides throughout
the country. Twenty years previous to 1848 such an
opportunity for the development of Sims Reeves's

genius did not exist, and it may be questioned whether it exists at the present day. When the Sacred Harmonic Society was established in 1832 there was but one choral society in London of any standing, for the Antient Concerts, for reasons already given, did not count. This was the Cecilian Society, which met in London Wall. With the advent of the Sacred Harmonic Society under Mr. Surman a new musical era commenced.

In an obituary notice of Mr. George Perry, the leader of the Society's orchestra in its early days, the *Norwich Argus* (1862) threw the following interesting sidelights on the difficulties encountered at the beginning of the enterprise :

" At the formation of the Sacred Harmonic Society, 1832, Mr. Surman, who filled the double part of conductor and librarian, invited Mr. Perry to come and lead, as the prospects of the society were favourable. Perry consented, and the members, about sixty in number, continued to meet for the space of two years in Gate Street Chapel, Lincoln's Inn Fields. In those days the difficulties with which amateur bodies had to contend and the pecuniary risk of getting up oratorios were so serious that the success of this society was perhaps almost without precedent.

" But it was not destined to be long uninterrupted. Some of the managers of the chapel all at once discovered that it was highly improper for young people to meet together there for the practice of sacred music. As there had been no indecorum or misconduct of which these pious people could complain or to which they could have been indebted for their illumination, they must have been ' inspired.' However, they ejected the society from their chapel, and then the practice meetings were held in Henrietta Street Chapel [now called Handel Street], Brunswick Square. Here two performances were given with moderate success, but the attendance of the weekly rehearsals was thin on account of the inconvenience of the locality. The society was at length reduced to so low an ebb that not one of the members paid any subscription for an entire quarter. It happened upon one wet night when Mr. Perry made his appearance with his violin under his arm and Mr. Surman arrived with a load of music in his bag that they found only one other member to join them in a rehearsal of Handel's *Messiah*. Men less determined and less enthusiastic would at that crisis have deserted their posts. But no ; they preferred adjourning to a neighbouring tavern, where they drank ' Success to the Society ' and seriously bethought them what now could be done. Mr. Perry had three miles to walk to his home, but they would not separate until they had resolved upon endeavouring to get twenty members to put down one guinea each for the purpose of carrying on the Society's business at their own risk in some more central situation. This was eventually done, or there would have been an end of the infant Sacred Harmonic Society."

After holding meetings in the hall of the Scottish Corporation, Crane Court, Fleet Street, the Society sought to obtain a room in Exeter Hall, which had not then long been built, but there were difficulties in the way. The founders of Exeter Hall had dedicated it solely to religious bodies ; the regulations regarded the introduction of music as a profanation of its sacred walls, and the application of the Sacred Harmonic Society sent a shudder through some of the committee. In any case the constitution under which the hall was governed had to be modified before permission could be granted even for the performance of an oratorio. But eventually an agreement was arrived at, and the Society transferred its operations to the building with which for many years it was identified.

The spurt the Society's concerts gave to oratorio was enormous. Until its foundation, the performance of an oratorio in its entirety, saving *The Messiah*, was unknown. Only selections were heard. When *Israel in Egypt* was performed at Westminster Abbey in 1834, " The enemy said " was omitted. Braham selected his show Handelian solos and nothing more, and he did not hesitate to treat Handel after his own ideas, joining, for instance, " Waft her, angels," from one oratorio (*Jephtha*) to " Deeper and deeper still " from another. It may be admitted that the union was very effective, and Sims Reeves doubtless thought so, as he accepted Braham's innovation. With the exception of singing " But Thou didst not leave," which before his time had always been allotted to a soprano, Reeves took no material liberties with the

Handelian text. The few emendations he permitted himself—in one case an omission, and in the other the transposition of one note an octave higher—were insignificant. It must be remembered that with the Sacred Harmonic Society's rigid adherence to its principle of giving an oratorio from beginning to end, the whims and caprices of soloists could not be tolerated. It was everything or nothing, and in this respect the claims of Braham as an exponent of Handel are not to be compared with those of Sims Reeves.

It was characteristic of the aristocracy in those days that they should look down with lofty disdain upon the Sacred Harmonic Society. There were no bishops upon its committee, and Exeter Hall had about it a strong leaven of Dissent. But throughout the provinces the example set in London was eagerly followed, and lesser Sacred Harmonic Societies sprang up everywhere. In the metropolis, musical societies such as the Choral Harmonists devoted themselves to Handel, Mozart, and Haydn, and so also did the Melophonic Society. The City Classical Harmonists followed in the same wake; in fact, to quote Mr. J. E. Cox (*Musical Recollections*), about 1840 " the metropolis witnessed the most frantic efforts to make its inhabitants suddenly proficient in musical as well as other arts." By 1847 the Sacred Harmonic Society had firmly established itself, and when in that year Mendelssohn conducted his *Elijah* in Exeter Hall and the Queen and Prince Albert were among the audience, its admission into the highest musical circles could not be gainsaid.

In 1848 the Society entered upon a period of disruption and transition. The merits of Mr. Surman as a conductor were being questioned. The principle with which the Society had started of having only voluntary efforts was found to be inadequate to that perfection at which it now aimed, and professional leaders of the various choral parts, and especially professional instrumentalists, were introduced. Mr. Surman was deposed, and the baton fell into the hands of Mr. George Perry,[1] the leader of

[1] In the early sixties Mr. Perry was a regular visitor to my father's house. I remember him an old man of eighty with a shock head of hair perfectly white, stray locks of which were continually falling on his

the orchestra, who had written additional accompaniments to *The Messiah*, and who was the composer of two oratorios, *The Death of Abel* and *The Fall of Jerusalem*—long since forgotten.   Mr. Perry was a very clever musician, but neither his temperament nor his training fitted him to be a good conductor ; he was excitable to the point of eccentricity.   George Perry was superseded by Costa ; but in the meantime there was an interregnum in the affairs of the Society.

Truth to tell, its performances had fallen woefully short of its high ideals, or Mr. Surman, when on his defence, would not have made the following lamentable and curious confession : " In our orchestra we have amateurs, some of whom hardly know how to tune their instruments, and scarcely look at a music-book from one concert to another.   But they have been admitted members, and I don't know who has any right to find fault with them. . . . We have no one to teach the instrumentalists to bow and tune their instruments, or the vocalists to scale, and it is only a wonder, as Mr. Perry says, that they do as well as they do.   We can never get a full rehearsal of band, chorus, and principals."   This state of affairs gave Mr. Hullah and Sims Reeves their opportunity with *Judas Maccabæus*.

forehead, very dark bushy brows, and gleaming eyes—altogether a striking personality.   He had lost nearly all his teeth and spoke with such rapidity as to be at times quite unintelligible.   He was full of interesting reminiscences over which he worked himself into fits of excitement, finding relief in seizing a corner of the table-cloth and screwing it, dragging towards him the cups and saucers, plates, etc.   He was quite unconscious of what he was doing.   One of Mr. Perry's anecdotes related to C. E. Horn's " Cherry Ripe."   He was trying over with Madame Vestris a batch of new songs, among which was " Cherry Ripe."   " Really, Madame," said he, " that's a very pretty song."   " I think so too," said she.   It was introduced into the part she was playing in *Paul Pry*, and its success was instantaneous.—C. E. P.

CHAPTER X

1848 (*continued*)

Exeter Hall in 1848. Mr. Chorley's criticism of Reeves's singing in *Judas* and his demand for the Handelian " shake." Indifference of great singers to the composer's intentions. Reeves's " Adelaida " not in accordance with Mr. Chorley's ideas. Reeves's debut in Italian opera. His great success in *Linda di Chamouni*. His sudden rupture with Mr. Lumley. Jenny Lind suspected of jealousy. Gardoni's rivalry of Reeves. Mrs. Pitt Byrne's partisanship of Gardoni. Her version of a squabble at Her Majesty's Theatre.

THE Exeter Hall of 1848 was very different—save in one of its defects—from the Exeter Hall remembered by the last generation. It possessed every fault that a building for public gatherings could possibly have. Whoever were the persons responsible for its interior arrangements, they were either ignorant of or indifferent to the elementary principles which should govern such a structure. Its acoustic qualities were detestable, its accommodation for the audience was most stupid, and its solitary approach up a double staircase the two parts of which met about half-way and continued in bottle-neck fashion, causing a congestion of two struggling streams of humanity, was a veritable death-trap. Though the most spacious building in London, the auditorium was so cut up by deep recesses supported and masked by massive pillars that the un-obstructed portion only formed a square of 75 feet, above which was a deep lantern roof. Half the sound of the orchestra was absorbed by the lantern; the pillars and the architraves of the recesses interrupted and confused the tone, and shut out a large portion of the chorus from the sight of the conductor and audience; the organ, built as shallow as possible, was placed with its back against a wall and projected nearly twenty feet into the orchestra. Mendelssohn, when conducting *Elijah*, complained bitterly of feeling "crushed" by this projecting mass. It cut the chorus completely in half. So bad was it that in the double choruses in *Israel in Egypt* it was barely possible for one side of the chorus to hear what the other was singing.

It was amid these muddled surroundings that Sims Reeves first sang "Sound an alarm" and "Call forth, ye powers." The full effect of his clarion tones must have been marred and muffled, yet he produced an electrifying impression.

Glowing criticisms were heard and were to be read on every side, and that of the *Athenæum* may occupy the first place because of the interesting difference it indicates between the old and new Handelian renderings. "As to voice," Mr. Chorley, who was then the *Athenæum* musical critic, wrote, "it would be childish to measure him [Sims Reeves] with any tenor England has had since Braham, and we suspect his register upwards to be more extensive than Braham's was in its best days. . . . His use of it in the martial songs of which his part principally consists was excellent. There was a mixture of measurement and flexibility in his divisions such as in our time at least was never exhibited by his predecessor, who used to confuse and precipitate his passages to arrive at his great notes in a manner neither refined nor scientific. This was particularly evident in the groups of six semi-quavers in 'Sound an alarm,' and we note the excellence minutely because it is a sign from which musicians may draw good auguries. . . . On the other hand, the shake (indispensable as a Handelian grace) was missing. It must be forthcoming if Mr. Reeves intends to become our great oratorio singer. . . . Briefly, our admiration of and expectations from Mr. Reeves are much heightened by this performance."

On March 4th, in noticing with much appreciation Sims Reeves's singing in *Acis and Galatea* (again under Hullah's direction), Mr. Chorley returned to the charge, remarking that "Handel wrote in a day when the singer was called upon to exhibit his taste in ornament, as constantly as the organist was expected to display his control over fugue and thoroughbass, and if we dispense with every other embellishment there is no true version

of Handel without the shake—for which, therefore, on the part of Mr. Reeves we must again
' agitate.' ''

Of Sims Reeves's singing in *Jephtha*, produced on May
20th for the second time by Hullah (the first performance
with Reeves was on April 17th, but the critic was not
present), Mr. Chorley wrote: " He seems steadily
improving in this ancient music, although almost perverse
in denying to it that indispensable Handelian grace,
the shake."

Mr. Chorley was quite entitled to his opinion, but
considering that for years the strict observance of
Handelian traditions had been disregarded, his insistence
on the preservation of the shake, which, after all, was as
much a fashion as it was a grace, and certainly not
peculiar to Handel, suggests straining at a gnat. The
singers of Handel's day were permitted to introduce
their own ornaments, a licence of which they took full
advantage. It is probable that Handel's music was as
much trifled with in the composer's days as it was after
his death, and it is a fair argument to ask, if so much could
be introduced which Handel did not write, was it so great
a sin to omit an ornament (purely conventional) which he
did write ? If Handel's music was to be accepted in its
primitive purity, why was it considered necessary for
Mozart, Bishop, and George Perry to write " additional
accompaniments " for *The Messiah* ? Lindley's
extravagant burlesque of the concluding symphony of
" O Liberty, thou choicest treasure," was applauded,
and Braham's dovetailing " Waft her, angels," on to
" Deeper and deeper still " was accepted without a
murmur. The great singers did what they liked irre-
spective of the composer's intentions. Did not Madame
Catalani sing the martial baritone air " Non piu andrai,"
and not only sang it, but introduced an alteration in one
particular passage ? Against this Mr. J. E. Cox, who
records this Philistinism, has not a word of reproach,
though he could severely condemn Mr. Sims Reeves
for singing an upper A in " Thou shalt dash them," a
perfectly legitimate transposition to produce the effect
he wanted.

It is possible that in the days of trills and roulades too

8

much importance was attached to the attainment of the shake. Catalani's method was painful in the extreme. Henry Phillips thus describes it : " When she executed a roulade or shake, the mouth and chin moved violently at every note, which to me had not only a most extraordinary but most ludicrous effect—in fact, it appeared strange and unaccountable. I resolved to discover its cause, or rather why it was done, and soon found that by such means an inflexible voice might execute the most elaborate cadenza, so that I presume her voice by nature was not constituted for the execution it had by art attained." Mr. Cox says something to the same effect. One may venture to assert that when a purely ornamental excrescence is produced by distorting the features, it is better left alone, the composer notwithstanding.

It is not to be supposed that Sims Reeves could not have used the shake had he chosen,[1] but he had his own ideas of the interpretation of Handel, and these ideas did not happen to coincide with those of Mr. Chorley. Unfortunately, Mr. Chorley had a fixed notion that what he thought *must* be right, and his idiosyncrasies tinged his judgment. Hence because Sims Reeves did not accept his advice, he was " perverse." Great as Sims Reeves was as a singer in the direct interpretation of the word, he was first of all an artist. His rendering of Handel was a revelation, because he had ever the dramatic spirit in view. Many Handelian singers have regarded the Master's music too much as vocal exercises, and all they cared for was how best to display their skill in the execution of difficult passages. This was not Sims Reeves's aim.

In *Jephtha* is a tenor solo, " Open thy marble jaws, O tomb." It bristles with awkward intervals ; it is ungrateful to sing, and has a rugged character all its own. Maybe Handel desired in some way to depict the horrors of death. *Jephtha* was the last oratorio he wrote ; he had not long recovered from a severe illness ; he was threatened with blindness. It can easily be imagined that his mind was impressed by gloomy thoughts. It is to be presumed that when Sims Reeves first sang in

[1] Mr. Herbert Reeves says his father was a complete master of the shake and could perform it perfectly.

Jephtha he omitted this trying air, as was then the custom. In the late sixties, when Mr. Barnby produced *Jephtha* at the St. James's Hall, Sims Reeves gave it with an amazing effect. It may seem extravagant praise to say that no tenor before or since could have sung, or could sing, this solo with the astounding vigour and declamatory power which Reeves exhibited. It was, as I well remember, an astounding *tour de force*, and the singer seemed to revel in his triumph over the mechanical difficulties. If any readers of these pages were present at this memorable performance, I think they will support my contention. It may, at any rate, be safely asserted that if Sims Reeves desired to show his exceptional gift of flexibility and vigour of attack, he thoroughly succeeded. With a less accomplished singer, this solo would be wearisome and unmeaning.

After Reeves's successful debut in opera and oratorio, engagements came thick and fast. He sang at Allcroft's concert on February 15th " Oh, 'tis a glorious sight to see," which became one of his stock pieces ; at Thalberg's concert on March 6th ; in *Judas Maccabæus* with the London Sacred Harmonic Society, formed by Mr. Surman in rivalry with the old Sacred Harmonic Society, from which he had been ejected ; and on May 6th for the Society of Female Musicians, at which, in the opinion of Mr. Chorley, " he lost caste by singing such poor pieces of namby-pamby as Mr. Linley's ballad, and a certain patriotic song." On May 20th he took part in a concert given by Mr. Calkin and the Misses Pyne, the latter destined in after-years to do good service in the cause of English opera ; and on May 27th he appeared again at the Antient Concerts.[1] Reeves had already sung " Adelaida " in English, but this was the first occasion on which he gave it in Italian, and, said Mr. Chorley, "our English tenor sang better than any tenor has sung it before. Had his contrast between his full and delicate notes been less abrupt, there would have been little left to desire. The fashion was set by Rubini, but Mr. Reeves would do well to recollect that in Rubini's case it was a matter of necessity, owing to the impaired state of the great tenor's voice which rendered *mezza-voce*

[1] This relic of the past gave up the ghost in the following year.

phrases so many difficulties that by some sacrifice or other must be evaded. Happily, Mr. Reeves has no need of expedients, and he would do wisely to avoid them as affectations."

In a previous chapter, alluding to Reeves's love of strong contrasts, I ventured to suggest that in so doing he was influenced by Rubini's method. When making this suggestion I was unaware of Mr. Chorley's opinion, and now that I know it, I see no reason for modifying what I wrote. Whatever effect Reeves's rendering may have had upon Mr. Chorley's mind, I can only say, after having heard him sing " Adelaida " many times during the sixties, that nothing approaching excessive or abrupt contrasts was apparent. But this is not to contend that in those early days, revelling in the delight of using his glorious voice in one of the most impassioned songs ever written, he may not have been betrayed into an exuberance which Mr. Chorley conceived (erroneously, I submit) would become a habit.

The Italian operatic season of 1848 gave Reeves the opportunity for which he had long been working and for which his Milan training had prepared him. He accepted an offer by Mr. Lumley to appear at Her Majesty's Theatre, upon which the *Athenæum*, with a prescience of what might befall him, wrote : " The engagement of Mr. Reeves at Her Majesty's Theatre commencing this evening (May 20th) is good in two ways—as supplying Mr. Lumley's troupe with a singer eminently wanting to it, and as affording an English artist a chance of rising to a first-rate position. Since the days of Michael Kelly and Braham no British tenor has been heard at our Italian opera. The situation is an arduous one—but

> ' If great be the danger,
> The prize, too, is great.' "

The opera selected was Donizetti's *Linda di Chamouni*, chosen more for the sake of Madame Tadiolini, for whom the opera was written, than to give Sims Reeves a part in which to distinguish himself. Madame Tadiolini was new to London, but she had made a great reputation on the Continent. It cannot be said that she was an ideal Linda. She was but an indifferent actress, her voice was past its fullness, and she was "fat, fair, and forty"; still, she was an accomplished vocalist with executive brilliancy. Sims Reeves must have felt that he was slightly handicapped, but he triumphed over his drawbacks, as he had a habit of doing. His success was complete, and the newspapers were unanimous in their praise. The *Musical World* declared that "Mr. Reeves made a debut which, without exaggeration, may be recorded as triumphant. The part of Carlo is a small one, but Mr. Reeves showed what a good artist can do with a trifling character. His cavatina in the second act, which generally passes unnoticed, was encored with rapture. It was sung with the utmost grace and feeling. Mr. Reeves indeed proved himself worthy of his reputation, and stood his ground manfully among his Italian companions."

The *Athenæum* was equally complimentary, Mr. Chorley evidently appreciating the obstacles which were in front of the English tenor. "Mr. Reeves," wrote the critic, "passed through his share of the ordeal with entire good fortune. The part of the lover is not one of those best suited to him; great, too, are the difficulties of an appearance in a theatre where an English vocalist is sure to be exposed to carping behind, no less than before, the curtain. . . ." But Mr. Chorley was nothing if not critical, and he followed this praise with cautions and admonitions which may or may not have been justified, winding up with the remark that " nothing could be more gratifying than his reception or more complete than his success."

The obstacles foreseen by Mr. Chorley speedily presented themselves. On Tuesday, May 23rd, *Linda* was advertised to be repeated with Reeves's second appearance, but a thunderbolt descended in the shape of the following announcement on the door of the Opera-house: "Tuesday evening, 5 o'clock. Mr. Reeves having refused to sustain his part in *Linda di Chamouni*, the indulgence of the subscribers and the public are respectfully entreated in favour of Signor Gardoni, who at the shortest notice has, to prevent disappointment, most obligingly undertaken the part."

Sims Reeves at once wrote to the papers to state his version of the case, but the dailies did not insert it and it was left for the *Musical World* and the *Era* to publish the explanation. Reeves wrote :

" The facts are these : in my engagement with Mr. Lumley certain characters were expressly stipulated for by me—viz. Edgardo in *Lucia* (the nomination of which in the bond principally induced me to accept the offer), Percy in *Anna Bolena*, and Arturo in *I Puritani*, the small part in *Linda* having been undertaken by me at the request of the manager, who seemed to think my performance of it would strengthen the cast. . . . My debut being considered successful and the opera of *Lucia* having appeared in the playbills of Her Majesty's Theatre, I naturally concluded that my next part would be Edgardo.

" But alas for the faith of managers and the inviolability of agreements, the startling intelligence soon reached me that Signor Gardoni was to perform my part in *Lucia*, no rehearsal of which was called until after my debut. The intention of the manager was thus carefully kept from me until after my appearance in *Linda*, Mdlle. Lind's name having been the only one mentioned in the announced bills of *Lucia*. As soon as I became acquainted with the facts, I immediately informed the manager that in consequence of this direct violation of our engagement, I could not consent to appear again unless my part was restored to me. . . . It is most distressing to me that the public should have experienced any disappointment on my account, but I trust I shall be held blameless when it is considered that, under the circumstances, Mr. Lumley had no right whatever to announce me for Tuesday evening."

Mr. Balfe, who was Lumley's musical director, replied thus :

" The nature of Mr. Reeves's engagement was simply that he was engaged for five nights certain this season, one night at least in each week, with power of renewal at the option of the direction for an additional number of nights on the same conditions this year, and for twenty nights next season—nothing more was stipulated.

" The part of Edgardo which Mr. Reeves suddenly and imperatively demanded had been in the hands of that great public favourite Signor Gardoni six weeks before Mr. Reeves was engaged. But so far from any wish existing to prevent Mr. Reeves having the fullest opportunity of success, some of the best parts in the *répertoire* and those deemed most suited to his talents had been destined for him."

Sims Reeves was not the man to be silenced when he held he was right, and he rejoined that " it will not easily be credited by the public that I should consent to sing at Her Majesty's or any other theatre without the fullest assurance that the part of Edgardo—to a certain extent identified with any dramatic reputation I may possess both at home and in Italy—should not be taken from me and entrusted to one who, though he may be, no doubt, justly styled ' that great public favourite,' has never yet attempted the part and is perhaps not altogether adapted to the performance of it. It is, however, for the public to decide whether what decidedly assumes the aspect of a foreign cabal against an English artist shall, or shall not, be successful. . . . It would certainly appear hard that an artist should be driven from the public service not because he has been unsuccessful, but because he has had the good fortune to please the public too well."

The point in dispute could have been settled by the production of the contract, but this was not done by either side, and one can only come to the conclusion that the arrangement and promises as to *Lucia* were made verbally, justifying the *Athenæum's* dry comment that " engagements are far too loosely contracted on both sides." The matter lapsed so far as correspondence was concerned, but both the *Musical World* and the *Era* contended that Mr. Lumley was under the sway of his Italian company and that out of jealousy of the Englishman's success they had forced his hand. The biographers of Balfe (W. A. Barrett and C. L. Kenney) are silent on the subject; and in his *Reminiscences of the Opera* Mr. Lumley, who alone knew the truth, contented himself with a bald summary of what had appeared in the newspapers and took shelter under what he calls the " powerful counter-statements " of Mr. Balfe.

The *Musical World* hinted that Jenny Lind was at the bottom of the business, and that if it discovered that such was the case, something further would be said. Editorially nothing further appeared, but subsequently two letters from anonymous correspondents were published, the writer of the second one remarking : " I cannot help fearing that the matter originated in the jealousy of the ' Nightingale.' Gardoni, no doubt, is an agreeable tenor for a prima donna to sing with, and he is always pleasing, and there is no danger of his giving his part a *disagreeable importance*, while Reeves is ambitious and could, I suspect, *at least divide* the applause in *Lucia*." This, probably, hit the right nail on the head. The constant disputes arising out of the lady's engagements show that the " Nightingale " or her business manager could not endure the idea of any rival, male or female, coming too near her throne, and that the infatuation of the public gave her a power which she was not slow to use. Allowing this to be so, there is, however, no evidence to show that Jenny Lind had any personal antagonism towards Reeves nor he towards her. At all events, any irritation which either may have felt had passed away in after-years. He pays a warm tribute to her in *My Jubilee*, calling her " the most perfect singer I ever heard " (p. 143), while on p. 209 there is a passage which may be quoted in its entirety as indicating the sincere admiration which each entertained for the other genius. " No singer," Reeves writes, " was ever less vain than Jenny Lind. She was scarcely indeed satisfied with herself, keeping always before her an ideal which she found it difficult to attain. She appreciated praise all the same when it proceeded from anyone whose opinion she valued and whom she knew to be sincere.

" ' Otto,' she once said to her husband, ' I have sung well to-night.'

" ' My dear, you always sing well,' replied Mr. Goldschmidt.

" ' No, but Mr. Reeves says that I sang well," she continued, ' and he does not say such things too often,'

JENNY LIND.
From a drawing by P. G. Wagner.

" Had I told her how perfectly she sang whenever I felt impressed by that fact, my assurance would have been frequent indeed."

But on p. 105 we have a possible explanation of any objection which Jenny Lind may have had to singing in *Lucia* with Sims Reeves. The latter, as he states, had a great repugnance to the lowering of the curtain after Lucia's mad scene, as not only weakening the effect of the tenor's great final effort when he has to act alone, but cutting the opera in such a way as to make " Fra Poco " somewhat of an anti-climax. " Jenny Lind," Reeves points out, " but for one fault—in the shape of an unwarrantable liberty taken with the composer's design— would have been an ideal Lucia. Although I was once cast for this part of Edgardo to her Lucia, I, for reasons already mentioned, did not appear. Had I done so, I should have felt bound to object to a highly novel incident which she thought fit to introduce. At the end of the magnificent finale to the second act . . . Lucia appeals to the indignant Edgardo, who throws her back into her brother's arms, upon which the curtain falls. Jenny Lind, however, as if to concentrate all attention on herself, rushed to the front of the stage, indicated by her gestures and general demeanour that she was losing her reason, and remained as if demented before the footlights while the curtain fell behind her." If this point were discussed between them and if Sims Reeves expressed his opinion— vigorously, one may be sure—on the " business " the prima donna proposed to introduce, it can be easily understood that the lady meant to have her way and took the only possible course to secure it—the sacrifice of Sims Reeves.

The sudden collapse of his hopes must have caused Reeves intense disappointment. To succeed in Italian opera was his ambition, and to have played Edgardo to the Lucia of Jenny Lind would have been a crowning triumph. It was perhaps a slight consolation that Queen Victoria should have gone in state to the per- formance of *Linda*, and from an advertising point of view the talk arising out of the affair did him no harm, but Sims Reeves had a contempt for such adventitious aids. Nor could it have given him any satisfaction that Gardoni's

Edgardo, full of grace of vocalisation and beauty of voice as it was, fell short of his own powerful rendering of the part. He had not the slightest ill-feeling towards the Italian tenor, and the demonstrations manifested in his behalf by impulsive admirers on the night Gardoni sang could only have given him great annoyance. The biassed opinion of the supporters of Italian opera was reflected many years after by a well-known authoress, Mrs. W. Pitt Byrne, who, in the *Gossip of the Century* (1892), wrote the following piece of nonsensical sentimentality :

" Gardoni, whose Edgardo was considered perfection in Paris,[1] and whose experience in the music of that opera [*Lucia*] enabled him to make it the leading character whenever he performed it, was—to the astonishment, annoyance, and indignation of the respectable part of the audience—coarsely interrupted in the midst of his first cavatina by a cry from the gallery of ' Sims Reeves,' immediately taken up by similar cat-calls from confederates *ad hoc* in various parts of the house. . . . However, they had it all to themselves ; no respectable persons of course took any part in such a cabal, and if the English tenor had any personal wish to supplant the prepossessing young debutant, his ' friends ' (?) went to work very clumsily ; the result of the disturbance they had the bad taste to make was that the obloquy fell back on the artist they represented and rendered more remote any chance he might have had of success. It was the English tenor's name that was now hissed, and the uproar now took sufficient proportions to require the manager's intervention. . . . Gardoni could hardly have resented this malicious demonstration—a weak revenge from the tenor upon another who had obtained a coveted engagement—nor could he take offence at the method in which it was imposed, for there could be no possible rivalry between the Sims Reeves—even of that day—and the young, elegant, and fresh-voiced Italian whose obvious superiority drew heartily to him the sympathies of the public."

---

[1] Reeves's assertion is that Gardoni had never previously attempted the part.

Mrs. Byrne's homage to "respectable persons" and her hysterical outpourings over the "young, elegant, and fresh-voiced Italian" (he was but three years Reeves's junior) are amusing, and her insinuations as to a "weak revenge" on the part of Sims Reeves are ridiculous and unpardonable.

CHAPTER XI

1848 (*continued*)

1848—a remarkable year. The Worcester and Norwich Musical Festivals. Their peculiar features. Professor Taylor's tampering with *Israel in Egypt*. The Duke of Cambridge and Howard Glover's operatic season at Manchester. The captious critic of the *Manchester Guardian* and Sims Reeves. Reeves sings in *Sonnambula* in London for the first time. The Sacred Harmonic Society engages Costa as its conductor. His characteristics. His regard for Sims Reeves. Reeves's first appearance in *The Messiah* under Costa. Costa's reading of " For unto us." The Wednesday Concerts. Reeves's great success in ballad singing. " The Bay of Biscay " and its second verse. Curious cause of disturbance.

In some respects the year 1848 was the most notable in Sims Reeves's career. He achieved success in English opera, and his solitary appearance in Italian opera showed what he could do when pitted against Italian singers. He began in 1848 his connection with the great provincial musical festivals—a connection which lasted for many years; he identified himself as the best English ballad singer of his day ; and lastly, and most important of all, he first sang for the Sacred Harmonic Society and commenced the series of triumphs which placed him at the head of oratorio singers for all time. Thus within twelve months it may be said that he showed his genius in every direction.

His work, after his return to London from singing for Jullien at Birmingham, included, in May and June, concerts given by Seguin, a popular bass singer, by Henry Wylde, Brinley Richards, Louisa and Susan Pyne, W. Kuhe, John Parry, and others, and on July 1st he was in Liverpool at the concert of the Roscoe Club. At all these concerts his selections were either operatic or classical ; he did not take up simple ballads until towards the end of the year. In August he sang for the Birmingham Choral Society, Miss Lucombe's name also appearing in the programme. On August 7th he was at Drury Lane at a benefit performance of *Lucia*, Madame Castelan being the prima donna. The *Musical World*, in reference to this occasion, was moved to an enthusiastic laudation of native talent. " Who can say," it wrote, " after the flattering testimonials Mr. Reeves has received whenever he has appeared, that English artists are neglected ? The simple fact is that the English public are not such donkeys as some suppose, and that they have a national tendency towards anything superior which leads them to prefer Italian songsters to those of British manufacture, for no other reason than that they are more accomplished ; for let a true English artist arise, and it is notorious that he or she is as well received as any foreigner—nay, the English artist is better received, for the national feeling is superadded to the recognition of merit, and the two sentiments go hand in hand to heighten enthusiasm ! "— a conclusion which the history of British music and the experience of British musicians scarcely warrants without reservations.

There was no doubt of Reeves's position when in September he was engaged to sing at the Worcester and Norwich Festivals. These festivals had features peculiar to themselves. The management was autocratic, and the subscribers and the public accepted its veto, sometimes silently, and sometimes with murmurs. All three worshipped Handel, but in a blind, semi-religious sort of way, while their knowledge and appreciation of music other than his were extremely limited. Very odd things from a musical point of view were sometimes done at these festivals, especially when the ecclesiastical element or the idiosyncrasies of musicians asserted themselves.

The absurd conditions to which Costa had to submit at Birmingham in 1829, and the extravagant whimsicalities of Lindley the 'cellist, have already been told. Another unwarrantable liberty was the appropriation of " Comfort ye " by Catalani ; while Braham came in for severe censure over the fantastic ornaments with which at the Hereford Festival he once " improved " the same solo.

These excrescences belonged to the dark ages, but even in 1848 the Festivals had peculiarities not to be found elsewhere. The arrangement of the orchestra in Worcester Cathedral when Sims Reeves first sang there in *Elijah* may be instanced. The chorus was placed in front behind the solo vocalists and the conductor between the two. The 'cellos and double basses were in the rear of the chorus, farther on were the violins and tenors, still farther the wind instruments, and at the back of all the brass close to the organ. The *Times* critic at first did not know what to make of this disposition, but admitted after he had heard the *Elijah* that the effect was better than he expected. It is pleasant to learn that Mr. Done, the conductor, had chosen his chorus from " the humbler classes and had sedulously practised them in Mendelssohn's music for months previous to the Festival." Owing to the recent death of the composer, the oratorio excited more than ordinary interest, and the audience was very large. The tenor solos were divided—an inartistic arrangement which would hardly be tolerated nowadays—Lockey singing " If with all your hearts," and Sims Reeves " Then shall the righteous." Of Reeves's singing in Beethoven's *Mount of Olives*, produced under the title of *Engedi*, or *David in the Wilderness*, in deference to religious scruples, the *Times* said that " he never produced a greater or more legitimate effect. . . . The music admirably suited his voice and he sang with immense fervour and infinite purity of style." On the evening when *Oberon* occupied the first part of the programme, the hall was packed, hundreds being turned away.

Altogether the Worcester Festival of this year was unusually successful. The *Times*, however, did not forget to point out the absurdity of the nominal conductor having to quit the desk because of his inability to handle a body of instrumentalists when they played alone, the odd spectacle being witnessed of his sitting in the orchestra or among the audience, while the leader of the violins assumed the baton. But this was not the worst. Not infrequently, at such festivals, the conductor was seen waving his stick in one direction while the leader of the orchestra was beating time in direct opposition. Such incongruities, it may be hoped, are things of the past.

At the Norfolk and Norwich Festival, which took place the week following that at Worcester, Sims Reeves repeated his triumph in *Elijah* (which but for his death

Mendelssohn would have conducted). Several characteristics of the times are noticeable. A symphony of Spohr's was received with an amount of applause which drew from the critic of the *Times* approval and surprise. He regarded it as an awakening of the musical taste of the Norfolk people, seeing that at the Festival of three years before Beethoven's C Minor Symphony was played " without a hand being raised." On one evening Haydn's Symphony in C Minor (No. 5 of the Salaman 12) was given solely on account of the minuet, played as a sort of 'cello obbligato by Lindley, who for fifty years had attended the festivals. The critic shook his head at this, as the symphony otherwise is not very striking, but he reserved his wrath for the interpolations in *Israel in Egypt*, the egregious work of the Gresham Musical Professor, Mr. Edward Taylor. These interpolations were in every sense unwarrantable, and the fact that they were taken from other of Handel's oratorios did not make them any better. The critic was very angry with Benedict, the musical director, for accepting Taylor's version. He did not know that Benedict was totally against the interpolations but was overpowered by the Festival Committee.[1]

From the point of view of to-day the adulation of the Duke of Cambridge was the most ridiculous feature of the Festival. He was regarded as of equal importance with the music, and when he arrived during the performance of Beethoven's Eighth Symphony the audience cheered him, " arresting the progress of the musicians in the orchestra." The National Anthem was sung as soon as the distinguished party had taken their seats, and at its conclusion the symphony was resumed !

It must be admitted that the Duke did his duty manfully. He never missed a performance ; he sat through all in a sort of chair of state, and during *Elijah* had " the score in his hand, from which he hardly took his eyes." He also commanded the various encores, and what would have happened had the audience chosen to act on their own initiative one hardly dares to think.

In connection with the Norfolk Festival we get for the

[1] Robin H. Legge and W. E. Hansell, *Norfolk and Norwich Musical Festivals*, p. 122.

first time some idea of the fees which Sims Reeves commanded at this time. In 1848 he was paid 100 guineas,
Madame Viardot Garcia and Madame Alboni each
receiving £300 and Lablache 150 guineas. In 1852
and 1854 his fee was the same, but in 1857 he asked 200
guineas, terms which were refused. Miss Clara Novello,
however, could command £300, the committee evidently
attaching more importance to sopranos than to tenors.
This year great prominence was given to Italian singers.
In 1860 Sims Reeves's fee of 200 guineas was conceded.[1]
His fee for 1863 is not given in the records of *The Norfolk
and Norwich Festivals*, from which this information is
taken, and in 1866 Reeves was ill, W. H. Cummings filling
his place. The same ill-luck befell him in 1872, which
gave a chance to Mr. Edward Lloyd, who was then coming
into prominence. Mr. Lloyd sang in subsequent Festivals
up to 1893, the final year recorded by the annals. Fortune was equally kind to Mr. Lloyd at Leeds in 1872.
Sims Reeves was indisposed, Mr. Lloyd deputised for him,
and subsequently was always engaged.

In September Howard Glover announced a series of
Italian operas in English at the Theatre Royal, Manchester,
with Sims Reeves as the great attraction, and Miss
Rainforth as his leading lady. There may or may not
have been design on the part of Mr. Glover in choosing
this particular date. On the week previous to his opening
Jenny Lind and Roger, the famous French tenor, had
appeared at Manchester in the very operas he intended
to produce—*Lucia* and *Sonnambula*—and comparisons
between the two companies were inevitable. Miss
Rainforth, of course, had no idea of rivalling Jenny Lind—
in *her* case there could be no comparison—but with
Sims Reeves it was different. Roger, a fine singer undoubtedly, was inferior to Reeves in quality of voice, in
vocalisation, and in intensity of passion. The duel was
really between the rival stars, Jenny Lind and Sims Reeves;
and possibly Howard Glover, who was an experienced
entrepreneur, foresaw the excellent advertisement his
venture would receive from the close juxtaposition
of the two, especially after the rupture at Her Majesty's

[1] For singing at the four concerts of the Leeds Festival in 1858 his
fee was 200 guineas.

in the summer. At any rate, Sims Reeves must have been greatly gratified by the enthusiastic crowd which packed the Manchester theatre—a larger audience than that which greeted Jenny Lind. It is to be noted also that these audiences came from two very different classes of society. The landed gentry, the rich mill-owners and merchants, paid their guineas for the same seats for which the operatives were asked but a shilling, the five-shilling gallery becoming a sixpenny one. Of the first audience it may be said that the great bulk were present either out of curiosity or because it was the correct thing to do. Of the second, very few came if not with an anticipation of real pleasure.

The *Manchester Courier* hailed Sims Reeves's " Edgardo " with unstinted praise. The *Guardian* maintained the grudging, carping tone it sounded in 1843. The captious critic was, however, graciously pleased to approve of Reeves's Elvino in *Sonnambula* (anglicised as *The Sleepwalker*) and in *I Puritani* (transformed in similar fashion to *Puritans and Cavaliers*), in which Reeves appeared as Arturo.

Mr. Alfred Bunn on October 7th commenced a series of operas at Covent Garden with *Sonnambula*, Reeves as Elvino singing the part for the first time in London. It was an unequivocal success. Upon his entrance " he was received with immense enthusiasm, the whole house continuing to cheer him for several minutes," said the *Musical World* of October 21st, 1848. A most unusual compliment was paid him on this occasion, for on being called for after each act bouquets were thrown to him, " which with great gallantry he proffered to Miss Romer, the Amina of the evening." It is odd to read that Sam Cowell, afterwards identified with *The Rat-catcher's Daughter*, played Alessio. Auber's *Haydie* followed, and here Reeves's success was shared by his future wife, Miss Emma Lucombe, who took the title-rôle. Of Miss Lucombe the *Musical World* said she " promised to be our most accomplished female vocalist," and the *Athenæum* wrote that in her singing " there was more of the operatic artist than we have ever seen and heard from any cantatrice on the English stage since Miss Kemble left it." *Haydie*, however, did not prove a trump card, whereupon

9

Mr. Bunn lowered his prices and revived *Lucia*—a change which resulted in a bumper house. With this performance Sims Reeves's engagement at Covent Garden seems to have terminated.

Meanwhile, events in connection with Exeter Hall were following each other, rapidly leading up to the commencement of an epoch as important in connection with British musical history as in its bearing on the career of Sims Reeves. Although at the present moment little is heard of oratorio (not so much maybe from change of fashion as from the strange and lamentable dwindling of choral societies), its home is, and has always been, in this country. Never in Germany, the land of Bach, of Handel, of Mozart and Beethoven, of Mendelssohn, of Spohr, has oratorio found such favour as in Great Britain, and it is not too much to say that to Michael Costa, an Italian, is partly due the high standard of performance and the wide popularity attained by oratorio throughout the Victorian era.

During 1848 the Sacred Harmonic Society passed " through a critical period " under Mr. Surman, and the committee, taking their courage in both hands, engaged Mr. Costa as musical director, despite the fact that his experience as conductor of the Philharmonic Concerts and of the Covent Garden orchestra was mainly in connection with instrumentalists. It was a bold experiment, and there was some shrugging of shoulders when the decision was announced, as it was held that conducting a great body of choralists was very different from conducting an orchestra. There were those also who did not like the autocratic ways with which Costa was credited, nor the new rules he laid down as a condition of his assuming the baton. But it was clear that the old, sloppy, easy, go-as-you-please methods would not do, and if the new régime resulted in the resignation of some fossilised members, it was all to the good.

Costa was known to be a rigid disciplinarian, and a capital description of him which appeared in the *Morning Post* during 1848 will bring him back to the memories of the habitués, if any remain, of the opera in the fifties and sixties, for his characteristics never altered. "The members of the band," the writer tells us, " have taken their places, and Costa has ascended the rostrum. He looks round, his arm is erect, one hand holds the baton, the other extended ; he has one eye on the score—but it is almost unnecessary, for we would hold a wager that he could conduct the opera he has once studied from memory— the other eye is on the band. The beat has begun, and he twists his head and his neck with a nervous affectation, but woe betide the instrumentalist who is playing a note that is a vibration only in the rear, or who slips a *petite* note." [1]

Costa's punctuality and precision became by-words with the Sacred Harmonic Society, and Mr. Herbert Reeves, who had many opportunities of closely observing him, says that about a minute before taking his place in the orchestra he would enter the artists' room, and watch in hand would say, " Time, gentlemen," and with a rapid glance and a curious one-sided dropping of the lower lip—a habit which he had at the commencement of a concert, and which probably was an outward indication of inward anxiety—he would proceed on his way.

This lowering of the lip and the fixed look in his eyes gave him an aspect of austerity which was not part of his character. Few vocalists, however distinguished, dared to brave his anger by being late. Sims Reeves alone was an exception. Reeves was never careless in this direction, but there were times when unavoidably he arrived after the other artists had taken their places, but on such occasions there was never a scowl for him. It must, however, be recollected that whenever Reeves chanced to be late he had the art of slipping into his place so quietly that unless any of the audience had their eyes fixed on the vacant chair no one would know the precise moment when it was occupied. Costa had a sincere regard for Reeves, and an intense admiration of his talents. [2]

[1] Arditi, in his *Reminiscences*— writing of Costa thirty years later, says that Costa's " invaluable services were somewhat obscured by his auto- cratic ways. . . . As long as Sir Michael was at the head of the orchestra there was practically no chance of any other conductor being allowed to share the honours." Bottesini was engaged for the season as assistant conductor, but he was never once allowed his privilege. It is interesting to note the loyalty of Costa's band, martinet though he was. When he resigned, Sainton and others resigned too, and those who remained gave Arditi, his successor, a very cold reception.

[2] I remember when quite a child my mother taught me to sing " I

The Society opened its season under Costa on November 1st with *Elijah*, and on the 24th *The Messiah* was given, Sims Reeves singing the tenor music for the first time in London.   During the summer great improvements had been made in Exeter Hall.   The lantern roof, the recesses, and the death-trap staircase were still in being, but the orchestra had been reconstructed.   Formerly the chorus stood on the same level, so that many could not see the conductor ; the seats were now raised each row sixteen inches above the one in front.   The disposition of the band was that adopted at the Philharmonic Concerts, the organ was improved so as to be in unison in any key with the wind instruments, whereas in certain keys it used to be sadly out of tune (one shudders to think of it), and other minor defects were removed and omissions supplied.   There was but one note of praise for Reeves's singing in *The Messiah*, and the improvement in the choruses was welcomed heartily, the *Times* remarking that it was now possible to obtain a *pianissimo*.   " For unto us a child is born " was given perhaps for the first time, it remarked, " with the proper expression ; the theme was delivered *pianissimo*, and the gradual crescendo was made up to a grand burst of the whole choral and instrumental forces which produced a very striking effect."   Years after a certain critic raised objections to this rendering of the chorus, which he jocosely called the " Monthly Nurse " reading, and he never lost an opportunity of repeating the gibe.

Sir Charles Villiers Stanford takes a like view.   In his entertaining reminiscences, *Pages from an Unwritten Diary*, he writes : " No such monstrous caricature as the *pianissimo* start of the chorus ' For unto us a child is born ' was ever heard in Dublin.   The ludicrous suggestion which such a rendering gives of the necessity of ' hushing up the facts ' was enough to kill it in an Irish mind."   He adds that " Hans Richter, when he directed

dreamt I dwelt in Heaven " from Costa's *Naaman*, and on one occasion when he was visiting my father I was asked to sing it to him.   I was terribly shy and half afraid of the great man, and I think I took refuge behind the music stool.   However, I got through the solo, after which he said smilingly, " Yes, that's just how I wish it to be sung."   I believe that his imperiousness was only on the surface and that he was really of a kindly nature.—HERBERT REEVES.

it for the first time in his life at the Birmingham Festival of 1885, made such satirical criticisms upon this Costa-monger *nuance* that it could never be ventured on again by any self-respecting conductor." Nevertheless, the fact remains that in the facsimile reproduction of Handel's original score published in 1863 the word *piano* is written over the opening symphony and over the repetition of the words " For unto us " in the middle of the chorus ; *forte* is only marked at the passage " Wonderful, Counsellor, Prince of Peace."

The Messiah with Sims Reeves created a great impression, and it was given three times during December by the Sacred Harmonic Society, and once by Mr. Surman's London Sacred Harmonic. He also sang in *Judas Maccabæus* for Mr. Surman during the same month.

The enthusiasm shown for the advancement of music in London and the provinces is nowadays very refreshing to read. The tastes of the general public were homely and narrow, but they were willing to enlarge their knowledge. In 1848 they had much to learn, and only through Jullien's efforts were they permitted a glimpse of a world other than that of simple ballads. With a laudable desire to follow the example set by the " Promenades," a body of organisers with Mr. Willy, an accomplished violinist, as director, started the " Wednesday Concerts," the object of which was to provide cheap periodical concerts, chiefly of a popular character, with the best artists in the various departments.

Sims Reeves was engaged as the principal attraction on the " popular " side, and his extensive répertoire of ballads acquired during his provincial experience was largely called upon, he singing the public's favourite ditties in a way that invested the old songs with new charm. " Nanny, wilt thou gang wi' me ? " " The Pilgrim of Love," " My pretty Jane," " Farewell, my trim-built wherry," " The Thorn," " The White Squall," and many more delighted the thousands who packed Exeter Hall at the twenty concerts which comprised the series, and on one occasion when he sang "The Death of Nelson," Braham, who was in the audience, heartily applauded.

A " popular " musical audience of those days, like the

pittites of the theatre who could bless or damn a play on its first night, were great sticklers for their rights, and of their punctiliousness Sims Reeves had a curious experience when he first sang " The Bay of Biscay " at the " Wednesdays." After singing the first verse he was greeted with immense applause. Omitting the second verse, he proceeded to the third, and was stopped by a volley of hisses and groans amid which could be heard yells for the " second verse." Reeves paused for a few seconds and was continuing, when he was again brought to a standstill by the renewed uproar. He stood patiently for five minutes while the tumult raged, and at last walked off the platform, puzzled and annoyed. Then the manager came forward and explained that only two verses had been assigned to Mr. Reeves, but that in making up the book of words the second verse had inadvertently been inserted.

Another disturbance was beginning when Reeves again appeared, upon which Mr. Willy handed him a printed programme, from which he declaimed the second verse " with extraordinary vigour," and the applause at the end was " as unanimous as it was boisterous." Whatever may be said of their musical tastes, our predecessors were at all events not lacking in sincerity.

CHAPTER XII

1849

THE manager of the " Wednesday Concerts " was a shrewd business man who knew what his public liked. He announced the engagement of Braham, and as an additional attraction promised that the veteran should sing a duet with his youthful rival. This musical " event " was looked forward to with intense curiosity, for it was as though the setting and rising sun were about to shine simultaneously. Mr. Chorley, however, was outraged and he smote the project hip and thigh. But, as Beatrice said of Benedick, nobody " marked " the critic's indignation. Exeter Hall was crowded and Braham's reception was uproarious. " The most tremendous encore of the evening," said the *Musical World*, " was awarded to ' The Bay of Biscay,' which the veteran sang and acted in a most extraordinary manner. The whole audience rose as if by general command, and cheered, clapped, stamped, and waved their hats, handkerchiefs, and palms as if they were one infuriated animal."

When one learns *how* Braham *acted* " The Bay of

Biscay," the question arises whether the audience let themselves go out of pure admiration. But it would seem to be so. At any rate, they were not treated to such an exhibition as that with which Braham once favoured a fashionable audience at a Hereford Festival. The story is told by Henry Phillips : " The Shire Hall, where this particular comedy was enacted, had an orchestral platform with an exceedingly high front. On came Mr. Braham to sing his famous song, in the last verse of which he was to exclaim ' A sail—a sail—a sail ! ' at which point he always went down on one knee as if in thankfulness. On this occasion, however, on his putting in this dramatic touch, he suddenly disappeared from sight behind the high front. The audience was quite alarmed, thinking he must have dropped through some trap-door. They were rising to their feet in dismay when up jumped the little tenor to finish his song, which he did amidst a universal shout of laughter." The spectacle of the squat little man, in his unwieldy light brown wig, his unmistakable Israelitish countenance, and with his head cocked on one side, suddenly popping up above the obstruction must have been irresistibly ludicrous, and it speaks volumes for his genius that the audience should have admired the performance despite its absurdity.[1]

The duet " Gallop on gaily," from Braham's musical play *Family Quarrels*, was sung by Braham and Reeves in due course and created a furore. Mr. Reeves's description of this memorable occasion must be quoted. " Out of respect for Braham," he says, " I made no endeavour to outshine him by the display of those qualities of voice which as a young man I naturally possessed. The room was full of venerable amateurs, and many of them seemed well satisfied at the idea of their man whom they had applauded at a hundred triumphs eclipsing the young upstart of a later age.

---

[1] Some forty years later a critic wrote of Sims Reeves at the Albert Palace, Battersea : " I heard Braham, when he had been about the same length of time before the public, sing ' The Bay of Biscay.' I must acknowledge in perfect fairness it was not singing but shouting, and the applause he received seemed hardly to repay him for the effort. Mr. Sims Reeves has indeed been a careful man and his production of voice a perfect study. You hear still the same quality of tone, due as much to method as to natural gift."

At last I heard someone near me in the orchestra whisper to a neighbour, ' The old man has the best of it.' This, I confess, aroused me. I had no wish to humiliate, but I certainly did not desire to be beaten. I exerted all my powers ; and this outburst was followed by universal applause. I am happy to say that the first who congratulated me in private was Braham himself." Mr. Herbert Reeves says that once, when his father was recalling the rivalry, his words were, " I think I fairly sang him down," and one can well believe it. The duet figured at subsequent Wednesday Concerts, as also did others with Sims Reeves, such as Braham's " Albion," " The Father's Blessing " by Lavenu (a popular composer of the day, long since forgotten), and " All's Well." The duettists were dubbed the " two monster tenors," the " thunderers," and, to quote the *Musical World,* " which came off the victor it was hard to say."

The " Wednesday Concerts," which in consequence of their enormous success were prolonged eight weeks beyond the season originally intended, established Sims Reeves's reputation in London as the tenor ballad singer par excellence. The old favourites with which he then identified himself he repeated continually in after-years, and no tenor ever challenged him on his own ground. Song writers were only too anxious to have their compositions sung by the popular tenor, but few of their efforts have survived to the present day.

A new era in concert enterprise was initiated by the " Wednesday Concerts." One feature peculiar to the " Promenade " audiences was absent, and many who would gladly have attended Jullien's concerts but for having to face flaunting women whose presence it is to be suspected was by the management courted rather than repelled, had now the chance of hearing good operatic music, together with ballads of the purely English school, rendered in a fashion which lifted them above the commonplace. Not much that was severely classical was given, but the audience which weekly crowded Exeter Hall probably did not regret its paucity.

One of the last concerts of the series deserves mention as thoroughly typical of the narrowness of the musical taste of the times. It was Ash Wednesday, when the whole of the theatrical staffs in the kingdom were condemned by the Church of England to lose a day's earnings. The hypocrisy of the thing was completed by the restrictions imposed on those entertainments which conformed to the law. Thus when Rossini's *Stabat Mater* was performed on this particular day, an extraordinary adaptation of the words to Dante's story of Ugolino was chosen. The medley was the work of one Maggioni, described as " dramatic writer to Her Majesty's Theatre," and presumably one of the authors of the egregious English versions of the Italian operas which used to be the laughing-stock of those who invested their shillings on " books of the words." Signor Maggioni published his travesty of Rossini's " service " in 1842, explaining in his preface that " the great success of the *Stabat Mater* of Rossini and the general and just objection to singing sacred words in parties or public societies of amusement suggested the idea." Sims Reeves sang " Cujus Animam" presumably in the original Latin, the audience being left to make what they could of the English perversion attached.

The adaptation of " Pro Peccatis " may be quoted as a specimen of Signor Maggioni's versification. It ran :

> " It was the hour they expected
> Bread ; but vainly long they lingered,
> Till in doubt they hoped no more.
> As they listened vain conviction
> Of that Tower, the Tower of famine
> Heard they nailed the dismal door."

The acceptance of this rubbish makes one wonder whether we had any sense of humour in the forties.

One more reference and the " Wednesdays " may be dismissed. At these concerts commenced the encore nuisance which pursued Sims Reeves wherever he went, and which continued until the very end of his career. It was a mania which had no sense in it. He might sing " Adelaida " and no attempt be made to insist upon a repetition, but when later on he gave " The Bay of Biscay " or " The Pilgrim of Love," an uproar arose if he refused to acknowledge the encore. What the *Musical World* called a " regular row " was constantly taking place, and when after sharing in a selection from *Masaniello* Reeves was called upon to sing " The Bay of Biscay " twice, and he simply bowed, a storm arose, upon which he remonstrated with his tyrants, pointing out that they treated him with harshness, since he had already sung four times, adding that the song which they wanted again was " dreadfully fatiguing."

The *Musical World* summed up the question in ironical fashion, its argument being that because Sims Reeves was encored every time that he sang, not being encored in the Masaniello part of the concert, he had, therefore, sung a less number of times than usual. On the other hand, it is unreasonable, it admitted, for the public to expect two concerts for one. But this is what they *did* expect and what they continued to expect. Sims Reeves was very good-natured and gave way whenever it was possible. On a certain occasion the audience fell to quarrelling over that stormy petrel " The Bay of Biscay," one half calling for its repetition and the other half yelling for something else. Reeves told them to settle the matter among themselves and he would sing whatever they wished. The house divided and the majority were for " The Bay," which he accordingly gave.

In later years he was not so disposed to endure this species of persecution. An instance within my experience occurred at the Beaumont Institute, Mile End, where the audiences were invariably insatiable. Reeves had been encored, and as bows of acknowledgment did not satisfy, he at last yielded to the clamour and appeared. He walked across the platform with that peculiar walk of his (acquired probably from his stage training) and the characteristic nonchalant swing of his shoulders (the origin of silly and unfounded accusations), and had sat down to the piano to accompany himself, when some stupid person called out " My pretty Jane." This was too much. He gave one indignant glance around, shut down the lid of the piano with a significant bang, and strode away without a word. He was willing to oblige, but he was not to be dictated to. A storm of indignation descended upon the indiscreet member of the audience, but Sims Reeves was seen no more that night.

Besides the Wednesday Concerts, Sims Reeves during the

first half of 1849 sang at the Bristol Musical Festival,
at various benefit concerts in London, and in concerts at
Liverpool and Manchester, at which latter town *Acis and
Galatea* and selections from *King Arthur* were given,
and his old antagonist, Mr. Sever, had another chance of
ventilating his views. The severe critic remarked
pettishly of Reeves that " in London he is lauded to the
skies, in Manchester he is lauded to the skies, yet as the
college distich has it :

> " We do not like thee, Dr. Fell,
> The reason why we scarce can tell ;
> But this we know and that full well,
> We do not like thee, Dr. Fell."

This, at all events, is candid, and suggests that it would
not be unreasonable to assign some of Mr. Chorley's
early captious criticisms to a similar idiosyncrasy. From
time to time during 1849 the *Athenæum* critic considered
it his duty to give gratuitous advice occasionally or to
chide the vocalist who dared to go his own way. After
a performance of *Judas Maccabæus* by the Sacred Harmonic Society, he found occasion to find fault with Reeves,
considering that the declamatory method of the modern
Italian school was not suitable for the recitatives and airs
of the classical writers. Mr. Chorley had at that period
not shaken off his pedantry. The time came when he
admitted that Reeves in the dramatic spirit which he
infused into oratorio singing was right.

Mr. Chorley was in an unusually acid mood in this
issue (January 13th, 1849), as he fell foul of even Handel
for his shortcomings in *Judas*. The oratorio, he considered, is " strangely patchy." It does not contain
" one first-class song," it has " sequence of key and
movement as *un*sequential as anything to be complained of
in Verdi," and he asked whether " See the conquering
hero " " is not one of Handel's after-thoughts—thrown
in like ' Dal tuo stellato soglio ' by Rossini into his *Mosè* " ?
To share Mr. Chorley's blame with Handel must in a way
have consoled the censured tenor. However, on Reeves's
second engagement in Italian opera with Mr. Beale as
manager, which was run at Covent Garden in opposition

to Mr. Lumley's company at Her Majesty's, the critic by his praise in some respects made amends.

The Covent Garden Company was a very strong one, and included Grisi, Persiani, Dorus Gras, Catherine Hayes, Mario, Tamburini, Tagliafico, Ronconi, and other stars. Reeves was thus associated with the very highest artists and there is no evidence that other than good feeling prevailed. With Mario especially Reeves was always on the best of terms. Reeves's debut was in *Sonnambula* on May 22nd. The papers were unanimously eulogistic; the *Times* remarked that he shared the honours with Madame Persiani; and Mr. Chorley wrote that the evening was "a legitimate success for Mr. Sims Reeves, as besides his appearance as Elvino to Madame Persiani's incomparable Amina he did good service to his theatre by singing the Rataplan couplets in *Gli Ugonotti*. "Having loudly expressed our vexation at certain mistakes made by our best tenor for popularity's sake, it behoves us no less emphatically to call attention to every better advised and better executed step on his part. . . . The success of Mr. Reeves was complete, as indeed his singing of the part of Elvino deserved." But in a few weeks the critic's mood changed. Reeves's Roderick Dhu in Rossini's *Donna del Lago* (July 18th) came in for criticism. Reeves, however, may not have felt much sympathy with the part, which was certainly not suited to his style.

The Covent Garden operatic season finished with the end of August, and it must be confessed that it had given Sims Reeves very few opportunities. One performance in *Sonnambula* and one in *Donna del Lago* represented the sum-total. On the concert platform, however, he was busy enough, and in the autumn he was engaged to sing at no less than three provincial Festivals— Liverpool, Birmingham, and Hereford. One notices even in these days his frequent indispositions, partly caused by his sensitive vocal chords and partly due to his extreme desire to give the public none but his best. A singer, however, is not necessarily the best judge of when he *is* at his best. The nervous system plays an important part in the artistic temperament, and a vocalist may consider himself in wretched voice in the morning and sing gloriously at night. It may be that Reeves at times suffered from want of confidence in himself. Anyhow, at the Liverpool Festival he was unable to sing in *The Messiah* owing to illness.

The Birmingham Festival (September 24th) is notable, as Mario sang for the first time in English, and in " Then shall the righteous " he surprised everyone by the distinct and intelligible manner in which he pronounced the words. He repeated this venture at Hereford, Sims Reeves in each case having to be contented with " If with all your hearts." There is an indication of the loosening of the bonds of prejudice in the fact that Beethoven's Mass in C and Rossini's *Stabat Mater* were given in Hereford Cathedral, but the absurdity of the President of the Festival determining when there should or should not be an encore still remained. The *Musical World*, in recording that Reeves's singing of " In native worth " made a sensible impression upon the audience, added that had the noble President given the signal it would doubtless have met the general wish. In the case of " Still so gently " the President yielded, but fixed the encore to be taken at the end of the concert, thus anticipating Mr. Henry Leslie, who on one occasion when worried by an incessant demand for repeats, told the audience that as the performance was long and as doubtless many present had to catch trains, if those who wished to hear the piece again would wait to the end it would then be repeated. There were no more requests for encores on that evening.

By this time Reeves was associated with Miss Lucombe whom he subsequently married, and this attachment had probably something to do with his formation of an operatic company under the business management of Mr. Whitworth, the baritone, with which he toured the provinces, Miss Lucombe as leading lady. He opened in October at Liverpool, at the end of the month he was in Dublin, and on November 6th, after his own " run " had concluded, occurred an episode the story of which deserves record at full length.

The remoteness of Dublin in those infant days of telegraphy is responsible for what at the present time would be impossible, or Mr. Willert Beale, who was on tour with a company of operatic singers, all foreign with

SIMS REEVES IN 1849.
From a drawing by Alfred Crowquill.

the notable exception of Miss Catherine Hayes, would have known that at the very theatre he had engaged, Sims Reeves had the week previous anticipated him with Italian opera, the series ending the week before Mr. Beale was to commence. On learning this, Mr. Beale called on the Reeves party at their hotel and had a friendly chat. " There had been some misunderstanding," Mr. Beale writes, " between Catherine Hayes and Reeves, which interfered unpleasantly with their professional pursuits, during which they were frequently engaged to sing together. At her request I attempted a reconciliation between them. In compliance with a note he had written me earlier in the day I had sent him a box for *Lucia*, which he used."

At the rehearsal Paglieri (Beale's leading tenor) showed signs of stage-fright, but in the evening all promised well until Edgardo appeared. He came on to the stage in an enormous flat black hat, still more enormous top-boots, and a black cloak. He was a short man, and the cloak and boots apparently met the spreading hat, which terminated on high with a black cock's feather. The gallery received this apparition with yells. " He opened his mouth," continues Mr. Beale, " threw out his arms from under the hat, and went ' quack ' on the high B flat ending the first recitative he had to sing. Catherine Hayes appeared and began the duet, which Edgardo turned into a burlesque ; the tumult increased, and at last Lucia bowed politely to Edgardo and disappeared behind the scenes, Edgardo following her example on the opposite side." Calcraft, the manager, in vain endeavoured to console Miss Hayes, and Damcke, the reserve tenor, was sent for, after which Calcraft made a speech explaining that Paglieri was seized with illness, but that Damcke would take his place. Unfortunately he called Damcke " Herr Donkey," and this sent the audience into convulsions.

In the meantime Reeves had been recognised by the audience and was called for. Mr. Beale went to his box, but could not induce him to come to the rescue. " Catherine Hayes," writes Mr. Beale, " had urged me to ask Reeves to sing, but was not disturbed at his refusal more than to remark how tiresome it was."

" During the performance," says the *Dublin Freeman's Journal*, " Mr. Sims Reeves . . . was loudly called for. . . . The excitement of the house continuing, . . . Mr. Calcraft addressed the audience and said :

" ' The gentleman who was to have filled the part was unable to appear, and Signor Paglieri in that emergency kindly took the part without, as must be admitted, preparation. I have asked Mr. Reeves to sing, and he has declined. (Loud groans.) ' Mr. Damcke will be here very soon, and I trust you will be then satisfied.' (Renewed confusion and calls for Mr. Reeves.)

" Mr. Reeves here presented himself in front of the box he occupied amidst a scene of terrific uproar, . . . and said, ' Ladies and gentlemen, permit me to say a few words in my own defence.' (' Come down to the stage,' and great confusion.) ' Ladies and gentlemen, I *will* sing to oblige you, but not to . . . ' (Here the remainder of Mr. Reeves's observation was drowned in the storm of cheering uproar that followed, but what he said was that he would not sing for Mr. Calcraft.) Mr. Reeves then retired from the box. Meanwhile the performance was suspended and the house was a perfect Babel."

Despite the compliment that was paid him, Reeves was evidently much irritated, and as he walked across the stage he met Julius Benedict, " who," says Mr. Beale, " was standing with his back to the curtain indulging in that kind of action so familiar to all who knew the kind-hearted maestro, as though he were washing his hands with invisible soap in imperceptible water. ' You will take care of me, Mr. Benedict ? ' said Reeves as he passed. ' I always do my best,' was the reply, to which Reeves answered irritably, quite excusable under the stress and strain of the unforeseen situation."

Naturally this upset Benedict. He left the theatre, and the opera was conductorless. Mr. Beale hurried off for Lavenu, whom he found. At length the curtain rose, and Reeves came on from one side of the stage and Catherine Hayes from the other. The two artists met and greeted each other cordially and gracefully, amidst pealing and deafening thunder of applause from the entire house.

It must have been a curious moment for both singers. True, they had sung together since the never-to-be-forgotten *première* at Milan, but they had recently had a difference. It is not unlikely that their reconciliation under such novel circumstances had much to do with their dual triumph that night, for the performance went splendidly.

The curtain fell at 1 a.m., but the comedy was not played out. Mr. Calcraft made a speech to the effect that he thought it right no misconception should arise in reference to the words of Mr. Reeves that he would sing to oblige the public, but not to oblige the manager. So far from any unkindly feeling, as a matter of fact he had engaged with Mr. Reeves to sing for him the week before Christmas.

At this juncture Mr. Reeves, dressed in his stage costume, came forward and, again to quote Mr. Beale, " stood with folded arms looking tigerish " at Mr. Calcraft, when a voice from the gods shouted, " Make it up, both of you," an appeal greeted with cheers and laughter. Reeves then gave his version—practically that everybody all round lost their tempers—upon which Mr. Calcraft, after saying he was obliged to Mr. Reeves for singing in the opera, extended his hand, which Reeves took, and the matter ended. On the whole the Dublin audience had a night's enjoyment quite after its own heart. Years after (says Mr. Herbert Reeves), Sir Henry Irving, referring to Reeves's *tour de force* on this occasion, said that to go through such an undertaking at a minute's notice and in a foreign tongue was nothing short of a stroke of genius.

From Dublin the company went on to Belfast, where an awkward contretemps occurred which was not wholly unconnected with Reeves, but with which personally he had nothing to do. Mr. Cunningham, the lessee of the Belfast theatre, had arranged with Mr. Whitworth to open in November, " but as there had been " (to quote Mr. Cunningham's explanation of the affair in the *Northern Whig*) " disappointments lately in engagements where Mr. Reeves was concerned, I could not take the risk of advertising and preparing for the opera unless Mr. Whitworth would agree to pay a moiety of my

10

expenses should any disappointment occur in this arising from *illness* or other causes." Mr. Cunningham was evidently a cautious Scot, and the emphasis he laid on the word " illness " shows that thus early in his career Reeves was looked upon—in sporting language—as a " doubtful starter."

Mr. Whitworth seems to have agreed to these conditions, and at his wish the date of opening was altered from December 12th to the 5th. It so chanced that Mr. Cunningham had business at Dublin in the early days of December, and found, to his astonishment, that Sims Reeves was billed to appear there on the 5th, the very day he had been announced to sing at Belfast, and he was naturally irate at having had no intimation from Mr. Whitworth that he had reverted to the original date. It seems, however, that Mr. Whitworth *had* written, but Mr. Cunningham, having left for Dublin, did not get the letter.

The reason of Reeves singing in Dublin on the 5th was this : *Ernani* was one of the operas in the series of six performances to be given by Sims Reeves, but owing to the tenor's illness in Liverpool he had not been able to study the part sufficiently, and consequently on the evening on which the opera should have been given the theatre had to be closed. Mr. Calcraft insisted on his rights and the deficiency was made good by a performance on the 5th. Possibly some disagreement on this point may have accounted for Reeves refusing to sing for Calcraft on the following evening.

However this may be, matters were arranged between Cunningham and Whitworth and the company opened at Belfast, things going smoothly until the final night, when at the close of the performance a heated dispute arose in consequence of Cunningham claiming his moiety of the expenses from Whitworth, as the series failed to start on the 5th. Whitworth contended that this condition applied only to the 12th, and the date having been altered the condition ought not to be observed. Mr. Whitworth cut the Gordian knot by appealing to the audience, and enlisted their sympathy so much that when Cunningham attempted to explain, they refused to hear him. He took the refusal much to heart and announced in the *Northern Whig* that henceforth he would have nothing more to do with Belfast or its theatre, and he cancelled his contract with Macready, whom he had engaged for a series of performances. How the matter was settled does not appear ; the important point to be remembered was that in Reeves's future engagements his health was a factor not to be overlooked.

The tour in Ireland concluded with performances at Cork, *Ernani* figuring in the series, and a return visit to Dublin, where Reeves's unlucky star of indisposition was once more in the ascendant. He was announced to appear on December 17th in *Ernani*, but was ill with influenza, as his doctor certified. On the 19th he was billed to sing in *Sonnambula* ; but on the 22nd, his benefit night—he was doomed to be ill-fated—he had again to disappoint. On the whole the Irish tour of 1849 was marked by mishaps.

CHAPTER XIII

1850

The encore nuisance. Reeves a victim. English and Italian tenors. The favouritism shown to the latter. Puritanic Exeter Hall managers. St. Martin's Hall opens. A doubtful success. Reeves's second entry into Italian opera. His triumph in *Ernani*. The *Morning Post's* denunciation of Verdi's music. Reeves sings with Catherine Hayes in *Lucia* and with Sontag in *Sonnambula*. *The Messiah* given for the first time in Wales. The " Monster " concert mania. The pretentious " Grand National Concerts." The " Berlin Choir " ruse.

THE beginning of 1850 saw Reeves back in London, where on January 2nd he was given an uproarious welcome at the popular " Wednesdays." He still excited the close attention of the critics, and we find the *Morning Post* and *Chronicle* condemning what they called the " liberties " he took in his singing of " Adelaida." The *Musical World*, however, could not discover a single alteration, and went on to say that his voice was "stronger, clearer, fresher, and more equal than in the previous season." He had lost " none of his energy and force, while his taste seemed more refined and his portamento improved." Reeves continued to appear at the " Wednesdays," where, it may be remarked in passing, the encores had become a " positive nuisance," and he interspersed these engagements with flying visits to the provinces, singing with great success at Norwich, Plymouth, Bath, and Bristol.

It is hard to avoid coming to the conclusion that Reeves overtaxed his strength by these far-afield commitments in the risks to his health incident to the long journeys of that time. It was in the winter, the railway-carriages were close, stuffy, unwarmed, and withal draughty. The trains were slow and jolting ; delays at junctions were frequent ; refreshments were bad, often there were none at all ; and the jaded passengers not

seldom arrived at their destinations in the early hours
of the morning when the inns were closed. Travellers
had to chance damp beds and other discomforts, and
this ordeal to a singer with a delicate throat and a nervous
temperament, sensitive to climatic influences, meant
asking for trouble. Sims Reeves in all probability laid
the foundation of innumerable illnesses by the conditions
attending his arduous work of those days.

But what was he to do ? He could not, like the
Italian tenors, the favourites of fashion, the pets of the
aristocracy, fatten on the few months of the opera season
at the best time of the year, and accept engagements at
exorbitant fees to sing at private concerts. He was not
the " idol " of the rich like Mario, Gardoni, Tamberlik,
and others, but of the great shilling public. The call
upon him was strenuous and incessant. Mr. Willert
Beale says : " It is much to be regretted that one with so
much influence at his command has not done more for the
art he represents. In oratorio singing he was unsurpassed.
Being recognised, and justly so, as the leading tenor of the
day, he could have advanced English music, had he been
so disposed, to an incalculable extent ; yet his practical
encouragement of composers has been limited to writers
of ephemeral compositions."

Mr. Beale did not explain what he meant by " art."
Was it to sing only at the Italian opera, in oratorio, and
at high-class concerts like the Philharmonic ? Reeves
was always anxious to appear in the first. It was the height
of his ambition, and in the few opportunities he had at
Her Majesty's and Covent Garden he maintained the high
standard he had fixed for himself. That these opportunities were not more numerous was not his fault. He
had to combat the jealousy rather than the rivalry of
Italian singers. Surely his singing in oratorio had
elevated art ; had never lowered it—Mr. Chorley's
prejudices notwithstanding. Unlike Braham, he never
descended to tasteless ornamentation ; and if he chose to
regard oratorio from a dramatic rather than from a purely
vocal standpoint, he was justified. As a ballad singer he
was unrivalled, but even here, where licence might be
permitted, he did not, like Braham, play to the gallery.
All that can be said is that he gave to many songs of the

day an importance they did not deserve. It is hardly fair to judge of the music which appealed to a mid-nineteenth-century audience by the taste of fifty or sixty years later. Scores of compositions made popular by Reeves are defunct, it is true, and will never be exhumed; but the old English, Scottish, and Irish ballads in which he excelled are never-dying, and art does not despise them. To be just, Mr. Beale should have given some examples of the English music which he infers Reeves neglected, but the fact is these examples do not exist. Reeves always did his best with the materials at his disposal. More he could not do.

One of the most significant commentaries on the " Art for Art's sake " cry occurred in connection with the newly erected St. Martin's Hall, opened on February 11th, 1850. The hall was the outcome of Mr. Hullah's meritorious efforts to further the progress of choral singing, and in view of the narrow-minded management of Exeter Hall[1] great things were expected from the new venture—expectations which, from various causes, were not altogether realised. The building was in after-years converted into a theatre, subsequently it became a warehouse, and is now a printing establishment. The British public at first did not take kindly to the new home of music, and on February 24th a high-class vocal and instrumental concert attracted only some 300 people. The small attendance was the more noticeable because the conductor was Mr. Willy, the well-known orchestral leader of the " Wednesdays," and Sims Reeves sang. The truth was the programme had nothing of the " popular " character of the " Wednesdays," and the public had no interest in " Art for Art's sake."

Mr. Chorley, who was nothing if not critical, made some remarks apropos of Reeves's singing (*Athenæum*, January 12th, 1850) which may be challenged. " Mr. Reeves," he wrote, " is obviously taking great pains,

[1] During 1850 the bigoted managers decided that Shakespeare could not be tolerated within its sacrosanct walls, and a series of readings from Shakespearean plays was sternly prohibited. As a set-off, it may be noted that in this year chanting the Psalms was introduced at the Weigh House Chapel—an innovation which caused some shaking of heads among the congregation.

drawing more largely on his falsetto than he used to do—
a device which it will require more practice to perfect
him in, seeing that the natural and factitious tones of
voices so robust as his have an essential difference in
timbre which it requires much art and experience to
harmonise, but his articulation of English has improved."
Now, did Reeves ever use falsetto ? Among the hosts of
critics who have passed judgment on his voice not one
save Mr. Chorley has ever made such an assertion. I
have heard Reeves sing scores and scores of times, and I
do not remember an instance. Mr. Herbert Reeves says
emphatically that his father never employed falsetto.

During February Reeves sang in *The Creation* at Exeter
Hall, and in *Judas Maccabæus*. Of the first a most
exceptional incident may be recorded—Miss Birch was
actually hissed ! She had introduced a tasteless cadenza
into " With verdure clad " which excited the ire of the
audience. Mr. Chorley condemned this demonstration
against a lady singer as " unbecoming men," adding,
" As much out of taste as Miss Birch's cadenza was the
elongated G with which Mr. Reeves chose to conclude the
recitative ' In splendour bright,' thus singing the word
' power ' on two notes of the octave—a thing impossible
to do without a jerk, awkward and totally indefensible.
Having (for illustration's sake) noted this mistake, we are
bound and glad to say that Mr. Sims Reeves displays
increased care and clearness of utterance." Mr. Chorley,
as the Rugby schoolboy said of Dr. Temple, was a
" beast," but at times was " a just beast."

After a successful operatic tour in the South of England
came, at the end of March, Reeves's third, and most
important, entry into Italian opera with a purely Italian
company. Mr. Lumley had secured for his season at
Her Majesty's a prima donna in Mademoiselle Parodi, a
pupil of Madame Pasta, whose advent was heralded
in a way which the result hardly justified, and Reeves
made his appearance with her in *Ernani*, on March 21st.
Mr. Chorley was once more in his critical mood, and his
dislike to Verdi's music accentuated his objections.
He started, however, with being complimentary. " Mr.
Reeves," he remarked (*Athenæum*, March 23rd), " was in
his best voice, and sang not merely with praiseworthy

care which is due to every occasion, but also like one who loves his occupation. Verdi's music in its solo passages and closes gives him scope for that slackening of tempo and elongation of favourite notes which are considered by 'Young Italy' as the style dramatic. But for the interest of art—rather than under any hope that our remarks will be heard amid so many plaudits—we must point out that Mr. Reeves's methods of producing his tone and phrasing stand in need of refinement and restraint—and that something of facility *must* be acquired by him ere his voice will either blend or tell in concerted music. . . . So no more at present, we hope and trust, of Verdi's music."

Mr. Chorley's brother-critics were by no means of his opinion. The *Musical World* enthusiastically spoke of Reeves's " delicacy and purity of singing " and of his " breadth of style, power of voice, and manly vigour for which he has been celebrated." Mr. Lumley (*Recollections of the Opera*) characterises the whole performance, " dramatic as well as vocal, as one of eminent merit in the opinion of all unbiassed harmonists."

Mr. Chorley was as prejudiced against Verdi as he was subsequently against Schumann and Wagner. And he was not alone. Verdi in the early fifties seemed to madden those who could not accept anything that was different from what they had been accustomed to hear. There was something absurdly personal in their violence. The *Morning Post* critic habitually lashed himself into frenzy whenever he had to write anything concerning the new Italian composer. With *Ernani* he expressed his " disgust." He hotly denounced the " wretched conventionalities, mawkish sentiments, and insipidities of the modern Italian school, rendered doubly offensive by being bellowed into one's ears by trumpets, ophicleides, and other species of noisy instruments making up the sum of excellence with which Verdi has purchased his popularity from the ignorant. . . . Signor Verdi may be popular with drivelling dilettanti, but the dull god of his inspiration shall never have our homage, for we scorn to bow our knee to the ' iron idols ' of the day, although the highest in the land may be among their worshippers." More " criticism " in the " Ercles " vein equally virulent could be quoted, but this sample will suffice. Yet the critic was not oblivious of Reeves's charm. " We never," he observed, " heard him in better voice. His chest notes came out with perfect clearness and with a full-ness of power little short of marvellous, nor was his *mezza-voce* less remarkable for its delicate purity."

The *Musical World* kept an open mind on the subject of Verdi's music, and in alluding to the public impression that Reeves the previous year had not been fairly treated by Mr. Lumley records how this impression found an outlet in the demonstration which followed the tenor's appearance on the stage. " Hands clapped, hats and handkerchiefs waved, and throats vociferated . . . nothing could be more unanimously boisterous, nor could anything more plainly exhibit the position in which Mr. Sims Reeves stands before the British public."

On April 2nd Reeves and Catherine Hayes, now friends again, renewed their triumphs in *Lucia*, to the disgust of the *Athenæum* critic, who plaintively asked, " How long will singers continue to be so depressingly fond of this sickly work ? " On April 28th he sang with Sontag in *Sonnambula*—Sontag of whom Berlioz wrote : " *Elle est absolument la première dans son genre, mais son genre n'est pas le premier.*"

What with the opera, the Sacred Harmonic concerts, and other engagements, Reeves was very busy during the first half of 1850. One concert at which he sang—that given by Macfarren and Loder at the Princess's—may be mentioned as illustrating the difference between those days and ours. " Second price " was the rule at all theatres, and was not relaxed in the case of a concert, with the result that on this occasion the second pricers swarmed in when Ernst was playing, and were so noisy that the great violinist brought his solo to an abrupt conclusion, walked off the stage and was seen no more. Excepting the soloist, no one seemed to care.

The " Monster " concert, initiated by Jullien, was a popular musical function at that time. But Jullien's " Monsters " were genuine ; this can hardly be said of those of his imitators. Too often the " Monster " concert was an *olla podrida* of gigantic dimensions—a sort of come-and-go-as-you-please affair, full of surprises and disappointments. The surprises were in the abundant contretemps and the disappointments arose from the failures of " stars " to appear. The *entrepreneur* invited all the artists with whom he had a speaking or even nodding acquaintance, and took his chance who turned up. It may be considered a mercy that *all* did not, or the concert would have lasted throughout the night. But their names appeared on the bill, and this was the great thing. The audience fluctuated like the tides, but not with the same regularity. The room might be crammed at one time, half empty at another, and crammed again before the function was over. Anything might happen and lots of odd things *did* happen. At a concert given by George Barker at the Princess's at which Sims Reeves and Miss Lucombe sang, some of the singers were *non est*, which perhaps did not matter very much ; but it was a different affair when it was discovered that the three " conductor-accompanists " — Loder, Lavenu, and Schira—were missing. Barker was not equal to the task of filling up the vacancies, and had not Madame Mac- farren, who was among the vocalists, volunteered her help, the concert must have come to an untimely end. The prodigious ordeal commenced at seven, and it was midnight before it was over.

In July Reeves sang at the Free Trade Hall Popular Concerts, Manchester (again to the distaste of Mr. Sever, an anti-Verdian), several times, and in September took part at Gloucester in the Festival of the Three Choirs, singing, among other things, " Adelaida " to Mr. Done's accompaniment on a piano woefully out of tune. After Gloucester came a celebration of the Welsh Eisteddfod at Rhuddlan Castle, notable as the occasion on which *The Messiah* was given for the first time in Wales. Sims Reeves completely won the hearts of the Welsh by his oratorio singing. One of the concerts was marred by an unfortunate accident, a gallery giving way, when several people were injured.

The notion that the British public were yearning for high-class music was exploited in the most pretentious and impudent way towards the late autumn of 1850 by the organisers of what they called the " Grand National Concerts," for which Her Majesty's Theatre was engaged.

Who the " Committee of Management " were and what were their qualifications for their self-imposed mission was not stated, nor did it appear by whom the enterprise was financed. The only certain thing was that someone skilled in advertisement's artful aid was in the background, and to his efforts were due the magniloquent promises displayed in the prospectus. The " Committee " claimed that they had " endeavoured to form a union of talent never hitherto witnessed in any country " and " to present an intellectual entertainment of the highest order, embracing the Greatest Works of the Greatest Masters illustrated by the most eminent artists in Europe." To justify the word " National," " original and instrumental works by native composers " were to be produced, while " entire works in an operatic form will be given somewhat after the manner of short secular [sic] oratorios." Macfarren and Loder were stated to have completed " two one-act serenatas," and Howard Glover was supposed to be engaged upon a similar work. The " Committee " were " in communication with the great master, Spohr," and Félicien David would " personally attend and conduct the production of portions of his opera, *Christophe Colomb*." " The renowned *chef d'orchestre* Signor Pilodo from the Jardin Mabille will have the entire direction . . . of the Light or Dance music," especial stress being laid on two novelties, " A Quadrille of all Nations, composed by Musard in celebration of the Great Exposition of the year 1851," and the " Grand National Polka "—save the mark ! Apparently these " intellectual " concerts were to combine the chief features of the Philharmonic, the " Wednesdays," and Jullien's " Promenades." The " Committee " succeeded in accomplishing none of these objects, and never got beyond a weak rivalry of the clever Frenchman then in the height of his glory at Drury Lane.

On the opening night the theatre was crammed with an audience for which the arrangements were as inadequate as those for the music. " The mountainous prospectus," to quote the *Athenæum*, resulted in " nothing much greater than pieces of mousework," and though the succeeding performances were better, " mousework " prevailed. It is true, all the best instrumentalists in

London were in the orchestra, but the " Committee " never gave them a chance, and Mr. Balfe, who conducted, was content to let things go as they pleased. The " Greatest Works of the Greatest Masters " were given in scraps ; Spohr sent a dreary symphony called " The Seasons," Félicien David never appeared, nor was any portion of his opera given. The " most eminent artists in Europe " were represented vocally by Sims Reeves and Mlle Angri, and instrumentally by Charles Hallé and M. Sainton ; the other artists (with one exception) did not rise beyond mediocrity.

Of the three compositions by British musicians, two only were produced : a cantata by Macfarren, two hours and a half of decorous music which must have tried the patience and the feet of the promenaders sorely, and fragments of another cantata by Howard Glover. Macfarren's cantata was entitled *The Sleeper Awakened*, and was based upon the story in *The Thousand and One Nights* which Weber used for his opera of *Abu Hassan*. Sims Reeves and Mlle Angri did their best, but it cannot be said that the work was attractive. However, it achieved one meritorious thing : it fulfilled a cherished hope of Mr. Chorley in regard to Reeves. " Let us," he wrote, " congratulate him on the shake which we have been long wanting to hear."

Howard Glover's cantata was, so far as the title and subject were concerned, little better than a fraud. It was entitled *Hero and Leander*, but it proved to be an overture to Lord Byron's *Manfred* and a series of vocal pieces dovetailed anyhow and having very little connection with the story. The critics and the public were completely taken in and the " Committee " did not consider it necessary to give any explanation. Loder's cantata was not produced at all.

Something of a " hit " was made by the Berlin Choir, who sang by the " gracious permission of the King of Prussia." Their répertoire consisted chiefly of hymn-tunes, volkslied, and a few part-songs, and, as the *Musical World* remarked, there was no reason why London should not have provided choral singers quite as good. The advertising genius who compiled the prospectus had a splendid opportunity of displaying his talents when the engagement of the Choir was drawing to a close, and he seized upon it. The public were informed that " in consequence of the disturbed state of Prussia the celebrated Berlin Choir has been ordered to return forthwith. Two of them being officers and several of them soldiers, no excuse can avail, and, their regiments being under orders to march, they are most anxious to rejoin their respective corps." But the Choir did not go to battle after all, and accepted several offers to sing in the provinces instead. The whole thing was a ruse to advertise a " Battle Chorus " with which they tickled the ears of the British public.

The Grand National Concerts came to an inglorious end in December, and the most notable thing to be recorded in connection with them is the successful debut of a girl pianist some fourteen years old, a pupil of Thalberg. This was Arabella Goddard, who in after-years became a great favourite of the public. The school in which she studied is now past and gone, and though one would hesitate to place Miss Goddard among the great pianists of the nineteenth century, that she possessed immense talent is undoubted. She would probably have gone further but for her training and the limited taste of the day.

CHAPTER XIV

1851–1852

Reeves's marriage. Another unlucky Irish tour. Sings in opera in Paris. Jealousy of Italian singers. The musical muddle at the opening of the Great Exhibition of 1851. Reeves sings with Sophie Cruvelli in *Fidelio*. A curious chorus of " stars." Thalberg's opera *Florinda*. Alfred Bunn's curious enterprise at Drury Lane. Reeves at the Philharmonic concerts. The Birmingham and Hereford Festivals. Mr. Chorley's praise of Reeves's singing. The Norwich Festival and Mr. Hugh Pearson's *Jerusalem*.

AFTER the performance of Macfarren's serenata at the Grand National Concerts, Reeves was little in evidence for some three months. There were two reasons for this. One was the dullness of the musical season—the *Athenæum* speaks of it as " the most stagnant winter in respect to concert music which we recollect for a dozen years past " ; the other was his marriage to Miss Emma Lucombe some time in January 1851. The names of " Mr. and Mrs. Sims Reeves " appear for the first time in a programme on the occasion of Balfe's concert on February 12th.

By an odd coincidence, Reeves made his first appearance at a Philharmonic Society's concert at the same time as Miss Lucombe. The compiler of the Society's records, noting this, remarked upon the number of marriages in the musical world which had followed joint appearances at Philharmonic concerts. Among the number were the marriages of Mr. Francesco Berger[1] (once the Society's secretary) and Miss Lascelles, Signor Bettini and Signora Trebelli, Sir Henry R. Bishop and Miss Rivers, Mr.

[1] Mr. Francis Berger wrote three songs expressly for Sims Reeves— " Geraldine " (introduced at a " Monday Pop," accompanied by the composer), " Forgotten All " (sung at a Crystal Palace concert), and " Sunshine o'er my Soul " (which Reeves accepted, but did not find an opportunity of introducing). Mr. Berger also accompanied Reeves in " Adelaida," " My Guiding Star," " The Message," and " Come into the garden, Maud."

Charles Lockey and Miss Bertha Williams, Mr. Frank Bodda and Miss Louisa Pyne, Mr. Sainton and Miss Dolby, and Mr. Patey and Miss Jane Whytock.

In March, Sims Reeves accepted an engagement to sing with Madame Grisi in opera in Dublin. Irish tours seemed to spell mishaps for Reeves, and when the series should have begun, Grisi was taken ill. The opening night was postponed from March 10th to the 14th to allow Mrs. Sims Reeves to sing in the place of the great prima donna, but when the 14th came Mrs. Sims Reeves was ill at Harrogate. On the 17th it was announced in the *Freeman's Journal* that " Mr. and Mrs. Sims Reeves have arrived in Dublin," and on the following night *Lucia* was given with complete success. *Sonnambula*, *Puritani*, and *Ernani* followed. Then came the benefit of Mr. Calcraft, the manager, with whom Reeves had had bickerings on a former occasion as already recorded, and again the night was marked by great disturbance.

The ill-feeling extended to the representative of the *Freeman's Journal*, who in writing hot on the same night quite lost his temper. He spoke of the " apathy " and " nonchalance " of Reeves's " singing and acting in *Rob Roy*," and remarked that " it looked rather awkward and withal disrespectful to the audience that Mr. Reeves should have affected to forget the words of ' The Minstrel Boy ' and read them out of his hat ! " As he proceeded the critic's wrath increased, and he seems to have lost his head completely when he allowed himself to write of " the cool insolence and *insouciant* affectation that marked the stage conduct of a very clever and very foolish young man who personated or attempted to personate the character of Tom Tug in the after-piece of *The Waterman*."

The critic's grievance was that Reeves refused to sing " The Bay of Biscay "—that constant bone of contention ; how Reeves must have hated it !—twice, admitting, however, that Reeves " conducted himself marvellously well, considering, throughout the evening, until at length he came out to sing ' The Bay of Biscay.' " Part of the complaint was that two verses only were given and that he sang them " with evident carelessness as if he deemed such an audience not worth throwing away good

singing upon. Even this was borne with and an encore
was called for, but the somewhat *jolly* tar refused persistently to accept the call of the house." The stage
manager tried to explain, but was met by a tumult which
lasted half an hour. Then " Mr. Reeves came out with
the whole corps of performers, and the finale of the
piece was sung in dumb show amidst a perfect tempest of
yells and hisses."

There seems to be more Irish whisky than Irish wit in
this outburst ; however, all was forgiven and forgotten on
the following night, when *Puritani* was performed, and
Reeves, " who was in good humour," repeated " A te o
cara." The series concluded with Mr. and Mrs. Sims
Reeves's benefit, selections from *Lucia* and *Puritani* being
given, concluding with *The Beggar's Opera*.

Meanwhile, Reeves had been engaged by Mr. Lumley
for his operatic season in Paris, the enterprising impresario aspiring to mark the Great Exhibition year by running
the Théâtre Italien as well as Her Majesty's. To
Paris accordingly Reeves proceeded in March, and much
curiosity was excited as to what the Parisian world would
think of him. Mr. Reeves, in *My Jubilee*, says he was
" introduced to his new public at a concert," and that
Ernani was chosen for his debut. Neither of these
statements would seem correct. The only mention
in the French papers of a concert is one which was given
on April 2nd, *after* he had sung several times in opera.
He made his debut, not in *Ernani*, but in *Linda* with
Sontag. The *Journal des Débats* spoke of his pure tone,
which it pronounced to be " both beautiful and correct.
His method is that of the grand school, and in spite of the
emotion arising from his first appearance, he made
sufficient use of his means to arouse the desire of the
audience to hear him in a more extended exhibition of
his powers." *Linda* was repeated on March 20th, and
Reeves subsequently sang with Mlle Cruvelli[1] in *Ernani*

[1] Sophie Cruvelli's singing was regarded with mixed opinions by the
critics. She does not appear to have been always successful in the parts
she undertook. She studied when in her teens under Reeves's Paris
master Bordogni, and going to Milan she sang to Merelli with a view to an
engagement at La Scala. But when she opened her mouth before the
impresario not a sound came forth, and she was so mortified that she
resolved to return to Bielfeld in Prussia, her birthplace. She was about to

with great success. The *Musical World* regretted he had not a chance of singing in *Lucia* with Jenny Duprez, but his Edgardo would probably have been a triumph not to be endured by the Italian tenors of the company, and the part was taken by Calzolari.

One would like to have had from Reeves himself some account of his experiences in Paris, but there is very little in *My Jubilee* beyond the record that in Paris as in London he found himself constantly exposed to the jealousy of the Italians, " not necessarily tenors, but for the most part friends and partisans of tenors." This was not surprising. In Paris the *claque* was considered indispensable. It might consist of applause or hisses according to instructions, and was used either to damage a successful rival or to invest a singer with a fictitious popularity. A stranger had little chance under such circumstances. The Parisian operatic world has ever been a hotbed of intrigue, and that Reeves succeeded so well as he did is a tribute to his genius. Apropos of Parisian jealousy, Reeves pays a tribute to Mario, with whom, he says, he was always on the most amicable terms. Mario he described as " a gentleman in the fullest sense of the word and as such was incapable of meanness or any sort of pettiness."

Whatever the company of the Théâtre Italien may have thought of Reeves, there was no doubt as to Lumley's opinion. On April 7th he wrote :

" DEAR SIR,—Your letter crossed me on my road to Paris and has but this instant reached my hands on its return. I lost not a moment in sending orders in compliance with your wishes. You will have a great success in *Ernani*. I was delighted to observe the real hold you had obtained over the Parisians by your singing at the last concert.

" B. LUMLEY."

take her departure when Lamperti, the well-known Milan professor, waited upon her, refusing to believe that she had lost her voice. He was right. Her voice returned stronger and more beautiful than before. She made her debut in Vienna as Doña Sol, and was then not twenty. She was engaged at Her Majesty's in 1848, but the Jenny Lind fever was on, and seeing she had no opportunity of distinguishing herself, she went away without singing.

II

On Reeves's return to London he found the capital all agog with the Great Exhibition (it was at first called " The Crystal Palace ") in Hyde Park. Music had no place in the aims which the promoters of the Exhibition had in view. Nothing was thought of but industrial progress. For months previous official agents throughout Great Britain had been preaching the gospel of mechanics and manufacture, and more importance was attached to improvements in pianos than to the development of the music to be played upon them.

The ideas of the Exhibition Commissioners in regard to music are sufficiently shown by what they proposed to do on the opening day. They considered a combination of the choirs of the Chapel Royal, St. Paul's, and Westminster Abbey would suffice, accompanied on one of the exhibitors' organs, but it was urged by those who had the progress of English music at heart that such a meagre assemblage in so great a space would serve only to make the music ridiculous. Ultimately the situation was saved by the addition of the forces of the Sacred Harmonic Society. But at the best it was a scratch affair. The National Anthem and the " Hallelujah " Chorus formed the entire programme, and the band and chorus with the soloists and conductor were huddled into three sides of a square formed by the gallery of the great transept. Mr. J. E. Cox (*Musical Recollections*, p. 66, vol. ii) says : " As all the performers were on the same level, mixed up with exhibitors' cases and crowded up by unauthorised officials—who would take and hold possession for their friends of the best and most prominent situations—it is no wonder that the music produced little or no effect."

British music was at a low ebb in 1851, and little that was of native production can be found in the entertainments provided in London for all the world and his wife. Writing at the close of the year, Mr. Chorley remarked that though he was not to be numbered " among those who retrospectively reviewing the small amount of musical progress . . . in 1851 cry ' The Great Exhibition has done it all,' yet the past twelve months might be looked upon as a musical year neither very fruitful nor interesting." The critic, however, was hopeful. " A time of exhaustion," he admitted, " had set in," but he preferred to call it "a time of preparation," adding that the future would largely depend on the manner in which "its good influences are turned to account and its evil ones counteracted." No thought of the Exhibition's successor at Sydenham was then in anybody's mind, and that the second Crystal Palace should have proved the great choral capabilities of the country and should have afforded such opportunities for the development of instrumental music makes Mr. Chorley's words singularly apt.

But if in 1851 the British musician was not much in evidence, the Italian operatic campaign was unusually complete and extensive. Her Majesty's and Covent Garden were crowded nightly, and every foreign singer of note was heard in his or her most famous rôles. The Sacred Harmonic Society had a most successful season, but its efforts appealed exclusively to British tastes and it is doubtful whether more than a few foreigners were attracted. In any case, the concerts were not representative of British music. Nor was there compensation to be found in English opera, for in 1851, singular to say, English opera was entirely unrepresented, not a single performance being given.

One important fact, however, is to be noted. Amid the almost unparalleled galaxy of foreign operatic stars, Sims Reeves held his own. No singer, no matter of what nationality, commanded so much attention, and, rising to the occasion, he sang gloriously. One of his greatest triumphs was his appearance with Sophie Cruvelli in *Fidelio* at Her Majesty's on May 20th. Nothing but a pæan of praise was heard. The *Athenæum* considered he was at his best as Florestan, that he sang "with great care and less alternation between piano and forte than was his wont." The *Musical World* wrote that "in point of energy and dramatic feeling he could hardly be surpassed, while his singing betokens skill as a musician and sympathy with the classical inspirations of Beethoven."

In this connection may be quoted Reeves's own words, uttered in an interview he gave to a representative of the *Daily Chronicle* in 1892. "A man," he said, "must be an idiot if he does not get a lot of intellectual training from his experience in opera and oratorio. Take the great tenor scene from *Fidelio*, for instance. That is an intellectual business from beginning to end." Does not this give the key to Sims Reeves's mastery of whatever he undertook ? He thought out everything. To him singing was not merely a matter of correct vocalisation, but of intention and interpretation. His hearers were impressed because of his presentment of artistic truth.

The opening performance of *Fidelio* was unique in one respect—the chorus of prisoners was sung by the very pick of the principals : Gardoni, Calzolari, Parduci, Poultier, Scotti, Ferranti, F. Lablache, Lorenzo, and Massol. At first sight this subordination of personality to the interests of general excellence would seem exceedingly praiseworthy, especially as the principal figure in the picture was an Englishman, but great singers do not easily relinquish their dignity and superiority, and with the exception of F. Lablache no one took the trouble to learn the music, and the result was so bad that Mr. Ganz, the chorus-master, dispensed with the services of the "stars." But their names, which probably was all that the management cared for, continued to appear on the bills, to which the lowly tenors and basses who were called in probably did not object.

The concerts of Her Majesty's operatic company were made specially attractive, as Mr. Lumley had an over-whelming amount of material to draw upon. Reeves sang every time, and it was at one of these concerts that, as already mentioned, he joined with Gardoni and Calzolari in Curschmann's trio " Evviva Bacco." Another musical curiosity was Martini's laughing trio " Vadi via di qua," known to the English public as " Don't tickle me, I pray," with the parts triplicated, the soprano being taken by Sontag, Cruvelli, and Jenny Duprez, the tenor by Sims Reeves, Gardoni, and Calzolari, and the basses including Lablache. The effect of the rollicking music as given by these great artists—to hear Lablache's mighty guffaws was in itself a healthy tonic—must have been exceedingly stimulating.

A production which raised great expectations was Thalberg's opera *Florinda*. Thalberg had for years practically made England his home. He was here regarded as representing the last word in pianoforte playing. As a mechanical pianist he was a marvel, but his powers ended with his mechanism. His school inflicted upon long-suffering parents with musical daughters indescribable tortures and brought a contempt upon English pianoforte music which retarded its progress for more than a generation ; but it enriched the piano manufacturers. *Florinda* had the advantage of a powerful cast in Cruvelli, Sims Reeves, Coletti, and Lablache, but it only achieved a *succès d'estime*. It was an ambitious effort without charm or dramatic spirit.

Mr. Chorley's criticism is to the point. He says : " There is something in the ingenuity of pianoforte invention and exhibition essentially at variance with all power of thinking largely which is demanded by theatrical compositions," and in connection with this theory Mr. Chorley quotes the case of Mendelssohn, whose piano was of pronounced badness. " Yes," said the composer, when one of his friends remarked upon the fact, " even my children laugh at it ; but I never touch it save to try a chord or two sometimes. A good piano might seduce me to write mere finger-music." The productions of Chopin and Rubinstein and Liszt to some extent support Mendelssohn's opinion ; Chopin, it is said, composed only at the piano.

Apart from his engagements at Her Majesty's, Reeves's work during 1851 calls for no particular notice. He was in request at Exeter Hall, where during the year Madame (then Miss) Clara Novello began her long association with the Sacred Harmonic Society, and he sang at the Worcester Festival, but all this was simply a repetition of old successes.

At intervals in the Great Exhibition year the oft-repeated cry for " National opera " was again heard, but there was no response. Composers apparently were waiting for enterprising managers to beg them to write works of genius and managers were expecting composers to submit such works. The position was one of suspended animation. Hence a sigh of relief went up when at the end of the year it was announced that Mr. Alfred Bunn had determined to produce at Drury Lane not only " National opera " but " National drama." Mr. Bunn was not a genius. He had no notion of " Art for Art's sake." He was the author of several English operatic libretti, notably that of *The Bohemian Girl*; he had had considerable experience in theatrical management; he thoroughly understood the advantages of skilful advertising; had won an action against Jenny Lind for breach of agreement, and had replied effectively to the constant attacks made upon him and his lyrical efforts in *Punch* by publishing a satire in which the *Punch* contributors were mercilessly lampooned. The intimation " to be continued if necessary " was effectual. *Punch* never attacked him again. *Inter alia*, he was the husband of an actress and singer of moderate ability whom he did his best to puff into celebrity.

Mr. Bunn's scheme in its outline resembled Macready's combination of the legitimate drama and " National opera," but he wisely avoided the tragedian's grandiose promises. Bunn committed himself to nothing. He started with *Fazio* and Miss Glyn, followed by a pantomime, and on the opening night commenced the programme with " a few words " from himself. He told the audience in his genial airy fashion that the theatre was opened " for the performance of the legitimate and illegitimate drama, and for opera, ballet, farce—whichever the dear public seemed to like best." This, at any rate, was frank, and the result justified the " few words," for in quick succession he produced *The Belle's Stratagem*, *Macbeth*, *The Lady of Lyons*, *The Young Couple*, *The Spoilt Child*, *The Wonder*, and *The Hunchback*.

The days went by and no mention was made of opera. The *Musical World* loudly called for it, and early in 1852 the possibility of the production of *Fra Diavolo* was rumoured. *Fra Diavolo* was hardly national, but it was better than nothing, especially as Sims Reeves was to appear in the chief character, in which he was known to be excellent. Nothing definite, however, followed; the delay, it was whispered, being caused by Reeves's objection to perform during the run of the pantomime. The *Musical World* could not believe that Reeves would make " so futile and impolitic a suggestion," and the *World* was probably right, as on January 24th the opera was produced and the pantomime was in the programme as usual.

Sims Reeves's success in *Fra Diavolo* was instantaneous and Mrs. Sims Reeves's singing was also greatly admired. Miss P. Horton and Whitworth as Lady and Lord Allcash added to the completeness of the cast. Reeves regarded *Fra Diavolo* as one of his favourite parts. " It is musical," he once said, " so full of point, so interesting ; it always gives you something to think about." *Fra Diavolo* was followed by *Lucia*, Mrs. Sims Reeves taking the title-rôle, and the all-round efficiency of the production prompted the *Athenæum* to say that " when we count up the excellent material . . . that we now possess in Mrs. Sims Reeves, Miss L. Pyne, Miss Fitzwilliam, and other artists that could be named, it seems impossible that ere long our often-expressed wish for the formation and maintenance of some establishment corresponding to the Opéra Comique of Paris must be fulfilled." But it never was.

In addition to his opera work, Reeves was singing regularly at Exeter Hall, its architectural excrescences now removed, acoustics and convenience gaining in consequence. On March 6th a new opera by Balfe, *The Sicilian Bride*, was presented by Mr. Bunn, but it fell flat, partly because of the failure of the leading lady, Miss Crighton, who proved to be an immature vocalist. Sims Reeves worked his hardest, but all to no purpose. It was performed several times and then withdrawn, never to be revived.

Reeves's engagement with the Philharmonic Society, for which he sang for the first time on March 15th, was a recognition of the place he held in the estimation not only of the general public, but of musicians. The Society had long been subjected to severe criticism on account of its cheeseparing economy and adherence to old-fashioned methods. The appointment of Costa as conductor was of course a great gain, and its pulses were further quickened when it was rumoured that a rival Society under the name of The New Philharmonic was to be formed. As a beginning to setting its house in order, the old Society restored " the salaries of the orchestra, which had passed down during years of famine, to something like their former figure " (*Athenæum*, January 31st), and con- descended to notice the taste of the day by engaging Sims Reeves, doubtless at a figure more than double that of

Mr. Bodda and other lesser lights, who had hitherto been considered good enough. Méhul's *Joseph* was then being talked about a good deal, and Reeves selected an air from that oratorio and " Della vita " from *Fidelio*.

The aim of the New Philharmonic in contradistinction to that of the older society was novelty. Two conductors, Berlioz and Dr. Wylde, were engaged and " analytical programmes " were introduced, to the great indignation of the *Athenæum's* musical autocrat, who protested against " anticipatory criticism on the style of a master who had yet a reputation to confirm in England." This was apropos of Berlioz's overture " Romeo and Juliet," of which later on the same critic wrote in very favourable terms, thus differing from many of his confrères, who gave the work a cold reception. Sims Reeves sang at the Society's second concert, the Queen and Prince Albert being present. At this concert was heard for the first time in England singing through closed lips (an importation from Germany) as an accompaniment to a solo. The solo on this occasion was sung by Reichardt, a German tenor who gained a certain amount of popularity in England both as a singer and composer.

In May, in pursuance of its policy of enterprise, the " New " produced Beethoven's colossal " Ninth " Symphony with Clara Novello, Sims Reeves, Miss Williams, and Staudigl in the solo parts. In spite of the stupendous difficulties they had to encounter, the artists achieved a complete success. The older society probably would not have been wholly displeased had the result been otherwise. The old Philharmonic paid Beethoven a hundred guineas for the symphony, performed it once, and promptly shelved it. Costa revived it in 1847, but the performance was nothing like so good as that of the " New." Reeves must have found the music extremely trying, what with its unvocal obstacles and its overpowering instrumentation, and it is not surprising to read that in certain parts he " with all his voice could hardly make himself heard."

Throughout 1852 Reeves was showered with engagements, and could he have undertaken them the number might have been doubled. His amazing popularity was shown by the packed condition of Drury Lane Theatre at his benefit on June 18th, on which occasion he seems to have asked Mr. and Mrs. Charles Mathews to assist him, judging from the following letter :

" LYCEUM,
" *June 2nd*, 1852.

" MY DEAR SIR,—Marry how ! Our ' chain of events ' lasts from 7 till 11, and they are both in it—nay, not only both but *all* the company, every Jack and every Jill.   Mrs. Mathews would be too happy to oblige you—indeed without looking forward she owes you one for the past— but there's no hope, as you see.   Better luck next time. With her best compliments—Faithfully yours,
" C. J. MATHEWS."

Could Mrs. Charles Mathews (better known as Madame Vestris) have appeared, it would have been particularly appropriate, for one of the features of the evening was *The Beggar's Opera* (the other was *Sonnambula*), and it was as Macheath that Madame established her fame as an unapproachable impersonator of what was known in her days as a " breeches " part.

Apropos of Reeves's benefit, the *Athenæum* took occasion to remark that London now possessed sufficient artists to furnish from its own resources " a company adequate to the performance of anything save the highest tragedy.   But," it went on to ask, " where is the repertory ?   Betwixt our old English ballad opera, which is insufficient for the musical requirements of the time, and the translated foreign work—inexpedient alike because it is hackneyed and in its performance save to provoke comparison and because it is not written in the spirit of either our country's poetry or her music—where are the characters which can be played and the music which can be sung so as to attract and retain audiences ? "   The same question might have been asked half a century later, for we had not then gone beyond Gilbert and Sullivan ; but a comparison between English and foreign singers to the disadvantage of the former can no longer be drawn with such confidence.

The Festivals at Birmingham and Hereford call for no remark beyond establishing the fact that the public with primitive instincts had elevated Reeves into a sort of god to be reverenced when he pleased them and chidden when he failed to satisfy their desires. Thus at Birmingham he was down in the programme to sing in the duet "Sulla Tomba" with Mlle Anna Zerr, but in consequence of the lady's non-arrival the item was omitted. The audience jumped to its own conclusions, and when Reeves appeared to sing an air from *Euryanthe* he was received with a storm of disapprobation, so much so that he walked off the platform. The uproar increased, whereupon Costa, turning from the conductor's desk, made his maiden and probably his only public speech. He explained that it was not Mr. Sims Reeves's fault that the duet was not sung, upon which the audience extended their forgiveness and all was well.

Reeves also sang at the Norwich Festival, which this year was notable for the production of two oratorios by British composers : *Israel Restored*, by Dr. Bexfield, and *Jerusalem*, by Hugh Pearson. Dr. Bexfield was a painstaking musician who had his reputation to make, and to this his oratorio added very little. Mr. Hugh Pearson was a native of Norwich. He had studied much in Germany and he aimed at originality. Both *Israel Restored* and *Jerusalem* had the powerful assistance of Madame Viardot Garcia, Miss Louisa Pyne, Miss Dolby, Sims Reeves, Gardoni, and Formes, but they had no opportunities in either. The audience was respectfully cold towards Dr. Bexfield's work, but that of Mr. Pearson it received with exaggerated enthusiasm, stimulated no doubt by the feeling that it ought to encourage a fellow-townsman. The critics, however, for once were unanimous. They smote *Jerusalem* hip and thigh, quite a controversy arose about it, and, disgusted with England and England's want of *Kultur*, Pearson retired to Germany and did his best to put on a Teutonic nationality by calling himself Hugo Pierson. Whether *Jerusalem* was a work of genius or an example of vaulting ambition remains unsettled to this day and is likely to stay so, as a glance at the score too plainly shows.

The outstanding feature of the year so far as Sims Reeves is concerned was Mr. Chorley's changed attitude. Reeves, to quote the tenor's own words, used for a different purpose, "fairly sang him down." He was completely won over. Of a performance of *Samson* he wrote : " The finest piece of *bravoura* execution which we ever heard from an English tenor (because evener and less fitful in its passage than Braham) was the harassing air ' Why does the God of Israel sleep ? ' sung by Mr. Sims Reeves so as to make it evident that he is resolved to command every style of music, and not that alone to which his big voice is sympathetic. That his expressive singing also has by this improved flexibility gained in variety and delicacy might be heard in his rendering of ' Total Eclipse,' which was delivered with as much subtlety as the grand aria in question was brilliantly sung." Approbation from Sir Hubert Stanley is praise indeed !

CHAPTER XV

1853–1855

Development of music in 1853. Sims Reeves again in Ireland. " Good-bye, sweetheart, good-bye." Reeves's bumper benefit at Drury Lane. *Fra Diavolo*—Reeves's emendation. Choral societies everywhere. Operas in English at Drury Lane. An audacious impresario. Opening of Sydenham Crystal Palace. The scandal of the band. Shabby treatment of Mr. Manns. English opera at the Haymarket Theatre. Choral gatherings at the Crystal Palace projected. Sir Joseph Paxton's bigotry. Costa and the Philharmonic. *Eli* produced at Birmingham. Extravagant laudation. Reeves tours the provinces.

WITHOUT attempting to gain fresh laurels—for which indeed few opportunities presented themselves—Reeves in 1853 materially strengthened his hold over the British public. The year witnessed a wonderful development of the love of music among the great masses of the people. Concerts had never been so numerous. Jullien had educated his audiences to appreciate the beauties of classical music, and the pleasures of choral singing were firmly planted throughout London and the provinces. The Sacred Harmonic Society, the London Sacred Harmonic Society, and Mr. Hullah's classes did not suffice to meet the wants of musical aspirants in the metropolis, and early in 1853 a fourth choral organisation was added in the shape of the Harmonic Union under the direction of Benedict. Sims Reeves, fresh from a successful tour in the southern counties, took part in its first performance, when *The Messiah* was given. He subsequently sang in *Elijah* and in a selection from *Acis and Galatea* and *Alexander's Feast* for the same Society.

His triumphs with the Harmonic Union form an oft-told tale, and the same may be said of his engagements in Dublin, Belfast, and Manchester, where musical enthusiasm was greater even than in London. The tour was under the direction of Mr. F. Beale, with

J. L. Hatton (whom Sims Reeves dubbed " The Sultan") as accompanist. At the Rotunda in Dublin, Reeves first sang (on May 12th) " Good-bye, sweetheart," at that time only in MS., composed by Hatton for Mario and sung by him at Manchester. Dr. Spark tells how Hatton read the words to Mario from a piece of paper he took from his pocket-book. Then he played the music from memory, and Mario practised the song until he had got over the difficulties of the " th." Everyone prophesied that the song would make a hit, and it did. The Dublin critics were now most friendly, and Reeves was equally amiable. He was " evidently bent on pleasing," wrote one of the former; " to desire with him is to ensure success."

The " Festivals for the People " in Manchester (Reeves singing, among other ballads, "The Last Rose of Summer," which, one reads, " moved the audience to tears ") were so successful that the building of a concert-hall worthy of the city was loudly called for. Innumerable concerts in London and the country occupied Reeves's energies during the summer, and it is pleasant to record, as evidence of the cordial relations existing between him and Costa, a presentation to the latter by Reeves of an " elegant and costly orchestral baton[1] made of elaborately carved ivory with gold mountings " some time in July.

Fra Diavolo and *The Waterman* formed Reeves's benefit programme, and in regard to the first it is to be noted that he introduced an emendation which consider-

[1] Conductors' batons as items in musical history are not without interest. Spohr in 1820 was the first to use one at the Philharmonic concerts. " It was at that time," he writes, " still the custom there that when symphonies and overtures were performed, the pianist had the score before him, not exactly to conduct from it, but only to read after and to play in with the orchestra at pleasure, which when it was heard had a very bad effect. The real conductor was the first violin, who now and then when the orchestra began to falter gave the beat with the bow of his violin." " When Spohr," says Mr. T. R. Croger (*Conductors and Conducting*), " drew a baton from his pocket and gave the signal to begin, some of the directors were quite alarmed and would have protested against it, but when Spohr begged them to grant him at least one trial they became pacified." Spohr's baton, shown at the Musical Exhibition at the Crystal Palace in 1891, was a clumsy stick of less than a foot long rolled round with parchment. Mendelssohn's baton was of whalebone covered with white leather. Jullien's was highly ornamented.

ably strengthened the finale. In the original the curtain falls as Fra Diavolo is being borne away by his captor. Reeves, conscious of this lame and impotent conclusion, substituted an escape for the romantic robber, a leap from a precipice, his recapture wounded, and death while seizing one of the band who he believed had betrayed him. This dramatic and exciting end was admitted to be a vast improvement.

The musical activity of 1853 increased in 1854. Concert succeeded concert. Choral unions, orchestral unions, quartette parties, abounded. The Sacred Harmonic Society, the London Sacred Harmonic Society, Mr. Hullah's classes, the Orchestral Union, the London Orchestra, the Philharmonic, the New Philharmonic, jostled each other at every turn. Jullien was in America, or he would have entered into the fray with characteristic ardour. Nearly every provincial town had its choral class. The London suburbs were busy in establishing musical societies, and Camberwell, greatly daring, engaged Professor Pauer to conduct a choral body of 150 singers. The Literary and Mechanics' Institutes were centres of musical instruction. Glee clubs held in suburban taverns flourished.[1]

Mr. Chorley writes in this year: "Chorus singing, whether theatrical, sacred, or orchestral, has never before been carried to such high perfection in England— our country may now in this improved branch of musical execution challenge its rivals whoever they may be. Neither, we apprehend, has there ever before been such part-singing as the English Glee and Madrigal Union displays." What would Mr. Chorley say of the paucity of choral singing at the present day?

The choral societies of 1854, large or small, sang the music of Bishop, of Webbe, of Horsley, of Callcott, and other English glee and madrigal writers. Mendelssohn's part-songs had not then made their way into England, and the *Volkslied* was unknown. Musical enthusiasts took their pleasure very earnestly. The frivolous in music was confined to the comic songs of the saloons—

[1] One of these musical hostelries deserves mention—The Little Driver, in the Bow Road. Here the music and the singers (mostly St. Paul's Cathedral men) were of the best.

SIMS REEVES AS FRA DIAVOLO.

the Grecian and other like places. Mr. Charles Morton at that time had not built the Canterbury and introduced music-hall patrons to high-class music.

The influence of the Great Exhibition was seen in the new enterprises for the recreation of the people. Amusement was subordinate to instruction. The Polytechnic combined the two very skilfully. The Panopticon in Leicester Square was designed with similar intentions. It was especially proud of its large organ, and it made a brave effort to attract educated musical people by its production of *Acis and Galatea* with scenery. The Sydenham Crystal Palace was originally intended more for instruction than for entertainment, and well-meaning attempts were made to conceal the first under the cloak of the second. The projectors had no sense of humour or they would never have conceived the brilliant idea of inculcating a thirst for the study of geology by planting plaster models, life-sized, of antediluvian monsters in unexpected places about the grounds. Of music they thought little ; the great incentive which the Palace gave to the art was yet to come.

One department of music, moreover, was quite ignored —the unhappy English opera. It had been treated with so much indifference that composers regarded it as a negligible quantity. It was no compensation for the absence of English opera in England that Balfe's *Keolanthe* and *The Bohemian Girl* should at the early part of the year be playing on the Continent.

There had been no opening for Sims Reeves in opera since Allcroft's venture with the Lyceum in the autumn of the previous year, and he took refuge in an extended provincial tour, returning to London in February " laden," as the *Musical World* put it, " with banknotes and crowned with laurels." He sang once in English opera at a performance given by George Case at Drury Lane, and increased his reputation, if such a thing were possible, by his share in *Acis and Galatea* performed by the Harmonic Union under Benedict, when Mozart's additional accompaniments, of which Benedict had contrived to get a copy, were given for the first time. " Sims Reeves," said the *Musical World*, " gave the music as probably it has never been given until now in England

or elsewhere." His appearance at one of the
"Wednesday" concerts is worthy of passing reference, as
on this occasion he sang "La donna e mobile," a somewhat rare selection for him, probably because Mario had
made it his own. He sang it gloriously, "though,"
remarked a critic, "his reading was different from
Mario's." He must, however, have felt at home in the
famous air, for when a few nights later the audience at one
of Allcroft's concerts chose to lash itself into a rage
because a trio from *William Tell*, in which Reeves was to
have sung, was passed over (the parts not having arrived)
and would have nothing to do with Richardson and his
flute as a substitute, Reeves soothed it with "La donna
e mobile," but wrath was again provoked on his not
singing "Pretty Jane" as an encore, oblivious of the fact
that the ballad was in the programme assigned to Augustus
Braham. Verily the British audience of those days was
an erratic and unreasonable tyrant.

In May came Reeves's chance in English opera, a Mr.
Jarrett entering into rivalry at Drury Lane with Italian
opera at Her Majesty's. Mr. Jarrett's scheme to alternate English (that is to say, Italian opera in English)
with German opera did not promise success, and some
incongruities resulted. Thus the German soprano Agnes
Büry not speaking English, *Lucia*, with Reeves, had to be
given in Italian. *Fra Diavolo* and *Sonnambula* were
also performed, the only novelties of the series being
Mozart's *Il Seraglio* (in which Reeves had no part) and
Masaniello. The cast was Reeves, Weiss, Leffler, Madame
Rudersdorff,[1] and Louisa Pyne. J. H. Mapleson, who
afterwards distinguished himself as an impresario, had
a small part, but was so "terror-stricken that he failed to
do himself justice." Reeves made a hit as Masaniello,
and it looked as if opera in English was going to be a
success, but somehow financially things went wrong, and
the theatre was suddenly closed. Whatever might have

---

[1] This was Madame Rudersdorff's first year in England. She afterwards
made a reputation in oratorio and was much in request at concerts. She
was a careful and painstaking singer and possessed a very powerful voice
which she did not scruple to use. She had an enormous mouth and she
opened it as widely as its limits would allow. One would rather listen
to than look at her. She ended her days as a teacher of singing in America.

been Mr. Jarrett's defects, want of audacity was not one of them, for it was asserted in the course of the liquidation proceedings which followed that he started his hazardous enterprise with a capital only of £150! An interesting point is that every night when Sims Reeves sang the treasury showed a profit of £60. Mr. Jarrett attributed his failure to the illness of the great tenor preventing him appearing oftener.

One of the events of the year was the inauguration of the Sydenham Crystal Palace on June 10th. If people anticipated that the occasion was to be marked by a great musical festival such as took place later in the year at Liverpool when St. George's Hall was opened, they were destined to be disappointed. The Sacred Harmonic Society, one reads, " monopolised the job," and the imagination of the directors could not rise above the National Anthem and the inevitable Hallelujah Chorus. Some 1,500 voices were got together, but how many of the 1,500 could distinguish between the two pieces they were called upon to sing is doubtful. Officialism was rampant, and its friends came from all parts of the country to take their places in the chorus, not because they knew anything about music, but because they wanted to see the show for nothing! As the *Musical World* indignantly pointed out, many of these " deadheads " were well-to-do, and but for favouritism would have paid their two guineas subscription, and the Crystal Palace coffers had to bear the loss.

An outcry was raised in musical circles over the engagement of Costa, a foreigner, as conductor. But no efficient English musician accustomed to control a large body of singers could be named as a substitute, and as the Sacred Harmonic Society (to put the point correctly, Mr. Bowley, who subsequently became the secretary of the Crystal Palace) had the management of affairs, they had a perfect right to select their own conductor. A more substantial grievance in regard to foreign musicians was the appointment of Herr Schallehn as conductor of the Crystal Palace band, with a salary of £500 a year and a residence. Schallehn[1] had been the bandmaster

---

[1] Schallehn's appointment was regarded at Sydenham with great disfavour. A few weeks after the opening of the Exhibition the following

of the 17th Lancers, and why he should have been picked
out it is impossible to say. His qualifications were not
remarkable, and his Teutonic peculiarities made him
anything but a desirable person. Briefly, his notions
were those of a drill-sergeant, with an eye to his own
pocket. The critics had ample reason to find fault with
the performance of his band at the opening ceremony.
It was admitted that the tone of the massed voices was
wonderfully fine, but, remarked the *Musical World*, " the
new brass band was seldom in time and always out of tune
with the choir, and the parts added from all sorts of brass

skit was circulated in the neighbourhood : " Five hundred pounds reward.
Lost on the road from the Crystal Palace, the entire recollection of what
the tunes were played by the Brass Band. They are supposed to have
been discovered in the ruins of Nineveh and formed a part of the famous
symphony of which the old winged bull died. Any clever theoretical
high-art musician who hates popular melodies and can recall their names
so that they may be hermetically sealed up for ever in one of the courts
will be cheerfully rewarded by ' The People ' whose palace it is." Herr
Schallehn's characteristics were best shown by the shabby way in which
he treated his sub-conductor, August Manns, whose name first came under
the notice of the public in connection with the transaction. Mr. Manns,
in detailing his grievance, wrote : " I was engaged to be sub-conductor
of the band of the Crystal Palace ; my duty was to play E flat cornet and
conduct the band when the conductor was not present. I have done so,
and besides, corrected the mistakes in music played, the palpable inefficiency of the proper party not being able to discern whether the parts
were correct or not. I have tried also to put into some correct shape the
collection of useless music not suitable, nor will it ever be, for the said
band purchased at the expense of the Company. On the occasion of the
Fête in aid of the Patriotic Fund I arranged a set of quadrilles suitable for
the occasion, combining English, French, and Turkish melodies, together
with some original matter of my own, and christened them the Alliance
Quadrilles. . . . I arranged them for the pianoforte and gave them to
Mr. Schallehn, who said he could sell them for me. What was my
surprise to perceive in a day or two my quadrilles announced to be
published in the city as ' The Alliance Quadrilles ' composed by Henry
Schallehn. I went to Mr. Schallehn and demanded the reason for so
acting, when he coolly offered me one pound, telling me that that sum
would pay me, and rudely informing me his name would sell them better
than mine. I spurned his offer ; when he said for my impudence I should
then and there be dismissed. . . . I have served in some of the best orchestras
in Europe, and I have never heard of such uncalled-for and futile vengeance
from a party in power. . . . I have made a full and true statement to the
Chairman of Directors of the whole circumstances, and it rests with them
whether artists who join their band are to be thus treated for merely
protesting against appropriation of their property by their conductor."

instruments helped rather to mystify than assist the effect." The singing of Clara Novello alone pleased the *World*, but with this exception " the music was unworthy the occasion." The comment of a contemporary on the police taking off their hats (hard, shiny-looking chimney-pots they were in those days) when the National Anthem was sung, that it was " an unconscious compliment to Miss Novello and Mr. Costa," moved the *World* to mirth and it derisively asked " Was it too much for them ? Did Costa compose the National Anthem ? Did Costa sing the National Anthem ? "

Jesting and controversy apart, it is certain that the singing of the 1,500 foreshadowed wondrous effects to be achieved. The *Athenæum* went so far as to say that Handel had in his mind possibilities of a vast augmentation of sound when he wrote his massive choruses, and added : " The opening of the New Palace thus has made its mark in music—by working out certain problems from which conductors and composers may deduce much that is useful, as well as to those professors who busy themselves over the curiosities of acoustics." In regard to the latter point Mr. Chorley did not overstate the case, for the difficulty of hearing properly in the great transept was for years a source of trouble and required many experiments and contrivances to overcome. That it was overcome, all who have heard Sims Reeves's clarion-like tones in " Sound an alarm " ring through the vast arena will readily admit.

Reeves's concert engagements in the first half of the year 1855 were very numerous, but they present no novelty, and all that is to be noted is his increasing popularity with the masses of the people. An instance of this may be given in what occurred at Allcroft's concert on Ash Wednesday. He had been encored in " Oh, 'tis a glorious sight to see," and on his returning to the stage half a dozen sections of the audience called out for as many different songs. He preferred, however, to adhere strictly to a repetition, and an uproar was beginning when a man in " a loose frieze coat " bounded from his seat in the pit and shouted in a voice that overpowered every other sound, " Sing what you like, my boy." This naïve appeal restored good-humour, and Reeves,

sitting down to the piano, to the satisfaction of everybody gave the inevitable " Pretty Jane."

During the summer Reeves sang in English opera at
the Haymarket, repeating his old triumphs, and in
The Bohemian Girl, giving to the music of the hero
" a charm of sentiment which no other tenor ever im-
parted." Towards the end of the season a new opera,
Bertha, by Henry Smart was brought out, but had no
prolonged run. It was considerably hampered by a
foolish libretto. Reeves, as usual, did his best, but the
part gave him no opportunities for effect. His benefit
as of yore drew an enormous crowd, a noteworthy
feature being *Guy Mannering*, in which Miss Cushman,
the famous American actress, played Meg Merrilies.

Meanwhile many musical men were seriously contemplating the possibilities of the Crystal Palace as a centre
where the art might be fostered, but it was too clear
that the great transept was full of defects, acoustically
speaking, which would have to be remedied before it
could be used as a concert-hall. To Mr. Willert Beale
belongs the credit of making the first practical suggestion
to lessen the defects. His idea was the construction of
a shelving platform at one end for orchestra and singers
and a similar arrangement for the audience at the other,
with seats rising tier upon tier possibly as high as the
first gallery. Full of his project, he obtained an introduction to Sir Joseph Paxton, and the account of his
interview given in his *Light of Other Days* is both amusing
and instructive, as showing the " swelled-headedness "
and narrow mind of the distinguished conservatory builder.

Mr. Beale tactfully complimented him on the success
of the Palace in its various departments, and Sir Joseph
graciously assented. Deeming the moment propitious,
Mr. Beale submitted that there was one art which he
thought had been strangely neglected. " And what may
that be ? " inquired the great man. " Music," was
Mr. Beale's reply. " Music ? Have we not Mr.
Schallehn's band in the music court ? " Mr. Beale
acknowledged the fact and went on to explain his idea.
Sir Joseph was horrified. " Never with my consent," he
burst out. " Never shall this place be turned into a
bear-garden such as it would become were we to have

more music than there is at present." "You will not, then, support my proposal to the directors?" "Most certainly not," was the gruff reply. Mr. Beale, however, was not daunted. He approached Mr. Scott Russell, who gave the notion a favourable reception, though he saw difficulties so far as the audience was concerned. The result was that Mr. Beale was allowed to give a concert, the singers standing on a species of dais erected for the occasion. It was a new experience for the artists whom he engaged; an attack of nerves seized Madame Alboni when she saw the vast space in front of her, and she was unable to sing. But the concert was a success, and when it was followed by a second one given in the Tropical Department, it was recognised that the first step had been gained. Undoubtedly Mr. Beale paved the way for the tremendous musical triumphs which were to come.

Costa was much in evidence in 1855. First came his resignation in the early days of the year of his conductorship of the Philharmonic Society's concerts. The exact cause of the rupture was never make known; probably it was due to a number of causes, one of which dated back to 1848. The incident, which gave rise to much comment in musical circles at the time, has its droll side. An overture by Sterndale Bennett was to be played, and at the rehearsal it was taken slower than the composer intended. Just before it was performed at the concert Bennett wrote on a piece of paper, "Fast—fast—fast," or what he thought were these words. When his hurried scrawl was handed to Costa the latter read "Fuss—fuss—fuss," and the conductor, always ready to stand on his dignity, was offended and he refused to conduct the piece. From that time Bennett played no more at the Society's concerts.[1] Had this incident been regarded simply as an outbreak of temper on Costa's part, the matter would have been forgotten, but in reality it exemplified what many of the directors held was an objectionable clause in Costa's contract with the Society—namely, his right to refuse to conduct any piece of which he did not approve, and when Bennett was elected a director it was felt that trouble might arise. Throughout 1853

[1] *Memorials of J. W. Davison.*

and 1854 there was a simmering of discontent, some of the directors alleging that it was due to Costa's extravagance that the finances showed a loss, while others objected to Costa bringing out his oratorio *Eli* at the Birmingham Festival. When, however, certain gentlemen who were believed to be inimical to Costa were elected directors, he resigned. The difficulty the directors had in filling Costa's place, leading to their unfortunate selection of Wagner, is a matter which most students of musical history will recall.

The event which brought Costa into public prominence was the production of *Eli* at the Birmingham Festival. The oratorio had been heralded by confident predictions that the composer would by this work be elevated to the same plane as Mendelssohn, if not indeed to that of Handel. Everything was done to bring about a success. The chorus was rehearsed again and again, and the soloists, Madame Viardot Garcia, Madame Castellan, Sims Reeves, and Formes, represented a quartette hardly to be bettered. The enthusiasm shown by the Birmingham audience was unprecedented. Had Costa been a heaven-born genius there could not have been more excitement. The memorable occasion when Mendelssohn conducted *Elijah* in that same hall was overshadowed. Many of the numbers were encored, and Sims Reeves, by his heroic rendering of " Philistines, hark ! " created a sensation of which those who heard him spoke almost with bated breath. The most magnificent tribute ever paid to an English singer was that of Mario, Gardoni, and Tamberlik, who were among the audience. Mario, the greatest, as Sims Reeves said, of the three, acted as spokesman, and after warmly complimenting Reeves, turned to Costa and said jokingly, " But you have insulted us." " How ? " demanded the astonished conductor. " By giving the tenor part to an English singer, . . . but you were right after all, for no Italian could have done justice to it."

The scene at the end of the performance was beyond anything ever witnessed at any festival, and the height of adulation with which Costa was overwhelmed was reached when four ladies of the chorus were deputed to demand as a memento from the composer the gloves he wore when conducting *Eli*. Having secured the coveted treasures, the deputation cut them into small pieces and distributed the fragments among the other ladies of the chorus, to be worn as a decoration during the rest of the Festival !

The local Press notices were excessively laudatory, a few of them absurdly extravagant. The London papers were not unanimous. The *Athenæum* expressed approbation in its lofty, judicial fashion, but if there was a lack of warmth in Mr. Chorley's criticism he made ample compensation in a letter to Reeves which exhibits the acid critic in a mood he did not often show in print.

"My dear Reeves," he wrote on August 30th,— " Business is business, and so I hereby acknowledge with thanks the £30 for the libretto. I hope you have one of my best works, for I should like *you* to have such an one from me in token that an artist and his *executioner* can get on well together. I know how disagreeable I *must* be sometimes, too thoroughly well, not to feel a very great pleasure in the cases where I know I am not misunderstood and not thought to be disagreeable out of a wicked disposition. Wishing that you may long live to sing and I to cut you, and with sincere and cordial wishes for your success and the happiness of yourself and belongings, believe me to be, affectionately yours,

"Henry F. Chorley."

Most of the other critics, London and provincial, were complimentary, but the palm for pure idolatry must be awarded to the *Birmingham Gazette*. " The name of Costa," it proclaimed, " even if he write no more, will by this work become a household word in the mouths of generations to come. . . . The great charm of *Eli* consists in the fact that it is not merely art expressed in a new form, but that it is something new in art. . . . *Eli* is a great and grand work of art, and if it is not at once a favourite with musicians and amateurs, it is because it is too lofty for their comprehensions. As years roll on his fame will only become more and more established. . . . Founded on Handelian strength, it combines much of the picturesque sublimity of Beethoven with the delicious harmony of Mozart, and the graceful beauty of Mendelssohn," and a good deal more inflated writing to the same effect. The culmination of rhodomontade came when it was gravely proposed that *Eli* should find a place in all the musical festivals throughout the provinces!

Time has not justified these wild predictions. Who knows anything of *Eli* now beyond the " March " which is occasionally to be found in cheap musical reprints? *Eli* is the work of a very clever musician who knew how to write for the soloist, for the chorus, and for the instrument, but whether it will ever be revived in this or the next generation is extremely doubtful. All that the present public know of oratorio may be summed up in two words *Messiah* and *Elijah*, and there does not appear to be a desire to hear any others. Even if choral music were again to come into favour, " Philistines, hark! " would present a formidable obstacle only to be overcome by a second Sims Reeves.

The remainder of the year was spent by Reeves in touring the English provinces, Ireland, and Scotland.[1] Jenny Bauer was the leading lady and Weiss the bass. There is nothing which calls for special remark beyond a statement in the *Dublin Freeman's Journal* that " it is said that Sims Reeves will shortly proceed to America with an operatic company." Whether Reeves had any such intention it is impossible to say. He certainly never carried it into effect, nor does he seem to have had much fancy for crossing the Atlantic.

On the whole the year 1855 was not marked by any musical event of importance apart from the production of *Eli*. There were, however, ample signs that the taste for music was widening, and even those who would not go to the theatre or to the opera, and who looked upon oratorio

---

[1] According to a paragraph in a semi-theatrical paper of some thirty years ago, Irving was appearing at Edinburgh in *Rob Roy* as " Captain Thompson [*sic*] with Sims Reeves as Francis Osbaldistone. Reeves was taken ill, and Wyndham suddenly swooped down on Irving and said, " Look sharp, the curtain's going up and you must take Reeves's place." " What, with all the songs? " returned the astonished actor. " Yes, all of them." " And I sang them," Irving used to say. " Yes, 'My love is like a red, red rose,' ' Though I leave thee now in sorrow,'—everything." It is difficult to accept this statement. The last time that Reeves sang in *Rob Roy* at Wyndham's theatre was November 19th, 1855 (J. C. Dibdin, *Annals of the Edinburgh Stage*), and Irving was not in the cast. Irving in fact did not play in Edinburgh until 1856. The blundering substitution of " Captain Thompson " for Captain Thornton also throws doubt upon the story.

MR. AND MRS. SIMS REEVES IN "BERTA."

H. Smart (1855).

as the only form of music to which " respectable " people like Sir Joseph Paxton should condescend to listen, were being catered for. In 1855 Miss P. Horton (afterwards Mrs. German Reed), an old associate of Sims Reeves in his Macready operatic days, started her " Illustrative Gatherings " in the small St. Martin's Hall —an enterprise which developed into a permanent institution so long as its foundress lived. The " German Reed " entertainments were welcome additions to the amusements of the metropolis, and their cessation has left a blank which might well be filled up.

CHAPTER XVI

1856–1857

A mania for organ building. St. James's Hall. Prim ideas concerning music. Sims Reeves and Bessie Palmer. The Bach-Gounod " Meditation." An *Eli* epidemic. Sims Reeves at the height of his powers. The Surrey Garden Music Hall opened. Jullien's success with oratorio. Remarkable acoustic qualities of the Surrey Gardens Hall. Oratorio in a Halifax factory. Clara Novello " improves " Handel and Haydn. Sensational incident at Exeter Hall. Projected gigantic choral gathering at the Crystal Palace. Weeding out the " old brigade " of chorus singers. Henry Leslie's choir. Part-songs displace glees. " Come into the garden, Maud." Sims Reeves sings at Windsor Castle. The first Handel Festival. Extraordinary preparations. Mr. Chorley enthusiastic over Reeves's singing. Acoustical defects of the great transept. Reeves in opera at the Standard Theatre. The coming of Santley.

A MUSICAL ferment marked the year 1856 which in these days of amateur soloists one can but regard with astonishment. A passion for choral singing on a large scale had set in. The principal towns in the Midlands—Liverpool, Manchester, York, Leeds, Bradford, Birmingham— rivalled each other in the building of halls large enough to accommodate hundreds of choral singers with orchestras to match. Each hall had to have an organ—the bigger the better. The whole country seemed to have gone organ mad, and both cathedrals and churches caught the infection ; old instruments were overhauled and new ones built where sufficient funds were forthcoming. The descendants of Jubal had the time of their lives. The sole object of this enthusiasm was the exploiting of oratorio, and the organisers of provincial festivals were fully alive to their responsibilities.

In London equal activity was shown. The *Athenæum* took occasion to remark that " the distance in which London has shot ahead in the matter of choral performances during the past twenty years can hardly be overestimated." The big-hall mania would not be denied. The gigantic Surrey Gardens Music Hall was well on its way to completion and St. James's Hall was in embryo. The *Athenæum* approved the general scheme contemplated concerning the latter, but shook its head at the restaurant proposed to be attached. It told its readers that " the changes that must be passing over the public in their appetite for entertainment are numerous and rapid enough to bewilder the most hopeful of persons. . . . Whether the cooking part of the Air Street castle in the air may be a wise thing in the scheme claims some consideration which may be reserved for a future date." Apparently it feared that eating and drinking on the ground-floor would have a deteriorating effect on the music performed in the hall above. Could Mr. Chorley have foreseen the reputation which the restaurant and buffet (when the rendezvous was affectionately known as " Jimmy's ") achieved in their decadent days, no language would have been strong enough for him to use.

It would not be fair to say that the *Athenæum* was influenced by Mrs. Grundyism, but, unconsciously perhaps, it was reflecting the views held at that time by " respectable " people. The puritanic feeling in regard to music, rampant in 1856 and for some years afterwards, appears to us in the twentieth century truly amazing. Queen Victoria set the example. On New Year's Day, for instance, Méhul's *Joseph* was performed at Windsor Castle, Sims Reeves, Clara Novello, Weiss, and Lewis Thomas taking the solo parts ; but to give the work as it was performed at the Paris Opéra Comique, for which theatre it was written, would have been too " shocking," so a new translation was written by the decorous Mr. Bartholomew, with new recitatives composed by Mr. W. G. Cusins. The proposal that bands should play in the public parks sent the bigots shrieking at the " depravity " which would follow, and the production of Verdi's *Traviata* raised a controversy in which poor Mlle Piccolomini, who essayed the part of the consumptive and naughty heroine, was attacked with a stupid savagery which was as ill-founded as it was vulgar and brutal. Horror of the wicked opera was carried so far that at Birmingham Piccolomini played to an almost empty house!

Meanwhile certain fussy persons were busying themselves

about music for the working-classes. Henry Mayhew, who ought to have known better, seeing that he posed as a " specialist " in regard to the poor, had an idea that when humble people went to hear music, it was not sufficient for them to be amused ; they ought also to be instructed. He accordingly worked out a scheme, which had the *cachet* of Bulwer-Lytton and other prominent people, for a series of concerts (at one of which Sims Reeves promised to sing) to be given at St. Martin's Hall, each concert to be " improved " by the delivery of a lecture. The inaugural discourse was written by Leigh Hunt and was read by Mr. J. H. Stocqueler. The result may be imagined. The audience enjoyed the music, but when the lecture began they would have none of it. The experiment was a hopeless failure and was never repeated.

As a matter of fact, there was plenty of cheap and good music for those who cared for something beyond *The Rat-catcher's Daughter*, at that time the rage. The Panopticon was giving concerts ; Jullien's " Promenades " were flourishing ; and of the music-halls, two at least, the Canterbury and the hall attached to the Eagle (late the Grecian Saloon), aimed at something better than comic songs. At the first-named Mr. Charles Morton was revolutionising the old style of music-hall entertainments by his first-rate operatic selections.

So far as Sims Reeves is concerned, his record in 1856 is a repetition of old successes. He was the great " draw " at the Sacred Harmonic Society's and Mr. Hullah's oratorio performances, and at innumerable concerts in various parts of London, notably at the Beaumont Institution, Mile End, where he was engaged season after season and where he found a host of enthusiastic admirers. Of his work at this period there is not much to say ; but one concert in a series given by Mr. Hullah may be mentioned. On this occasion Henry Leslie's charming trio " Oh, Memory " was first sung, the exponents being Sims Reeves, Mrs. Sims Reeves, and Miss Bessie Palmer,[1] who had already been associated with Reeves in a per-

[1] Miss Palmer, in her *Reminiscences*, records an instance of Reeves's readiness to assist young singers. She was staying at the same hotel at Southampton as Mr. and Mrs. Sims Reeves, and after supper " Mr.

formance of Mendelssohn's *St. Paul* and Beethoven's Mass in C, and for whom Reeves entertained a strong friendship.

On the same evening was also first given at St. Martin's Hall Gounod's " Meditation " on Bach's Prelude, and concerning it the opinions of two leading journals are not without interest. The *Athenæum* wrote : " The ' Meditation ' gave the utmost delight, indeed, as a piece of suggested creation it may rank, however different in style, with the most masterly of those glosses on ancient *corales* produced by Bach." " Why it was encored," indignantly demanded the *Musical World*, " we are at a loss to know . . . a piece of more sheer stupidity was never perpetrated. . . . What next and next ? And yet this impertinence has been lauded and encouraged by critics who ought to know better or leave off criticising." Time, at all events, has been on the side of the *Athenæum*.

A noticeable feature of 1856 is the extraordinary popularity of Costa's *Eli*. The furore amounted almost to an epidemic. The Sacred Harmonic Society gave four performances ; it was sung at the Bradford Festival, and fairly revelled in by the lusty Yorkshire vocalists ; at Gloucester, at Liverpool, and at Birmingham, where a testimonial was presented to the composer. Selections were given at York, badly done, it would seem, as the " splendid new organ " was half a tone flat ; and at Norwich Mr. George Perren was courageous enough to emulate Sims Reeves. His " Philistines, hark ! " was no doubt meritorious, for Mr. Perren attempted nothing that he did not do well, but as a battle-cry it must have lacked the necessary fire.

Reeves asked me why I used chest notes so high. I explained that Mr. Hullah had told me that my middle register was not strong enough, therefore I had better take F and G in chest quality or I should not carry those notes well to the further end of St. Martin's Hall. Then Mr. Reeves took me to the piano and showed how to strengthen the middle register by bringing down the head quality carefully and mixing it with the middle register. By closely noting what he explained and by practising as he told me I soon strengthened the weak middle notes and only used the chest notes up to E flat unless there should be a real necessity for power on the E natural occasionally. Some time after I was singing at a musical evening at Mr. Hullah's, when he remarked, ' How much rounder and fuller your voice has developed,' to my intense delight."

For *Eli* Reeves was in great request, but the prominent fact is the unanimity with which the critics this year emphasised their appreciation of the wonderful perfection to which his singing had reached. He was at the zenith of his powers, and it is to be remarked that for years afterwards he maintained this high pitch of excellence. One cannot help regretting that he had not the opportunity of adding to his repertory in Italian opera. But the goodwill of Italian singers was necessary, and this, it may be safely hazarded, was not forthcoming. Neither the manager of Her Majesty's nor of Covent Garden ventured to offer him an engagement, fearing trouble with the company if they did so. All that was left for the great English tenor in the way of opera was a series of performances at Sadler's Wells at a salary of £50 a night. His triumph was a foregone conclusion, albeit nothing fresher than *The Bohemian Girl, Sonnambula, Fra Diavolo,* and *The Beggar's Opera* was produced. But the public was unwearied. Whatever Sims Reeves chose to sing was welcome.

In June Jullien, the enterprising and unconventional, opened the Surrey Gardens Music Hall. Probably not many nowadays could say off-hand where the Surrey Zoological Gardens were situated. They have long been lost under a maze of mean streets. But in 1856 Walworth was a pleasant, leafy suburb—Mr. Wemmick, it will be remembered, had a " box " in Walworth—and Camberwell abounded in small villas, admirably described by Miss Braddon in *The Story of Barbara.* The Surrey Gardens were among the last of the outdoor pleasure-resorts (Highbury Barn, I fancy, outlived them) once a distinguished feature of the metropolis, and for a time bravely resisted the change of taste and the rage for speculative building which had swept away Vauxhall and Cremorne. Jullien prolonged their life, and the concerts he gave in the magnificent hall, which held 9,000 people, were of the best. The Emperor of the " Promenades " was probably desirous of showing that he could wield the baton at an oratorio as well as he could in front of an orchestra, and he succeeded. Performances of *The Messiah* and *Elijah*, with Sims Reeves, Clara Novello, and Madame Rudersdorff, not only attracted great crowds, but were great successes musically speaking. As Jullien got his chorus from all parts of England, it could not be other than a scratch body, but all the same it was remarkably efficient. This efficiency was probably due to the fact that at that time an enormous number of choral singers, both in London and in the country, knew their *Messiah* almost by heart, and in a less degree *Elijah*. Would it be possible to get together nowadays more than a score or so of persons of whom this could be said ?

The acoustics of the Surrey Gardens Hall were perfect. Mr. Spurgeon subsequently within its walls held multitudes spellbound under the charm of his homely eloquence and his ringing, melodious voice, and there is little doubt that he gave the architect of his " Tabernacle " many hints derived from his experience of the good qualities of the Surrey Gardens edifice. Reeves must have revelled in the opportunity he had of displaying his gifts in an arena where they had the fullest scope. The critics were astounded. The *Athenæum*, while holding that the building defied all " architectural proprieties," admitted that in it " the solo singers sang at their ease " and that " no one could have expected a building so floridly decorated should have turned out so capital a music-room." The *Musical World* marvelled that " a tranquil piece of chamber-music should be heard so well in so vast a building," in allusion to the singing of Mendelssohn's part-songs " O Hills, O Vales " and " The Vale of Rest," and further remarked that " the most delicate sound from the smallest word penetrated to every corner of the building."

Apart from oratorio, there was very little opportunity for Sims Reeves in London, and the autumn months were spent in connection with what was known as the Boosey concert troupe, consisting of Madame Endersohn, Miss Fanny Huddart, Sims Reeves, Balfe, Miss Arabella Goddard, and Mr. G. Case. After an extended tour in the south of England the party visited the Midlands and thence proceeded to Ireland, where in Dublin he sang at the Rotunda, on November 12th.

One of Reeves's engagements during the tour in the Midlands was at Halifax, where a concert was given to

inaugurate the opening of a huge " shed " belonging to
Messrs. Ackroyd, the well-known cotton spinners. The
following letters were part of the preliminary arrangements. The first, from Sims Reeves, runs thus :
" Wednesday, 123 Gloucester Terrace, Hyde Park, June
18th. DEAR SIR,—My lowest terms for the performance
would be sixty guineas. Will you favour me with a
reply per return whether you accept or not, and oblige,
Yours truly, J. SIMS REEVES."

The second, from Mrs. Weiss, shows the friendly footing on which Mr. Weiss stood with his fellow-artists :
" 77 Great Portland St., Portland Place, June 6th, 1856.
MY DEAR SIR,—Will you be kind enough to put Mr. Weiss
down for the songs I send you, and he leaves the selection
of the other music to Madame Novello and Mr. Reeves,
as any they select will be sure to suit him. I remain,
my dear Sir, Yours most truly, GEORGINA A. WEISS.
1st part. Song, Mr. Weiss, ' The Wanderer ' (Schubert).
Early in 2nd part, new song, Mr. Weiss, ' The Village
Blacksmith ' (W. H. Weiss)."

The experiment of a concert in the new " shade "—
to give the Yorkshire pronunciation, a term which
puzzled Clara Novello not a little—was not an unqualified success. Halifax Fair was going on, and the fat
woman, the travelling wax-works, with effigies of the
latest murderer, the circus, the swings, and the round-
abouts were more to the taste of the Halifax folk than
Haydn's *Creation* which formed the *pièce de résistance.*
Moreover, the prices of admission were fixed too high,
and in spite of special trains from Bradford and Huddersfield the shed was by no means crowded. Indeed, the
Halifax Guardian describes the concert in the evening
as being given to " empty benches." The chorus was
a combination of the Haly Hall, the Halifax, and the
Woodside Choral Societies, of whose singing the *Guardian*
said " not a note was lost, but the waves [of sound]
seemed crushed in by the roof."

Yorkshire people in those days took their oratorios
very seriously. Like good Mrs. Battle in another connection, they were sticklers for the " rigour of the game,"
and of Clara Novello's rendering of the solos in
The Creation the *Guardian* critic remarked : " We have

had handed down from father to son and from mother to daughter the traditional style in which this class of music ought to be sung, and though the great Italian-taught singers are constantly studying to deviate from this style, all their deviations are detrimental to the proper effect. Miss Clara Novello at the Bradford Festival wandered from the text, but in Halifax she was better." It must be confessed that at times the Queen of Oratorio had a tendency to " improve " Handel and Haydn. Maybe, however, on this occasion she had been warned that Halifax preferred its oratorio unadulterated and that she trimmed her sails accordingly. Of Sims Reeves, he was, one reads, " in splendid voice " and proved himself to be " the leader of English oratorio singing." Said the critic : " Long may he preserve unimpaired the rich quality of notes that seem of music all compact."

Towards the winter Reeves was again in London, where his services in oratorio could not be dispensed with. An incident which happened at a performance of *The Messiah* at Exeter Hall, which formed a *bonne-bouche* of musical gossip at the time, may be recalled. Mrs. Hepworth, who had achieved some reputation in the provinces, undertook the soprano solos and broke down badly, whether through nervousness or incompetency it is difficult to say. She had scarcely commenced the recitative following the Pastoral Symphony when it became obvious that she could not sing a note in tune, and she was fairly paralysed in the air " Rejoice greatly," stopping short in the middle. Costa signalled to the band to stop playing and Reeves led the lady from the platform. The contretemps was very embarrassing, but Costa chanced to espy Miss Louisa Vinning[1] among

---

[1] Louisa Vinning was a born singer, but somehow she failed to reach the height her admirers hoped for her. She came out as a " prodigy," and could scarcely have been more than six years old when all London flocked to the Adelaide Gallery (now Gatti's restaurant) to hear the " Infant Sappho." The flexibility of her voice was wonderful and her imitative faculty not less so. Her performance consisted of florid passages played on the piano—passages which she heard for the first time and which she reproduced with marvellous accuracy. She ought to have succeeded on the English operatic stage, but she was either wanting in opportunity or in ambition. She was a great favourite at the Beaumont

13

the audience, and the rising young vocalist was asked to
fill the vacancy, which she did with complete success,
the *Musical World* remarking that if she had never sung
the music before "she must be a *rara avis.*" Such a
chance of distinction rarely comes to a vocalist, and Miss
Vinning had the ball of fortune at her feet, but she made
little use of it. Her taste and her powers did not lie
in the direction of oratorio.

During the spring of 1857 little else, musically speaking, was talked of but the choral gathering to be held
in the Crystal Palace as a preliminary to the great Handelian Commemoration Festival which was contemplated
for 1859. Mr. Robert Bowley, a prominent member of
the Sacred Harmonic Society and a man of unbounded
energy, projected the scheme in 1856, and it was warmly
taken up by the Society and by the Crystal Palace Company, the idea being to utilise the grand transept, Exeter
Hall not being considered large enough. Everything
was to be on a gigantic scale. Of course a huge organ
was indispensable, and to Messrs. Gray & Davison was
entrusted the task of building an instrument worthy of
the occasion. Such a colossal undertaking as was proposed
would have been impossible but for three things : firstly,
the widespread taste for choral singing ; secondly, the
exceptional vocal power of the three leading exponents
of oratorio—Sims Reeves, Clara Novello, and Charlotte
Dolby ; and lastly, the existence of so spacious an arena
as the Crystal Palace centre transept.

Meanwhile, choral singing was being developed and
refined in a direction quite apart from the study of
oratorio. Choral singers were of two classes, those who
believed that oratorio was the beginning and ending of
all things, and those who were capable of appreciating
the fine effects to be got out of works written in a lighter
vein for a limited number of voices. The first were of
a mechanical type and would attack " And he shall purify "
or any other of Handel's fugual choruses with the vigour
and precision of well-drilled infantry. The more ex-

Institution, where I heard her sing many times. She was very delightful
in " Cease your funning " from *The Beggar's Opera,* and would have
been an ideal Polly both as regards sweetness of voice and charm of
personality.—C. E. P.

perienced led their weaker comrades who were quite content to follow after the signal for action was sounded.[1] The second comprised vocalists of a more intellectual and sensitive class. Mr. Henry Leslie was among the first to recognise the difference, and the outcome of his efforts was his Madrigal Choir, afterwards called Henry Leslie's Vocal Choir, a redundant title which became the once familiar Henry Leslie's Choir. In 1856 it had already given concerts which promised a perfection of choral singing hitherto undreamt of. A similar enterprise was seen in the Polyhymnia Choir for male voices only, which was distinguished by the combined vigour and refinement and the purity of tone for which Leslie's choir was justly celebrated. Mr. William Rea, an organist of great talent, was its founder and conductor, and it attained a pitch of excellence not exceeded by the famous Cologne Choir.

Local choral societies became more numerous than ever. Mendelssohn's part-songs were the rage, and English composers hastened to follow in Mendelssohn's footsteps. Henry Smart, J. L. Hatton, Henry Leslie, and others produced many charming compositions, and the new kind of chamber vocal music began to supersede the glees of Bishop and those of older writers. The part-songs of Arthur Sullivan, Pinsuti, Barnby, and many more succeeded in their turn. Musical people trained in the big societies met at each others' houses, and these enjoyable evenings were features of social life which

[1] It is to be suspected that a large proportion of the Sacred Harmonic chorus would have found a difficulty in passing a sight-singing test. The worst of it was that these personages usually had very loud voices, which made the habit of waiting for a " lead " very objectionable. A story is told of a bass singer who could roar like a bull when once set going, but could only start by watching the mouth of his neighbour. The latter resolved upon revenge, and his chance came when the chorus " Populous cities pleased me then " from Handel's *L'Allegro e Penseroso* was being rehearsed. In this chorus is a bass lead on the words quoted, and half a bar before the passage commenced a stentorian " Pop " echoed through the hall. It came from the offender, who seeing his neighbour's mouth open followed suit. Unfortunately for him, the leader uttered not a sound, but merely moved his lips, and his victim had no sooner shouted " Pop " than he realised his blunder and stopped short. This story is told in rather a different form by Sir Charles Stanford, and the latter's version may be the true one.

apparently have passed away. The amateur soloist now holds sway, and must have his or her audience, who have to resign themselves to listen whether they are interested or not. The old camaraderie which part-singing brought about no longer exists.

While sopranos, altos, tenors, and basses all over the country were zealously rehearsing for the Crystal Palace performance, Sims Reeves, who was destined to be closely associated with this and future festivals, went on his way undisturbed. He, at all events, had no need of rehearsals. It was on March 2nd of this year that at a morning concert given by Brinley Richards he first sang the most popular of his songs, " Come into the garden, Maud," a ballad whose charm has not departed even now, hackneyed as it has been, and despite the hash which the composer, with his habitual indifference to poetic rhythm when it interfered with his melody, made of " Queen rose of the rosebud garden of girls," turning it into " Queen of the rosebud, garden of girls," and making it still further nonsensical by dividing the line into two phrases. From the time of Reeves first singing this song to almost the last year of his appearance in public, " Come into the garden, Maud," was the delight of thousands, and was always sure of an encore. In his *Art of Singing* Reeves takes it as one of his examples in the study of vocalisation.

Queen Victoria was a great admirer of Reeves's singing, and on her birthday in May we find him with Clara Novello, Miss Bassano, and Beletti in a performance of Mendelssohn's *Lauda Sion* at Windsor Castle. Beyond this he was not concerned in any musical event which requires record until the Handel Festival in June. For weeks previous to the 15th nothing else was talked of, thought of by the musical world. The Festival catered only for the well-to-do. The price of admission was 10s. 6d. and a reserved seat cost a guinea. The great shilling public had no share in the celebration. Jullien, however, came to the rescue and filled up the gap. He announced a " Great Musical Congress and Festival " to take place at the Surrey Gardens Hall during the Sydenham week, and promised performances of *The Creation* and *Elijah*, interspersed with Beethoven, Men-

delssohn, and Mozart nights, and right well did he fulfil
his engagements.

But of course the Crystal Palace enterprise overshadowed everything. It was in every sense a national
gathering. Bradford, Birmingham, Liverpool, Dublin,
Worcester, Hereford, Gloucester, Norwich, Canterbury,
among other towns, each contributed its quota, most of
the singers having had good training in the various
Festival Choirs. Oxford and Cambridge Universities
were represented, and the services of the boys and men
of the Chapels Royal were also enlisted. The strength
of the orchestra staging was a matter of considerable
anxiety, and to make sure five hundred workmen rushed
up and down at the top of their speed and then were
ordered to jump at the same instant. The testing must
have presented a queer spectacle ; anyhow, the structure
bore its ordeal very well.

A sidelight on the feminine fashions of the period is
thrown by a letter in the *Athenæum* of June 5th, the
writer calling to mind that when *The Messiah* was
produced at Dublin in the eighteenth century the ladies
were " respectfully requested to attend the performance
without their hoops," and he remarks that " an act of
self-denial in some degree corresponding to this would
add to the comfort of the vast audience that will assemble
at Sydenham on the 15th and the following days."
Crinoline skirts were not so enormous in 1857 as in 1860,
but they were still of prodigious dimensions. Whether
any lady paid the slightest attention to this appeal is
extremely doubtful.

The Festival was favoured with the brightest of
weather and the scene presented by the transept was
brilliant in the extreme. The nine hundred ladies of
the chorus with their " white shawls or visites or whatever
they may be called " (*Morning Post*) formed a delightful
contrast to the gay colours of the audience. A special
feature to be noted was the abundant use of parasols
both by audience and chorus, which the sun rendered
almost indispensable, and in some cases the selfishness
exhibited formed as great an annoyance as the matinée
hat of later days. An innovation, which in later re-
strictive times reads quite sybaritic, was refreshment

handed round in the interval in the shape of small bottles of wine, ices, and biscuits.

More in wonderment than in admiration, I venture to say, did the audience gaze upon the extraordinary scheme of decoration adopted in what was called the royal box. Nothing could be more typical of the taste, or rather the want of taste, in vogue in 1857. The colours were of a dull crimson and yellow relieved by cabbage-green, and the general effect was that of a gigantic Punch and Judy show. Some musical septuagenarians may recollect this marvellous effort for the reception of the Queen and her consort.

There are few musical persons of middle age of to-day who have not " assisted " at some time or another at one of the gigantic choral gatherings given at the Palace, and to enlarge upon that of 1857 would be wholly superfluous. As the first, and coming as it did as a perfect novelty, the " word-paintings " of the newspaper scribes are only what one might expect. If the performance did not attain the pitch of perfection reached at subsequent Festivals, it was sufficiently great to astonish the critics. " The performance of *The Messiah*," writes Mr. Chorley, " was splendid. The mass of choral and instrumental sound . . . seemed balanced to a nicety —real, glowing, sonorous, and of a certainty such as is not to be heard out of England." . . . The soprano, Miss Novello, the alto, Miss Dolby, the tenor, Mr. Sims Reeves, did the best of their best." Reeves, he said, " sang with more than his usual care and with something of the inspiration belonging to so august a celebration."

Judas Maccabæus and *Israel in Egypt*, the oratorios chosen for the other days, excited Mr. Chorley to unwonted enthusiasm. " With regard to two of the solo singers, Mr. Sims Reeves and Madame Novello, it would be difficult to say too much by way of praise. . . . Any such singing by any Englishman—so pure, so noble, so forcible, and so highly finished—we never heard before. The spirit of the day, of the master, and of the work seemed to have fallen on the artist and enabled him to enkindle his vast audience to an excitement rare in sacred performances." This whole-hearted praise concerned Reeves's singing in *Judas*. Over his rendering of the tenor music in *Israel* the once-fastidious critic was not less emphatic in his admiration. "Mr. Reeves deserves a separate line to himself," are his words, "for his brilliant and forcible delivery of the *bravoura* ' The enemy said,' which called forth an encore so vehement as not to be resisted."

The Press everywhere sounded the same note. What the *Morning Post* said deserves to be quoted, not only in regard to Reeves, but (though in a different sense) to Clara Novello. Of the first it wrote : " The singing of Sims Reeves was transcendently grand. We could not have believed it possible for any man's voice to sound in such a vast locale so rich and voluminous and at the same time so brilliant and penetrating. There was no mere brawling—no coarseness—no unmeaning display of physical force, but each vigorous note had a fine heroic ring with it—a soul-felt vibration—a dignified broadening of tone which revealed intellectual energy and lofty poetical passion as well as marvellous physical power." One feels in reading this that the writer had not mere praise in his mind, but that he had sought to analyse the effect wrought on his feelings, and that he had chosen his words with deliberate intent. It is only just that this should be pointed out, as the present generation who never heard Sims Reeves and those of the past one who only heard him in his last days are disposed to be incredulous and smile pityingly when Sims Reeves's name is mentioned as that of the greatest tenor of any age.

What the same critic had to say of Madame Novello was in a very different vein. He regretted " an unhappy little appoggiatura " which she introduced, causing " the voice-part to make consecutive fifths with the bass, but," he added sarcastically, " singers do not mind such trifles and audiences do not find them out." On another occasion " unacceptable liberties were taken with Handel's text." Truth to tell, as remarked elsewhere, the gifted vocalist was given to adding her own ideas to Handel's and not always with the happiest effect.

One would like to know what were Reeves's sensations on singing for the first time in so gigantic a concert-room —if such a term can be applied to the Crystal Palace

centre transept, which had but a back and a front, the
sides being open to the nave. Every singer or speaker
has, so to speak, to take the measure of his surroundings
when using his voice amid acoustic surroundings strange
to him, and he has to accommodate the tone to suit
them. Reeves had probably had a larger experience of
various concert-halls than any singer of his or any other
day, and no doubt this experience stood him in good
stead, but even he must have been anxious, depending
as he did so much upon the dramatic effect of his singing.
Yet the contrasts, the delicate *nuances* and the heroic
outbursts, which he beyond any other vocalist could
produce without seeming effort were as perfect in the
Crystal Palace transept as in the Hanover Square rooms,
the best concert-hall, musically speaking, which London
then possessed.

Acoustics have always been a difficult problem for
the architect to solve. The Albert Hall should have
been designed with a special care for the excellence of
its acoustical properties, but the result was an uncertainty
which has never been completely overcome. In its
inception no one thought of the Crystal Palace transept
as a concert-hall, and least of any Sir Joseph Paxton, whose
soul would have revolted at the very idea. Yet even in
its primitive days its acoustics were remarkably good.
The voice, given the proper pitch, certainly " carried."
I remember Phelps reading the text illustrative of
Mendelssohn's *Athalie*. I was seated at the corner of
the first gallery to the left of the orchestra, and despite
the distance, which was considerable, every syllable was
perfectly distinct. The tragedian spoke with the utmost
deliberation and the intervals between the words could
be reckoned by the watch, but there was no want of
continuity. Phelps simply allowed time for his voice
to travel. In the case of purely musical sounds such
deliberation was not possible and clearness of articulation
was all the more essential, and it cannot be doubted that
Sims Reeves studied with this object previous to his
wondrous performance at the first Handel Festival.

Various concerts, among them a remembrance concert
in connection with the death of Douglas Jerrold, occupied Reeves until the Worcester Festival, about which

nothing need be said. In September we find him, together with Mrs. Sims Reeves, in opera at the Standard Theatre, Shoreditch, an engagement of which the *Musical World* wrote thus : " Here is a public that knows what it likes and it especially likes Mr. Sims Reeves. . . . Mr. Reeves is not only heartily welcomed at the Standard and thoroughly appreciated, but he is respectfully admired." Reeves was truly the people's songster.

In the comments regarding an operatic enterprise at the Lyceum one gets some idea of the fees which in those days Reeves could command. The time-worn subject of National Opera was again discussed, and the *Musical World* regretted that Sims Reeves and Clara Novello could not be engaged on account of the cost. " At this moment," it observed, " Mr. Sims Reeves is receiving fees at the rate of £200 per week for singing in old ballad opera. What new company would be justified in offering over that sum ? On the other hand, why should a singer give up a large income for the remote chance of establishing English opera ? " The Lyceum project, however, was carried through with the assistance of Miss Louisa Pyne and Mr. W. Harrison, and during the season Balfe's *Rose of Castile* was produced and ran for many nights. From this undertaking sprang what subsequently became the Pyne and Harrison Company.

Up to the end of the year there was nothing notable in Reeves's engagements, but on November 18th came the debut of a singer who cannot be passed over. On that day, at a performance of *The Creation* in St. Martin's Hall, Charles Santley made his first public appearance in London, the Crystal Palace, at which he sang on October 5th, hardly counting as being within the metropolis. It is interesting to read in Sir Charles Santley's *Reminiscences* how, previous to his departure for Italy, he made the acquaintance of Sims Reeves, who gave him some valuable information respecting masters in Milan ; and on his return Mr. Chorley introduced him to Mr. Hullah, who had proposed to divide the bass solos in Haydn's oratorio. Adam was but a small part and Mr. Hullah could not offer the debutant " any terms," but Santley accepted the engagement for the sake of coming before a London audience. His singing at once impressed the critics. The *Musical World* spoke of him as " possessing a magnificent voice, and what is as good, a correct method of delivery, with style and expression to boot. Mr. Santley was eminently successful, and the duet ' Graceful consort ' was encored with acclamation. A new and valuable acquisition has been made to the concert-room in the person of this gentleman." How this fine singer justified the critic's opinion there is no need to say.

CHAPTER XVII

1858–1859

A Royal function—a " slight " to Sims Reeves. Foreign artists and English audiences. Grisi and Mario sing in English. Mr. Chorley's indignation. The taste for music broadening. E. T. Smith's experiment with the Panopticon. The pioneer of Sunday Concerts. Opening of St. James's Hall. Sims Reeves astounds an Exeter Hall audience in *Israel*. " Monster " concerts run mad. The advent of " black minstrelsy." Mozart re-cooked. Reeves at the inauguration of the Leeds Festivals. Mean ideas of the wool magnates. Reeves in English opera at the Standard. The Monday " Pops " started. Their democratic tendency. Extraordinary preparations for the first Handelian Festival at the Crystal Palace. The " encore " nuisance. A " scene " at the Surrey Gardens. Reeves wins the day. The Gloucester Festival of 1859 and the amazing blunders of its stewards. Clara Novello champions Sims Reeves.

THE marriage of the Princess Royal to the Crown Prince of Prussia took place on January 25th, 1858. There were great rejoicings in connection with the event and much comment was caused by the non-inclusion of Sims Reeves in the musical programme set before the wedding party. The *Musical World* called it a " slight," but the indisposition which persistently pursued Reeves during the early months of the year may have accounted for his absence.

The true reason probably was in the fact that for the moment the Pyne and Harrison Company were the only representatives of British opera. Balfe's *Rose of Castile* was all the rage and it was impossible to include Sims Reeves in the cast without displacing Mr. W. H. Harrison—a thing unthinkable from Harrison's point of view. The *Musical World* was of opinion that *The Bohemian Girl* might have been substituted and so have given a chance to both tenors. But this would have meant Harrison playing second fiddle, and would have invited comparisons more than " odorous." Mr.

Harrison was never strong where perfect intonation
was demanded and his nasal twang was at times
unpleasantly conspicuous.   Harrison, like Dickens's
biographer, John Forster, was a "harbitrary gent"
and could not fancy himself out of the limelight.   I
have it from Sir Charles Santley himself that during
his engagement with the Pyne and Harrison Company he
had more than one tussle with Harrison to maintain his
rights while on the stage, and more than once was the
victor, much to the chagrin of the tenor, who had to be
made to see the propriety of occasionally being subordinate
when the situation demanded it.

Whatever may be the explanation of Reeves's absence
from the Royal rejoicings, it was hardly a question of
foreign versus British artists.   It was at this time beginning
to dawn upon the former that the great British public
was worth cultivating.   The pit and gallery were much
easier to please and to rouse to enthusiasm than the vapid
aristocratic patrons of stalls and boxes.   Italian vocalists
now thought it worth while to try to sing in English.
Mario had accomplished the feat the previous year in
"Then shall the righteous," and Grisi followed suit
but with a difference.   The husband had for his audience
county bigwigs and landed gentry.   Madame sang to the
motley gatherings which Jullien's "Promenades" never
failed to attract.   Mr. Chorley was greatly shocked at
so distinguished a prima donna thus lowering herself.
"After five and twenty years' persistence against singing
in English," he writes, "the lady now condescends to
sing ballads.   We hear on every side epithets and
expressions which it is painful that one for a quarter of a
century so distinguished as herself should have courted."
If there is any argument in such a protest, it is a regret
that Madame Grisi did not begin to sing in English
twenty-five years sooner than she did.   But whatever
Mr. Chorley meant he did not mean *this*.

The critic was on much safer ground when he rejoiced
in the spread of choral music in England.   "Our cousins
in Berlin," he remarks, "have no longer their old
superiority over us in part-singing—in their Dom Choir
and their Sing-Academie.   In fact the old . . . taste
for vocal music is breaking out in England almost as if

SIMS REEVES IN 1858.

' the merrie days of good Queen Bess ' were come again."
He laments that hardly the same could be said of instrumental music.

English ballad music apparently did not appeal to
Mr. Chorley. Italian singers, on the other hand, found
much in it to their taste—so far, at all events, as Balfe's
melodious effusions were concerned. In February *The
Bohemian Girl* was produced in Italian at Her Majesty's
with Piccolomini and Giuglini, " who," according to our
super-critic, " outdid Mr. Harrison's greatest popularity
in the ballad in the last act by outdoing the long-drawn
sickly style of the old-fashioned stage tenor in England.
He was encored twice and pelted with bouquets—the
first appearance of flowers emitted against a gentleman on
the stage which we recollect." Evidently Mr. Chorley
was unaware that this unusual compliment was first paid
to Sims Reeves.

February is notable in the fact that in this month the
" Panopticon " in Leicester Square changed its name and
also its attempt to combine science with music. It had
worked bravely in the cause of the first and its organ
recitals were the best in London, but the two refused to
mix. Mr. E. T. Smith, who was then looming large in
the world of impresarios, saw possibilities in the place in a
" popular " direction and under his magic wand it
emerged as the " Alhambra." Mr. Smith was nothing if
not original, and his idea was to cater for the taste of
everybody. The entertainment was satirically described
as a mixture of casino, concert-room, and public-house,
with an extra novelty on Sunday in the way of a sermon !
A preacher of the name of Rutherford was engaged for the
religious part of the performance, and M. Henri Laurent,
the conductor of the Argyll Casino band, directed the
music. A London newspaper at once taxed Mr. Rutherford with inconsistency. After expressing himself
opposed to the Sunday opening of national institutions,
he " now lends himself to a palpable evasion of the law
forbidding Sunday amusements." Mr. Rutherford's
reply was that he consented to open the Alhambra because
he thought we couldn't have too many places for the
preaching of the gospel, and he stipulated that in the
morning all classes should be admitted free of charge. As

for the music, he thought it would be the choral music of the Church of England. In the evening, however, the singing was turned into " Sunday amusement " and he would not preach again. On which the *Musical World*, always on the look-out for the funny side of things, remarked, " So Mr. Rutherford backs out of the Alhambra. Still, let us hope that a plan so comprehensive and so beautifully symmetrical is not to be rendered abortive by the fastidiousness of a single preacher—he is evidently a man much behind his age. Do not despair, Mr. E. T. Smith. Look out for another preacher. There are as good fish in the sea as ever were caught."

Meanwhile Sims Reeves was through illness unable to fulfil his engagements. However, during February he recovered sufficiently to sing at Exeter Hall in *Elijah*. Santley for the first time essayed the title-rôle, Mr. Chorley observing that " since Herr Staudigl ' created ' the part (with the exception of Signor Beletti) we have not heard a first appearance as Elijah on the whole so satisfactory." In March, also at Exeter Hall, we have Reeves singing in *Samson*. " Finer singing and declamation have never been heard in the sacred orchestra than his rendering of ' Total Eclipse ' and that tremendous *bravoura* ' Why does the God of Israel sleep ? ' ; than his objurgation of Delilah . . . and his share in the admirable duet ' Go, baffled coward ' " (*Athenæum*). On March 25th was opened St. James's Hall, destined to be the scene of many triumphs both of Reeves and Santley. It was inaugurated with *The Hymn of Praise* by the Vocal Association, under Benedict. The hall itself met with general approval, but the arrangements for the chorus and orchestra were severely condemned.

Finely as Reeves was known to sing " The enemy said " in *Israel*, he captured everybody when he gave the famous air at a performance of the oratorio on May 1st. One reads that " he produced a sensation unparalleled in Exeter Hall. It was a real furore in which the whole band and chorus joined, and which by its vehemence and continuance fairly took the singer by surprise." At a concert at the end of May Reeves sang in St. James's Hall. The management was then feeling its way as to how far it might go in the direction of classical music. The

programme was based on the lines of the " Wednesday "
concerts which had been so successful a few years previous,
but minus the band and also the ballads of the " washy "
order. Reeves sang " Adelaida," delightfully accompanied by Miss Arabella Goddard.

Music in 1858 was in the ascendant, from oratorios
down to Mr. Howard Glover's " monster " concerts.
The " monster " had not yet been scotched, but if anything
could have killed the monstrosity it would have been
the impudent enterprise organised (if the word can be
applied to a haphazard thing which depended upon
unscrupulous advertisement) by the " Editor of *La Presse
de Londres* under the superintendence of H. St. Leger,
Esq." at St. James's Hall. The object was stated to be
the establishment of a club for artists. The programme
contained fifty-four items by artists known and unknown,
not one of whom, Mr. H. St. Leger proudly proclaimed,
was paid. The *Musical World* denounced the " monster
concert " in unmeasured terms, called it an intolerable
nuisance, and was rewarded by receiving an extremely
silly letter from " H. St. Leger, Esq." So far as can be
ascertained, no more was heard of the " club for artists,"
nor of the concert intended to inaugurate it.

The public was insatiable in its capacity for absorbing
music in every shape and form, and if ever there was an
opportunity for the founding of National Opera, now
seemed to be the time. But there was no agitation or any
such thing. Those who thought about it probably considered that ballad opera as given by the Pyne and Harrison
Company satisfied all reasonable requirements. The
English operatic theatre was packed nightly ; concerts
at Exeter Hall, St. Martin's Hall, St. James's Hall, and
other London centres attracted large audiences.
Suburban musical gatherings abounded, choral societies
were singing lustily everywhere with thoughts of the great
Handelian Festival the following year in their minds.

In addition to the supporters of operatic and classical
music, a large section of the population who knew little of
either found satisfaction in black minstrelsy, the rage for
which had just set in, and which, in spite of the indignant
protests of musical purists, was making its way. A
good many prophets were certain the craze would soon

die out. English people, they held, were far too sensible to patronise such silly and vulgar entertainments. But black minstrelsy lived on and established itself as one of the institutions of London. It found a home, of all places above others, beneath the roof of St. James's Hall, where crowds humming the latest " nigger " novelty mingled on the staircase with the devotees of Bach and Beethoven !

Italian opera, on the other hand, was not doing well owing to mismanagement and the unfair treatment of the artists. The *Athenæum* of July 11th comments thus : " We heard the other day on good authority that attempts have been made to invite Mr. Sims Reeves to Her Majesty's Theatre, to which our tenor has wisely turned a deaf ear. Who shall wonder at the caprices of artists themselves so capriciously treated—one month raised to the seventh heaven of a Fools' Paradise and the next it may be all but put to the door ? " Italian opera at this date really seemed topsy-turvy when so curious an incongruity could be perpetrated and approved as transposing the part of the Don in Mozart's masterpiece to suit Mario ! However, it was done, and hundreds rushed to hear Mozart re-cooked.[1] The thing was the more noticeable in that at that very moment Mr. Chorley was crying out for more tenors. " Who is capable," he asks plaintively, " of dividing duties or doubling them with Sims Reeves ? George Perren, Haigh—what has become of them ? "

The time of the musical festivals came on apace. At Birmingham Reeves sang in *Acis and Galatea*, to which Costa had written additional accompaniments ; and in November came a great event in Yorkshire, the establishment of the Leeds Festivals, for the opening of which Sterndale Bennett composed *The May Queen*. Sir Charles

---

[1] Lord Mount-Edgcumbe has a passage bearing on this question which is not without interest. It runs : " It has always surprised me that the principal characters in two of Mozart's operas should have been written for basses, namely Count Almaviva (*Nozze di Figaro*) and *Don Giovanni*, both of which seem particularly to want the more lively tones of a tenor, and I can account for it no otherwise than by supposing they were written for some particular singer who had a bass voice, for he has done so in no other instance." The noble amateur forgot that the operatic tenor of Mozart's day was generally a colourless, sentimental individual totally out of keeping with the amorous Almaviva and the dissolute Don. Mozart doubtless knew perfectly well what he was about.

Stanford (*Pages from an Unwritten Diary*) throws an interesting sidelight on the ideas of the wool magnates who managed the affair, concerning the commercial value of art. They rather shook their heads over the terms asked by the artists. One gentleman seriously proposed that though guineas were stipulated, pounds should be sent and the balance be retained for " commission." The management was saved from ridicule by Mr. Walker Joy, one of the prime movers of the foundation. The cantata, with Reeves, Clara Novello, Dolby, and Weiss, was a tremendous success.

The engagement of Sims Reeves in September at the Standard Theatre in Shoreditch was the occasion of the following enthusiastic outburst from the *Morning Star*. " Mr. Sims Reeves—and every Englishman who loves the divine art should be proud that such a distinction can be claimed by a compatriot—can say to the foreigner what no foreigner can say to him : ' I can play Edgardo, Fra Diavolo, and Florestan (*Fidelio*) as well as any of you, but not one of you can sing " Comfort ye, my people," " The enemy said, I will pursue," and " Love sounds the alarm," let alone " The Death of Nelson " and all the incomparable ballads and sea-songs of the immortal Tom Dibdin as well as I.' He would not say so, it is true, being too genuine an artist to boast of his achievements, but he might say so with none to contradict him." At the Standard he did nothing that he had not done before. All that need be recorded is that in *Guy Mannering* the pit, as was said of Edmund Kean, " rose at him." It may be lamented that his genius was wasted in continual repetitions of the Braham and Bishop ballad-opera, but what was he to do ? It was rumoured at this time that the Pyne and Harrison management had offered him an engagement, but if this were so, nothing came of it. As the *Musical World* pointed out, no adequate salary could be offered him when without effort he could earn £200 a week by singing at a remote theatre in the city.

Meanwhile the managers of the St. James's Hall had come to the conclusion that they could safely depend upon an audience which would support concerts in which high-class music formed the greater part of the programme. They had given many ballad concerts, at one of which

14

(December 11th) Reeves sang, and on Monday, January 3rd, 1859, the " Popular " concerts, which afterwards became a feature of music in London, were started. Reeves was to have sung, but he was ill, and Mr. Wilbye Cooper had to take his place. There was the usual storm of senseless indignation when the substitution was announced. Santley also sang, and many a time subsequently ; the great baritone delighted his audience, who looked for him as a matter of course at the Monday " Pops." It was not until February 26th that the " Pops " took the form with which the public became familiar.

The Monday " Pops " represented a thoroughly democratic movement. Not so many years before it was thought by many superior persons that the great shilling public did not and could not appreciate high-class music. They took care never to give that public a chance. The gallery at the Italian opera was as a rule 5*s.*, the cheapest seat at the Exeter Hall oratorio concerts was 3*s.* ; the lowest price at the Philharmonic was prohibitive. So was it with chamber music. The working population were shut out. Jullien and the promoters of the " Wednesdays " opened the door to the enjoyment of classic orchestral music at a cheap rate, and the St. James's Hall management essayed to do the same with chamber music. Once started, the Monday " Pops " for a quarter of a century never looked back.

So much for democracy and music in London. In the provinces much more than thought was bestowed on the matter. For a long time high-class concerts for the people, the prices well within their means, had been given at Manchester, and the Free Trade Hall was crowded with operatives who listened with intelligent appreciation to the performance of classical masterpieces by the best artists. An admirable example was set by some of the merchants and mill owners, who on one occasion subscribed for 4,500 tickets for a performance of *The Messiah* and distributed them among working people. It is safe to say that the great Handelian celebration held at the Crystal Palace in 1859 excited as much interest in Lancashire and Yorkshire as it did in the metropolis.

Preparations for the Festival were going on in every

musical centre throughout the country. It was a time of musical enthusiasm such as will never be repeated. Wild ideas were afloat. People saw no limit to numbers in choral gatherings. Paris, not to be outdone, talked of a chorus of 7,000 voices. Caen contemplated a performance of the famous septuor in *The Huguenots* by a thousand singers to a part! Improvements were made in the Crystal Palace orchestra by the addition of a solid boarded enclosure of " repellent material " running round the back ; and a special contrivance for the soloists was suggested. What this contrivance was no one knew, and the *Musical World* facetiously inquired whether the artists were to be provided with speaking trumpets or with movable sound-boards to be elevated or depressed at discretion. A double monster bassoon to descend an octave below those then in use and a kettle-drum 13 feet in circumference were among the gigantic addenda rumoured.

The Handel Centenary Festival came and went. There is no need to repeat the tale of Reeves's wonderful oratorio singing and of his welcome by the audience— all the warmer because of his frequent illnesses during the preceding months. He was at the height of his popularity, and he was never in more splendid voice. The improvements effected to overcome former acoustical shortcomings were successful. But no " contrivances " were introduced to assist the soloists and the mystery of the " invention" was never solved.

The Festival gave occasion for one of Mr. Chorley's typical letters, interesting because it shows that the writer was quite conscious of his own infirmities. On June 18th he wrote : " I saw your wife—and shook hands with her over you—yesterday, but I can't help writing a line or two to you in addition to the lines of you which the penny-a-liner who uses my name may think fit to print elsewhere, to express without flattery or nonsense the very great pleasure which your singing in *Judas* and its success gave me. It makes me feel young in spite of a hard life and worn-out feelings and many disappointments whenever I hear anything so true, so cordially appreciated. To admire and to see success is always, believe me, a greater honour and a pleasure than any occasion of disparagement can offer to your sincere *ogre* and faithful friend, HENRY F. CHORLEY."

The encore nuisance to which Reeves was constantly subjected was greatly in evidence during 1859. It is to be noted that this persistency became accentuated in the intervals between his periods of indisposition, as though the public had decided that the popular tenor should make up for the times when he was unable to sing by doubling the quantity when he *could* sing. A disturbance more outrageous than usual took place on July 30th at the Surrey Gardens Hall, arising out of this unreasonable demand. Reeves sang " Fra Poco," and shouts for an encore were heard. The vocalist declined to repeat the trying air, and for half an hour the concert could not proceed. When Reeves again appeared, the malcontents determined that he should *not* be heard. The singer endured the uproar for some time, then clutching his music-roll he exclaimed, " I'm too much of an Englishman to be beaten when I have right on my side," and coolly sitting down he faced the angry audience and calmly waited. Good sense at last prevailed, and when all was quiet he went to the piano and sang " Pretty Jane." It was received with enthusiasm, but not a voice was raised for its repetition. Just to show his appreciation of his victory he came back of his own accord and gave " The Bay of Biscay." Long experience had taught him how to deal with a British audience.

A curious delusion prevailed in regard to his frequent illnesses, even among those who ought to have known better. An instance of this stupidity occurred at the Gloucester Festival on September 17th, and the story is worth quoting in full if only on account of Madame Clara Novello's chivalrous conduct. " The indisposition of Mr. Sims Reeves was observed on all sides," wrote the *Times* correspondent, " during the performance of *The May Queen*, and no one ought to have felt surprise, however he may have experienced disappointment, at the omission of a ballad allotted to that gentleman in the second part of the concert. When, however, Madame Novello had sung ' Prendi per me ' out of its place and on her retiring there were no signs of Mr. Reeves, the audience began to be restive and would not be pacified until one of the stewards (Mr. T. G. Parry) came forward and addressed them. He said (as nearly as we can remember), 'Ladies and gentlemen, it seems to be the principal duty of the stewards to make apologies for Mr. Sims Reeves. The stewards have done all in their power, but as Mr. Sims Reeves has quietly walked off, the stewards cannot fetch him back and I hope they will not be blamed. He has found a good friend in Madame Novello, who has kindly consented to sing a song in his stead.' This somewhat disingenuous address was received with mingled applause and hisses. It did not, however, satisfy Mr. Reeves's substitute, who, protesting that it conveyed an erroneous statement of the facts, declared that she would not sing until it had been corrected. The Mayor of Gloucester (on the refusal of his colleague to set matters right) then volunteered a further explanation, which amounted to this :

" ' Ladies and Gentlemen, I have the pleasure to inform you that Madame Novello will give another song in place of Mr. Sims Reeves.'

" Cries of ' Not enough '—' We know that already,' greeted the ears of his Worship as he left the platform, having delivered himself of this weighty piece of information. Being apprised of the inadequate manner in which he had accomplished his self-imposed task, the Mayor returned to the charge and addressed his turbulent co-citizens afresh. ' Ladies and Gentlemen,' he said, ' I am to state that Mr. Sims Reeves, being ill, was compelled to leave.' This speech, a worthy pendant of the other, was answered by shouts of laughter, and it seemed unlikely now that the disturbance would be quelled at all.

" After a long interval, during the progress of which the Shire Hall threatened to be turned into a bear-garden, Madame Clara Novello made her appearance on the platform to fulfil, as was generally surmised, the task she had undertaken as deputy. Shouts, cheers, and plaudits greeted her from every part of the room, and when these subsided she opened her lips—but not to sing. Instead of ' Bonnie Prince Charlie ' it was ' Ladies and gentlemen.' Calmly, unaffectedly, yet firmly, Madame Novello, like a musical Portia, admonished her hearers. She spoke to the following purport : ' Before he went away, very ill, Mr. Reeves explained to the conductor his total inability to sing his ballad in the second part ; but with a desire that the audience might not be losers through his indisposition, which was not his fault, he applied to me to introduce something in its place, and even sent for a copy of the ballad I am now going to have the honour of singing to you with much less ability than he would have shown. Mr. Arnott, with whom alone the artists engaged at the Festival can communicate on business, was consulted and gave his approval, and not satisfied even with this, Mr. Reeves spoke with one of the stewards, who also consented to the change. Had this been stated, no fault could possibly have been laid to his charge. I thus take the liberty to address you, ladies and gentlemen, because I will not allow a brother-artist to be unjustly accused as Mr. Reeves was—of course unintentionally—in the explanation given this evening, or to be blamed when he is entirely innocent, and especially when he had taken all the precautions in his power to compensate for any disappointment.' The tones of the nightingale had more persuasive eloquence in them than the voices of the steward and the Mayor. The fair apologist (who speaks, by the way, quite as musically as she sings) was completely overwhelmed with the demonstrations of complete satisfaction that her quiet speech had elicited, and the peace of her ' brother-artist ' was made with the public."

The blundering of the stewards was unpardonable. The facts were these. Just before the Festival a fire broke out at the Oatlands Hotel, Surrey, where Mr. Reeves was staying. He had to turn out of his bedroom and encamp in the park. He caught a chill, the full effects of which did not make themselves felt until later on. He wrote at once to the stewards expressing his fear that he might not be able to fulfil his engagement, but getting better he went down to Gloucester, with the result detailed above. There were forty-four stewards, and probably all did not know the circumstances. " Had they followed," commented the critic, " the example of the stewards of the Hereford Festival, who, when an

MADAME CLARA NOVELLO.
From a photograph by Mayall.

explanation had to be made, ' came, one and all, hand in hand on to the platform like a party of Ethiopian serenaders about to sing " We are a band of Brothers," ' it would have ensured something like unity," but, as the critic goes on to say, " the appearance of the forty-four Gloucester stewards drawn up in line on the platform and fraternally grasping one another by the hand would have been too imposing a sight for the nerves of the public." However, subsequently, the stewards did their best to set matters right, and not only apologised to Mr. Reeves, but, what was much more to the purpose, sent him a cheque for the full amount of his fees.

And with this contribution to the long list of provincial festival peculiarities the chronicle of Reeves's doings in 1859 may well conclude. The fact that at the end of the year English opera in London was non-existent, while Italian opera in English was being played at two theatres —*Il Trovatore* with Santley at the Lyceum, and *Lucia* at the Standard with Reeves—to use the trite expression, needs no comment.

CHAPTER XVIII

1860

English choral singing " at the top of the tree." Rage for Gluck's music. Reeves superb in *Iphigénie en Tauride*. Italian opera in London at a dead level. Mr. Chorley's remarkable forecast as to music in Italy. Incongruity in public taste. A typical suburban concert. Reeves's popularity at the East End. The encore nuisance again. Oratorio at its zenith. Why it was favoured. Reeves's influence on oratorio. Scotland's first Musical Festival. Santley's *tour de force* at the Norwich Festival. Effect at the Worcester Festival of the freaks of fashion. English opera and English operatic singers in great favour. E. T. Smith's bold experiment at Her Majesty's. Production of *Robin Hood*. Reeves's enormous success. Italian opera yields supremacy to *Robin Hood*.

THE year 1860, without being in any way remarkable, maintained the high musical level reached in 1859. A performance of *Israel* moved the *Athenæum* to declare that " the stride made in English choral execution during the last twenty years is almost fabulous—we English are now at the top of the tree so far as the European nations are concerned." Another outstanding fact is that Reeves continued to sing magnificently, whether in oratorio, ballads, or in opera.

The Handelian style influenced musical taste. The florid, ornamental Italian school was neglected. Gluck suddenly came into high favour. A notable revival was that of *Iphigénie en Tauride*, produced by Mr. Charles Hallé at Manchester. The first performance of the opera in England was given by a German company at the St. James's Theatre in 1840, and served for the introduction of Staudigl to the British public. The second was that in the Free Trade Hall in 1860. The singers could not have been bettered. Catherine Hayes undertook the title-rôle ; Sims Reeves was Pylades and Santley Orestes, and both these incomparable masters of song added to their laurels. One can imagine that Reeves felt a particular pleasure at the opportunity of fulfilling an early ambition. *Iphigénie* was one of the operas Jullien contemplated giving during his 1847–8 season at Drury Lane, but, as already mentioned, circumstances stood in the way and the project was abandoned.

In his notice of the Manchester performance Mr. Chorley wrote : " The Pylades of Reeves was the best of Reeves at his best. The music suits him as admirably as the great oratorio music of Handel ; more intense, more pathetic rendering, and higher vocal art could not be imagined." The critic was equally enthusiastic over Santley, who, he remarked, had "made another step higher in his rapid ascent as Orestes." Later on in the year Gluck 's *Armida* was given at Norwich, with Reeves, Santley, and Clara Novello, and at Manchester the opera was again performed, George Perren taking the place of Reeves. In Paris the star of Gluck was also in the ascendant.

It seemed to be incumbent that Gluck should be heard in London in some shape or form, and a performance of *Iphigénie* at the Crystal Palace was announced. At the last moment either the hearts of the promoters failed or the necessary artistic material was not forthcoming, and *The May Queen* was substituted ! On this the *Athenæum* remarked that " the work demands not merely deliberate preparation difficult to ensure, but an audience willing to wait to hear and to comprehend a whole poem of some length." Yet these essentials were possible in Manchester !

In a forecast of music for the year Mr. Chorley as regards Italian opera was pessimistic. He hoped that Verdi's star was on the wane. " The attractions of Bellini and Donizetti," he declared, " are worn out, and it is hardly possible to assemble a troupe capable of doing justice to the less-known operas of Signor Rossini. . . . If Italy be in very truth and deed remaking herself, . . . we will forgive her should she make no music for years to come." By the light of the last quarter of a century Mr. Chorley's words read as a remarkable example of prescience. Until the advent of Mascagni, Leoncavallo, Boito, and Puccini, Italian music was for many years in comparative stagnation. Verdi, contrary to the critic's hopes, remained the sole representative, and his genius, instead of waning, showed its vitality in *Aïda, Falstaff, Otello,* and the *Requiem.* The fact cannot be overlooked, however, that before Verdi came into his own many musical critics shared Mr. Chorley's opinions—or prejudices. When the *Requiem,* Mr. C. L. Graves tells us (*Diversions of a Music Lover*), was first produced Hans von Bülow attacked it " with all the acerbity of which he was a past master. But before he died he had so far changed his mind as to indite a spontaneous palinode confessing that on further acquaintance he had learned to admire what he had originally condemned. Verdi acknowledged the compliment with grave irony, hinting that perhaps after all von Bülow's first thoughts might be better." Save for Verdi, composers in Italy in 1860 were almost non-existent, and it is significant that three talented composers of Italian birth—Pinsuti, Tosti, and Tito Mattei—should have domiciled themselves in England and written entirely to suit English taste.

Mr. Chorley was equally pessimistic about Germany. " Never," says he, " has any great school died out in such disappointing nothingness as that of its instrumental composition seems to have done." Wagner and Schumann he does not condescend to notice, and he is equally silent about English instrumental composers. But in truth with the solitary exception of Sterndale Bennett they could hardly be said to exist. Since 1860 England, like Italy, has remade herself, thanks to the long list of earnest instrumental composers headed by Elgar. And while Russia has gone ahead with giant strides, Germany, the birthplace of Bach, of Handel, of Haydn, of Beethoven, lags behind despite Richard Strauss.

Sixty years ago the musical taste of the British public was strangely mixed. While one section had gone oratorio mad, another was devoted to chamber music and the Monday " Pops " ; a third clung tenaciously to the banal drawing-room ballads of the period ; a fourth found its delight in the Balfe and Wallace operas ; and a fifth had all the gratification it wanted in negro minstrelsy. Some concert directors took their cue from the programmes popularised by Jullien, leavening an intolerable quantity of commonplace with a ha'pennyworth from

some of the great composers. Others favoured the division
of a concert into " sacred " and " secular " parts—a
stupid idea happily long since consigned to limbo. But
whether one plan or the other was adopted, the main point
was the pleasing of everybody, and the result in many cases
was an *olla podrida* which to-day would be impossible.
A writer in a musical paper of 1860 held up to ridicule
the programme of one of the concerts of an annual series
given at the Beaumont Institution, at which concerts
Reeves was always the great attraction. The *Oberon*
overture, played on the organ, was cheek by jowl with
" Sally in our Alley " ; " We were boys together," by
Weiss, came next to a trumpet solo ; " Let the bright
seraphim " was sandwiched between " The Wolf " and
" Tom Bowling." Flotow's " Spinning Wheel " quartette finished the first part, and the second began with
an organ selection from *Acis and Galatea*. The rest
of the twenty-four items which constituted the programme was an equally incongruous jumble. That the
singers included Reeves, Madame Lemmens Sherrington, and Weiss made the mixture more unpalatable.
The critic exclaimed indignantly that " an institution
like that in Mile End Road ought to set a better if not a
graver example. Why should they look at every other
subject from a dignified point of view and treat music as
a toy with hardly skill enough in its construction to
attract the curiosity even of thoughtful children ? "

To this rebuke the Beaumont Institution directorate
had a right to say : " Thoughtful children or not, we
did attract ; the hall was packed, the audience encored
half the pieces, and—we paid our expenses." The
suburban concert is practically a thing of the past, but in
the sixties the fringe of London was a long way from the
centre. The suburbs had mainly to depend upon what
music was brought to them, and it had to be adapted to
their own standard, which, it must be confessed, was not
very high. If a schoolgirl could scramble through
Thalberg's " Home, sweet home," she was considered
a prodigy. The Beaumont Institution was not concerned
about " dignified " music ; their object was to give its
patrons what pleased them, and they certainly succeeded
whenever Reeves's name was in the bill. Bitter was the

disappointment—a disappointment which we of to-day cannot measure or even understand—when slips were found posted stating that " owing to severe indisposition, etc., etc." Not often did this happen, for Reeves liked his hearty, boisterous East End audience, who were never tired of hearing over and over again the old ballads which they already knew by heart, and he had to be ill indeed before he failed to appear.

I have before me the programmes of the Beaumont Institution Concerts from July 15, 1849, to May 6, 1861, at many of which I was present. They number forty-seven, and Reeves took part in every one. He sang later than the year last mentioned, but of these performances I have no record. At these forty-seven concerts Reeves sang seventy different songs without reckoning an " intolerable quantity " of encores. The selections most favoured by the audience, and maybe by Reeves himself, were " Still so gently," " The Death of Nelson," " The Pilgrim of Love," and " Deeper and deeper." " My pretty Jane " and " Tom Bowling " do not figure in the programmes so often, but this was because they were so frequently given as encores. Operatic selections, " Fra Poco," " Oh, 'tis a glorious sight to see," " La Donna e Mobile," and others are to be found at intervals, and the rest were made up of ballads long since forgotten.

Throughout his long career Reeves never put in more work and never sang better than in 1860. He was in excellent health and rarely was an audience disappointed. His appearances at the Monday " Pops " were frequent, and notable occasions were those when he gave the "Lieder Kries," which he sang with an intensity of passion which no other singer could rival. One evening when a vocalist announced to appear failed to arrive, Reeves filled up the gap with "Adelaida," Benedict playing the accompaniment from memory. Some singers would have considered it beneath their dignity to " oblige " in this manner, but Reeves never suffered from " swelled head," and when he stood up for his rights he was amply justified in so doing.

This year at the end of April Reeves selected St. James's Hall as the scene of his annual benefit, and the hall was packed to overflowing. His programme was one which showed to perfection the versatility of his genius.

" Deeper and deeper " and " Waft her, angels,"
" Adelaida," " Dalla sua pace," and Beethoven's " The
Stolen Kiss," were not merely sung, they exhibited all
the highest resources of art. Each one was a lesson in
methods of vocalisation ; each one required different
treatment. It should not be forgotten that on this
occasion Mrs. Sims Reeves emerged from a long retirement and sang Mendelssohn's " Fruhlingslied " and in a
duet from Spohr's *Jessonda* with all the musicianly
qualities by which, as Miss Lucombe, she was so well
and favourably known.

Oratorio was now at its zenith and provincial festivals
made a feature of a branch of musical art which is at the
present day practically extinct. The support of oratorio
and what was termed " sacred music " was derived from
the conventional religious ideas of the Victorian age. The
greater portion of oratorio audiences in the days of
Sims Reeves made up for their lack of musical knowledge
by their submission to orthodoxy. They considered that
listening to an oratorio was in a way a religious observance.
Applause was regarded as out of place, not on æsthetical
grounds, but because it savoured of irreverence. Reeves
probably is the only oratorio singer whose dramatic
passion shattered artificial restrictions and awoke human
feeling. The groans of that dreary instrument the
harmonium were quite typical of the sentiments of a
large section of the public sixty years ago. In 1860, so
far as London was concerned, few suburban houses were
unprovided with harmoniums, and Sunday was made
lugubrious by their dismal strains. Then arose Moody
and Sankey, when the harmonium enthusiast became
surfeited and the American organ drove its precursor
out of the field.

But far beyond the influence of religious
conventionality in maintaining the taste for oratorios
was the powerful support of the thousands of choral
singers all over the country. Every provincial town
of any pretension had its choral society, and it is not to be
supposed that choral singers, whether of that or any other
day, are to be fobbed off with practice only. They must
have the concert to crown their efforts. The Handelian
chorus had a weakness for hearing their own voices, and

their favourite composer gave them plenty of opportunities. In *The Messiah*, in *Judas*, in *Israel* they had full scope for their lungs. Part-songs did not so appeal to these lusty singers. Softness, delicacy, expression, accuracy of intonation were not easy to acquire. These qualities meant the subordination of self to the general effect, whereas in a Handelian chorus one had only to shout.

Another advantage did the oratorio concert possess. It gave choral singers a chance of learning how the solos for which their hearts yearned ought to be sung. It was a lesson which cost them nothing, and they could in the recesses of their own homes show how they had benefited. Their delight in the great Handelian choral gatherings at the Crystal Palace and the pride of singing under the machine-like baton of the autocratic Costa were also to be reckoned with.

All this was part of the joy of the oratorio, and little wonder that it was popular. To-day the great Handelian soloists are silent, the occupation of the choral singers is gone, oratorio is dead. Whether anything has taken its place which contributed so much to the harmless pleasure of the musical public may be doubted. The conclusion one cannot help coming to is that Reeves not only created the taste for oratorio, but he upheld its existence while he was in his prime. Braham is identified with one or two solos, but his répertoire was nothing so extensive as that of his successor, and, judging from the opinions of his contemporaries, it may be questioned whether his renderings did not sometimes tend rather to the theatrical than to the dramatic. He was certainly apt to play to the gallery. This Sims Reeves never did.

It is to be noted that in 1860 Scotland succumbed to the craze for musical festivals and held its first at Glasgow. It lasted four days, and, following the English fashion, was not without its special novelty. Horsley's oratorio *Gideon* was produced, with Reeves and Clara Novello as the chief exponents. Beyond this nothing need be said. *Gideon* has long been forgotten.

Reeves was, of course, in great demand for the various autumn festivals in England. With the exception of Norwich and Worcester, these functions call for little notice. In the case of Norwich, Santley's *tour de force* in Spohr's *Last Judgment* ought not to be left unrecorded. Owing to a change being made in the programme without apprising the soloists, Santley had to sing the bass solos in Spohr's oratorio at sight. One can imagine that to so accomplished an artist the task presented no difficulty. Worcester is mentioned not because of anything exceptional in a musical sense, but because it exhibited in a ludicrous light the prevailing feminine fashion of the day—crinoline. " The elegantly dressed ladies," a musical critic wrote, " would perhaps feel offended if they were told that their devotion to fashion sadly interfered with the charitable objects of the music meeting and could not think it possible that their skirts amplified by crinolines (which, huge as they were in the metropolis, became positively gigantic in the provinces) should be enemies to the Festival to the extent of more than £200, but so it is, for this time there are 230 seats fewer than last to allow room for the present outrageous height, or rather width, of fashion ! "

The autumn of the year saw a revival of interest in operas in English and in English operatic artists. The Pyne and Harrison Company were making a great success of *Lurline*, not only vocally but financially, if it be true, as Dr. Grattan Flood says, that Wallace sold the opera to them for £10 and they made £50,000 out of it !

At the Pavilion Theatre in the Whitechapel Road a very efficient body of English singers—notably Madame Florence Lancia—were nightly drawing big crowds. Their programme consisted mainly of Italian and French operas in English, with now and again old favourites of native production such as *The Bohemian Girl* and *Maritana*. At the Canterbury Music Hall Mr. Morton was giving selections from opera after opera, and probably was stimulated to further excellence by the prospect of a rival in the heart of London, the Oxford Music Hall, where it was proposed to run entertainments of a kind similar to his, being well on its way to completion. At the Philharmonic, Islington, Bellini by an English company was in favour, and *Norma* and *Puritani* drew big audiences for many weeks. The greatest change in the popular taste was seen at about the last place in the metropolis where one would expect it—Evans' supper-rooms. Here Mendelssohn's *Walpurgis Night* and selections from Weber, Auber, Rossini, the finale to *Fidelio,* and other classics were sung to an audience of men while they devoured chops, sausages, Welsh rarebits, and other supper dainties. The " men about town " of the forties and fifties, had they visited the hall, might have fancied from the decorum which now occupied the place of the old freedom and coarseness that they had strayed into some conventicle.

The last and most important step in the direction of English opera was taken by Mr. E. T. Smith, who, nothing if not audacious and original, conceived a scheme of running Italian and English opera on alternate nights at popular playhouse prices at Her Majesty's. The stars in the first were Tietjens and Giuglini, and in the second Lemmens Sherrington, Santley, and Reeves.

To institute a rivalry, for such indeed it was, between the English and foreign schools was a bold experiment, and some of the musical prophets shook their heads over the project. They were inclined to think that the attraction of Italian opera at low prices would overpower that of English opera, despite the commanding personality of Reeves. The English programme was to some extent a leap in the dark. The opera—Macfarren's *Robin Hood*—was a new and untried one ; the prima donna— Madame Lemmens Sherrington—had to make her first appearance on the stage. Reeves and Santley were, of course, towers of strength. Despite the support of these two, there were elements of doubt, and the first night in October of the new opera was looked forward to with much anxiety.

The result completely upset the prophecies of the pessimists. The opera proved an unequivocal success. Lemmens Sherrington, already known as a brilliant and sweet singer in oratorio and ballad, showed that she possessed also true dramatic feeling, and her impersonation of Marian undoubtedly added to the attraction of the opera. Santley could not be bettered, but the singer whom the audience went to see and hear was Reeves. Save his annual appearance at the Standard Theatre in his well-worn operatic rôles, he had not been

SIR CHARLES SANTLEY.

seen on the stage for some years, and the Press was unanimous in its welcome and equally unanimous in praising his singing and acting. "He never was in finer voice," wrote one critic. "Sims Reeves has gained abundantly both in action and in articulation since we last saw him on the stage," declared another. "Mr. Sims Reeves," pronounced the *Times*, "was never better suited. . . . He gives the arduous scene of the prison, late as it appears in the opera, with an enthusiasm that imparts itself to his audience and encourages the belief that he could go through the whole of the music again with the utmost ease, so fresh and vigorous is his voice, so unabated is his energy." Reeves at this time and for long afterwards was so associated with Santley that one can hardly think of one without also thinking of the other, and it is but just to quote the words of the *Times* critic. "Mr. Santley," said the writer, "whose voice alone would attract even were he a less consummate vocalist, shared and deservedly shared the applause with Mr. Sims Reeves."

As for the opera itself, it was of its time ; a ballad-opera essentially, but with more attempt at elaborate orchestration and dramatic effect in its concerted pieces than is presented by the Balfian and Wallace school. The demands of the music publishers influenced the composer. As the *Athenæum* sarcastically remarked, "every English opera must have *the* ballad for the tenor—and the shops." Reeves was looked upon as the gold-mine to be worked, and the publishers lost no time in preparing for the golden shower. On the night of the first performance the whole of the music was in the hands of the music dealers, and when Reeves brought down the house with "My Guiding Star," there was a rush for the song before the week was out. This was only to be expected. Reeves had the supreme art of investing the commonplace with romance and individuality, and the result was the elevation of much that was worthless into an ephemeral popularity. Time has had its revenge, and hundreds of songs with which Reeves did so much and which helped to line the pockets of the publishers are now forgotten, "My Guiding Star" among the number. Macfarren had not the melodic genius of

15

either Balfe or Wallace. He could follow, but he could not initiate. Lasting power does not belong to imitation, and it is extremely doubtful whether *Robin Hood* will ever be revived. Yet there is still vitality in *The Bohemian Girl, Maritana,* and *The Lily of Killarney.*

When *Robin Hood* was produced, no one troubled about the future. Reeves was singing gloriously and this was all that mattered. He could always command his public—a tremendous asset in the eyes of an impresario—and every night the English opera was performed the theatre was packed. Reeves was in excellent health, and on only two occasions was he indisposed and unable to appear, when Mr. Swift deputised for him. On December 8th he suffered a bereavement in the death of his father. The event was duly announced, and it was stated that in a few days Reeves would resume his part.

When that resumption came it meant but a few performances. To everybody's astonishment, E. T. Smith brought his operatic enterprise to an end and substituted pantomime! His daring enterprise had failed not because of shortcomings on the English opera side, but because of those on that of the Italian opera! It was a revelation. Yet the Italian débâcle was inevitable. The salaries of the Italian stars far exceeded those of the English ones. The aristocratic patrons, without whom Italian opera could not exist, were out of London. It was not the orthodox opera season, and maybe it was thought that low prices were derogatory to the dignity of the Upper Ten. Be the cause what it may, the curious and unexpected fact remained that English opera virtually drove its foreign rival out of the field.

In justice to Mr. E. T. Smith's business capacity it is only fair to say that he was compelled to run English and Italian opera side by side owing to the impossibility of putting on *Robin Hood* throughout the week. Reeves would only sing three nights in the week, and he was right in thus stipulating. No voice, and especially his, could stand a greater strain, to say nothing of the demands upon physical energy generally.

Pantomime supplanted *Robin Hood,* but it was scarcely a success, and on February 5th the opera was once more put on and lasted until February 23rd, when the production of Wallace's *Amberwitch* was announced, and Reeves never sang in *Robin Hood* again. It was played by the Pyne and Harrison Company at Covent Garden in 1861 with Madame Guerrabella (Miss Genevieve Ward), Henry Haigh, Santley, Patey, and George Honey, and by Turner's opera company at the Princess's Theatre in 1889. Since then it has been allowed to rest, and that rest is hardly likely to be disturbed. *Robin Hood* was composed for Reeves so far as its principal tenor music was concerned, and probably herein was its weakness. Reeves shone pre-eminently, as in many other instances (Costa's *Eli* notably) where he created a part written for him, and no other tenor cared to challenge a comparison. The opera has a sad association, for it was while composing it that Macfarren was afflicted with blindness, necessitating the dictation of every note. It was a superhuman task, which, however, the determination and patience of the composer enabled him to accomplish.

The unexpected has a way of happening on the stage more frequently perhaps than elsewhere. Mr. Walter Macfarren, in his *Memoirs*, tells how on one occasion Madame Sherrington rushed from the back of the stage with such energy into the arms of Reeves that Marian and Robin both fell over and rolled down to the footlights, and the audience went into convulsions. Madame, it is no crime to say, though short, was by no means a light weight.

CHAPTER XIX

1861–1862

The first oratorio performed in St. Paul's Cathedral. Extraordinary objection to *The Messiah*. Reeves's magnificent rendering of " But thou didst not leave." *The Amberwitch* produced at Her Majesty's. The advent of Wagner. The love of music spreading in England. The Crystal Palace Saturday concerts started. The English Opera Association. The International Exhibition of 1862. The muddling musical arrangements. Verdi's cantata rejected. Costa and Sterndale Bennett revive their old quarrel. The first Crystal Palace Triennial Festival.

ON January 25th, 1861, Reeves took part in a performance of *The Messiah* in St. Paul's Cathedral, the first time an oratorio had been given within its walls, while twenty years had passed since an orchestra had been heard there. It was the custom for the Royal Society of Musicians to supply annually the chorus and a band of forty stringed instruments for Handel's *Dettingen Te Deum*, but the custom had fallen into abeyance and the announcement that *The Messiah* was to be given somewhat alarmed a group of worthy souls, on the curious ground, according to Canon Povah, that " it is a service which does not promote the ends either of prayer, praise, or religious instruction." The Canon was amazed by the objection, as well he might be, and he remarked that an answer would be found by a " reference to the words of the oratorio, all of which are taken from the Scriptures," and lest any of the timid ones should not be convinced, he pointed out as a further precaution to ensure reverential behaviour that " the clergy connected with the Cathedral will appear in their robes "—on the same principle, it may be supposed, as that in the mind of the Lord Mayor in *Barnaby Rudge*, who when appealed to for assistance during the Gordon Riots suggested sending an alderman " to awe the crowd."

To make assurance doubly sure, a further proof of decorum was promised in the announcement that no books of the words should be sold within the Cathedral walls, but only at the outside rails or the Chapter House. What a pother over nothing this now appears to our twentieth-century minds !

But conventional orthodoxy was a serious matter in the early sixties, and the Dean and Chapter had qualms of conscience over the *fons et origo* of the performance itself. A new organ was wanted for the Cathedral. Mr. E. T. Smith had one to sell, and as it was really a magnificent instrument the clerical authorities resolved to buy it, despite the fact that it had worldly, not to say sinful, associations. The organ was in truth the one built for the Panopticon in Leicester Square, the Moorish building afterwards transformed by Mr. Smith into the Alhambra.

The Dean and Chapter, having come to terms with Mr. Smith, had to raise the purchase-money and decided upon a performance of *The Messiah*, charging of course for admission. This charge was at variance with their religious scruples, and instead of boldly announcing that the oratorio was to be given in aid of the organ fund, they adopted the roundabout method of calling the gathering a festival to celebrate the " opening " of the " new organ." The statement was hardly ingenuous. The organ was second-hand, and the unpleasant truth (to some persons) that it came from the Alhambra was carefully concealed.

The " opening " of an organ can only have one meaning : it implies an organ performance. But the Dean and Chapter had their own ideas on the matter. The organ was not played upon, no mention of it was made—possibly to avoid the awkward questions of its " past "—and the accompaniments to *The Messiah* were orchestral throughout. Probably the audience were indifferent to these niceties. They had paid their money to hear Reeves, Madame Lemmens Sherrington, Mrs. Lockey, and Mr. Weiss, and they were more than satisfied. If the chorus of 600 voices was here and there a little rocky, the soloists amply made amends. Reeves, influenced by the occasion and the surroundings, sang like one inspired. " Finer musical declamation," wrote the *Times* critic, " was never listened to," and commenting on his rendering of " But thou didst not leave," in former years generally assigned to a soprano, the writer said, " The most triumphant proof that it should never be wrested from the tenor (for which voice it was originally intended) is the faultless manner in which it is given by Mr. Sims Reeves, who enters into it heart and soul as if he meant to convey that while he continued to sing in oratorio no soprano should ever rob him of this song, his own legitimate property."

As the Dean and Chapter got the money they wanted, all ended happily. In due time the organ was " opened " by being played upon and nobody said anything, and there it is to this day, its origin safely buried ; and probably at the present moment not one person in a score or so of congregations knows that it once had its home in that " wicked " place the Alhambra.

While the pantomime at Her Majesty's was running towards a somewhat inglorious end and pending the production of Vincent Wallace's *Amberwitch*, Reeves had sufficient engagements to keep him constantly before the public. Exeter Hall, the Monday " Pops," miscellaneous concerts, saw the repetition of old triumphs and call for no special mention. Then came the *Amberwitch*, which from the high standard set by Madame Lemmens Sherrington, Santley, and Reeves, albeit the latter had no outstanding part as in *Robin Hood*, ought to have succeeded better than it did. The musical judges termed the *Amberwitch* Wallace's best work, and from a technical point of view it may be so, but it did not appeal to a ballad-loving audience like *Maritana*, which still remains a certain attraction to a large section of the public. The *Amberwitch* ran for a little more than a fortnight, when it was withdrawn, the " season " being " finished," which probably was another way of saying that Mr. Smith's resources were exhausted.

The scores of *Robin Hood* and the *Amberwitch* show that both Macfarren and Wallace were conscious that something more than ballads with Donizetti-like accompaniments were now wanted. The musical knowledge of the average English audience was growing, and so also was their discrimination. Meanwhile a force was slowly, if not silently, making its effect felt, and like every other innovation in art was meeting with great opposition. This force was represented by Richard Wagner, who was maturing his ideas of opera. The reception of *Tannhäuser* in Paris in 1861 was very discouraging, but Wagner was not disheartened and his novel ideas were beginning to cause much perturbation and controversy. The story of Wagner's early struggle is now ancient history and need not be dwelt upon in these pages. Yet it cannot be ignored, as it marks the beginning of a phase of musical revolution which few musicians sixty years ago could foresee. The words of a French musician relative to *Tannhäuser* may be quoted, as his epigrammatic summary probably expressed the opinion of the musical world at that time, at all events in Paris. " A libretto like *Tannhäuser*," he wrote scornfully, " capable of killing a good score, and a score like *Tannhäuser* still more capable of killing a good libretto. Judge what must be the effect of the two combined in action ! " The *Athenæum* wrote : " The work brought to judgment remains intrinsically bad— a series of uncouth sounds and ungracious combinations, with the scantiest amount of beauty to relieve them. . . . Having long thus deliberated the *Tannhäuser*, while we can enter into the disappointment of its composer and his enthusiastic friends, we are glad for the sake of Art that the verdict has been so condemnatory." And to-day *Tannhäuser* is part of the répertoire of most operatic enterprises, and is even regarded by the advanced school as almost a decadent example of the once so-called " music of the future."

So far as London was concerned, Wagner in 1861 had not begun to trouble the experts. The *Musical World*, looking around complacently and admiringly, found in the metropolis the hub of all that was good and elevating. " In no city in the world," it remarked, " is so much really good music to be heard as in London. . . . Where do we find any societies corresponding in magnitude, importance, and number to our Sacred Harmonic and Philharmonic Societies—we speak not of London alone, but also of the many provincial associations bearing the

same name ? Can Paris, Vienna, Berlin, or anywhere
else show a tithe of the concerts and various musical
entertainments that are given in London every season—
to say nothing of the two large opera-houses open throughout the greater part of the year and provincial concert-
opera tours ? And though last, but by no means least,
is there any place where classical chamber music of the
highest order is brought week after week within the reach
of the shilling paying masses as it has been now no less than
fifty-two times at St. James's Hall, to say nothing
of eleven similar concerts in the provinces quite recently,
swelling the total of the Monday Popular Concerts to
no less than sixty-three within two years of their
foundation ? Such a result is unparalleled in the history
of musical entertainments."

In confirmation of this opinion may be quoted the
remarks of Mr. Chorley, who, in noticing the London
Promenade Concerts (one series at Covent Garden
conducted by Alfred Mellon and a second at St. James's
Hall under the baton of M. Musard), wrote : " Music
has of late become nearly as indispensable to the Briton as
to his ' Cousin German.' The Crystal Palace cannot
get on without it ; Canterbury Hall presents it, and
well, too, to its smokers and guests desirous of ' stout ';
Mr. Smith invokes it, for his Alhambra playgoers sup at
Evans's to the sound of glees exceedingly well sung ;
Mr. Weston cannot open his evening lounge in Holborn
without the presence of the ' heavenly maid.' What is
better, some experience justifies the statement that not
merely is the music of a better order than it was formerly,
but in the selection of the words the rule seems to be to
avoid offence, whereas formerly it was to touch on questionable ground to the last and beyond the last permissible
limit." Had Mr. Chorley been writing a month or two
later doubtless he would have recorded the significant
fact that the Oxford Music Hall had opened, and that
two of the artists who took part in the inauguration
were Madame Parepa and Charles Santley.

It may be admitted that there was then much in the
spread of the love of music in England to justify this
jubilation, but progress did not include musical
composition. English composers were still stereotyped,

yet probably no more so than those of other countries, Wagner excepted. Gounod, it is true, was fluttering his wings, but Gounod was some distance from Wagner, and was not looked upon as a revolutionist. *Faust*, when it was first given in Paris, was damned with faint praise, and of it was written that it " really could not be considered as anything more than respectable."

The important point to be noted in the musical activity seen in England at this period is that it was paving the way for the acceptance of instrumental compositions, the proper appreciation of which demands a higher standard of musical knowledge and a more elevated taste that that which is satisfied by mere ballad singing. It is clear that this effect was even then beginning to be evident, for in 1861 Mr. Manns commenced his famous Crystal Palace Saturday Concerts, which, it is hardly too much to say, acted as a stimulus and encouragement to orchestral performances and compositions, for which one should be ever grateful.

Reeves's activities during the greater part of 1862 were mostly confined to provincial tours, notably one in the spring of the year, when he joined forces with Madame Lind-Goldschmidt. There was no opening for him in opera, either English or Italian. The success of the Pyne and Harrison Company in the first had led to a revival of the oft-repeated demand for " National opera," and the response was the formation of the " English Opera Association." Members were enrolled, a long list of names of prominent musicians who approved the idea and were willing to assist in carrying it out was published, and the capital was to be £50,000, but its future was hardly promising.

The pre-eminence of Reeves was really the stumbling-block. It was felt that without the attraction of the prince of English tenors the performances would lack the element essential to success, but Reeves was over-whelmed with engagements ; he could command almost any fee he liked to ask, and it was unreasonable to suppose he would make such a sacrifice as devoting himself to " National opera " would entail. Moreover, the wear and tear of his voice had to be considered, and to such wear and tear Reeves would never consent. Having this contingency in view, the "Association" was faced with insuperable difficulties.

In Italian opera Santley was more fortunate than Reeves. On April 15th he made his debut at Covent Garden as the Conte di Luna in *Il Trovatore*, which proved to be the beginning of an operatic career in conjunction with Italian artists which is unequalled by any other English singer. Mr. J. E. Cox (*Musical Recollections*), who is not given to exuberant praise, writes that the date must by no means be left unnoticed, " because of its having introduced to the Italian stage the most genuine [baritone] singer that England has produced since the days of Bartleman."

Eighteen hundred and sixty-two was "Exhibition" year, when an international gathering of arts and crafts similar to that in 1851 was held in a building specially erected at Kensington, conspicuously ugly and irreverently termed the "Brompton Boilers." Two episodes in connection with the musical arrangements for the inauguration are worth recalling. The "Commissioners" invited four composers of different nationalities to "assist" with original works. England was represented by Sterndale Bennett, France by Auber, Germany by Meyerbeer, and Italy by Verdi. In those days Russian music was an unknown quantity.

Trouble at once arose over the cantata submitted by Verdi. It was, to the amazement of the musical public, rejected! The reason put forward was that shortness of time did not permit the work to be adequately rehearsed. This was a palpable misstatement and some other cause had to be sought for, but this cause was never discovered. As the matter stood, it was an insult to the great Italian musician, who received the slight to his genius with a calmness and dignity quite in keeping with his character. English musical opinion was outraged and the "Commissioners" came in for severe criticism. It was suggested that a special performance of the cantata should be given at Covent Garden, but the suggestion never materialised.

The excuse put forward by the "Commissioners" in the case of Verdi stands out in strong contrast with what happened over Meyerbeer's "Exhibition Overture."

SIR MICHAEL COSTA.
From a photograph by Mayall.

Meyerbeer had bestowed upon the work all the elaborate orchestration of which he was so great a master and told Costa that it would require at least *ten* rehearsals. " I can only give it *two*," was the answer of the despot of the baton. Meyerbeer was dismayed, but submitted. He attended the first rehearsal and was astounded. Costa's band played the overture at sight without a single hitch ! " No other orchestra in the world could have done it," exclaimed the composer enthusiastically.

The second episode must have vexed the souls of the " Commissioners," although they had nothing whatever to do with it. The issue was a narrow one, simply the opening of an old sore between Costa and Sterndale Bennett, going back to the days of the Philharmonic Society when Costa was appointed its conductor. The story has been already told in these pages. Though many years had elapsed since the dispute, Costa's bitter memories of it were still fresh. He refused to conduct Dr. Bennett's cantata, and as the composer declined either to conduct or to nominate anyone to occupy the post, a very pretty deadlock arose, which was ultimately solved by the baton being placed in the hands of M. Sainton, the leader of the orchestra. *Punch* summed up the situation with equal humour and common sense in this effusion :

A REVIVED POET

(See Mr. Punch for ever so long ago)

I am the Poet of the Philharmonic,
Who some years back composed in *Punch* a Tonic,
Which I hoped would bring peace between Bennett and Costa,
But regret animosity has been permitted to foster.
Surely it is time that Costa should alter his demeanour
And forget all that mistake and nonsense about Parasina.
Sterndale is not stern and they state has made a sign
That he will forget and forgive if Costa behaves Benign.
Now Michael should trample on the Devil of Wrath and Spleen,
Apologise like a gentleman and let all be serene,
And as has been suggested by an able Contemporary
Make some Amends as *humanum est semper errare,*
Request the gracious Mr. Gye to ask Dr. Bennett
To produce his Ode at Covent Garden, the Musical Senate,
Mr. Costa conducting it firm and brilliant as Marble,
What might indeed be Deemed making Amende honorable ;

Then the Public will rejoice at the reunion of the gifted Secessioners
And with one heart turn round and cordially kick the International
  Commissioners.

Reeves's benefit concert this year at Exeter Hall was a
little out of the common, and was of especial interest.
He provided band and chorus, chiefly with the object of
giving a performance of a new cantata by Balfe, *Mazeppa*.
The music was melodious and picturesque, and the
interpretation by Madame Lemmens Sherrington, Miss
Palmer, Reeves, and Santley was perfect. This seems to
have been the one and only performance of *Mazeppa*,
and apropos the temptation of quoting the well-known
epitaph on a still-born baby :

> " If I am so quickly done for,
>   I wonder what I was begun for,"

is irresistible. But possibly the music publishers could
answer the question.

The year 1862 was made memorable by its association
with the first of the Handel Triennial Festivals, which,
extending as they did for over thirty years, constitute
an important epoch in English musical history. Since
the " Commemoration " in 1859 the acoustic properties
of the central transept had been vastly improved by a
boarded roof covering the whole of the orchestra, and
the effect of the solos was considerably enhanced. Nothing need be said about the executive excellence of all
concerned in the first Triennial Festival which does not
apply equally to its successors, but one item in what
was called the " Selection Day " calls for special mention.
This was the fragment from the *Ode on St. Cecilia's Day*,
a slow chorus interspersed with solos for soprano (un-
accompanied), " As from the power of sacred lays,"
succeeded by a fugued chorus, " The dead shall live, the
living die." Mr. J. E. Cox claims to have been the
means of inducing the Festival Committee to revive
this fugued chorus, which, he remarks, " was equally
unknown both to themselves and Mr. Costa." Mr. Cox's
assertion in this respect was doubtless true. The two
numbers are not to be found in any modern edition of
the Ode, and one has to go back to the score published
in 1770 to find these two examples of Handel's wonderful

conceptions of effect. The contrast between the un-accompanied soprano solo and the choruses is a touch of genius which only a great musician could imagine or portray. The singing of the solos by Madame Tietjens, the trumpet obbligato of Mr. Harper, and the triumphant grappling with the fugual difficulties by the massive chorus " The dead shall live " made a profound impression and induce one to echo the words of a contemporary critic, who asked, where can the *Ode on St. Cecilia's Day* be heard ? " Nowhere, alas! " he was forced to answer, " and yet it contains passages that may be placed side by side with the most remarkable in Handel's un-forgotten works." If this wish was vain in 1862, it is still more so to-day.

CHAPTER XX

1863–1864

Reeves and the Sacred Harmonic Society fall out. He sings for the National Choral Society. The dispute settled. Absurdities of oratorio concert restrictions. " Sound an alarm " received in silence at the Norwich Festival. Mr. Alfred Mellon's curious experiment at the " Proms." Reeves joins an Italian company at Her Majesty's. *Oberon* and *Faust*. Great success of *Faust* in English with Reeves, Santley, and Lemmens Sherrington. Mr. Chorley's grievance concerning his libretto. The Royal English Opera Association produces *Helvellyn*. The opera a failure. The Pyne and Harrison Company engages Reeves. He sings in *Faust* with Louisa Pyne. Production of Costa's *Naaman* at the Birmingham Festival. Enthusiastic reception.

In spite of Reeves's long association with the Sacred Harmonic Society and his many triumphs at its performances, an estrangement came about in the early part of 1863 and in consequence he transferred his services to the London National Choral Society.

The change was regarded by some as one not altogether to be regretted if it led to an increase in the older Society's staff of tenor soloists. Here indeed was a chance for some hitherto unknown vocal phenomenon. But the efforts to unearth this rarity only went to prove that there was but one Sims Reeves and that nobody could stand in his place. Mr. Henry Haigh, the possessor of a lovely tenor voice, was tried, but Mr. Haigh had not had the requisite vocal training, and it is safe to assume that had he provided himself with this essential he had not the genius which constitutes a great oratorio singer. Mr. George Perren, an accomplished vocalist, also essayed to fill up the gap, but nature had denied him the requisite organ.

Faced with the difficulty of finding a substitute for Reeves, the Society did its best, but its resources financially decreased while those of its rival were considerably bettered. Naturally the National Choral Society made

the most of its newly acquired treasure, but the announcement of Reeves's first appearance at its concert on April
25th was the cause of a mild rebuke by Mr. Chorley,
who thought the Society, by trumpeting forth the attraction of Sims Reeves, was departing from the object for
which it was founded—namely the furtherance of choral
singing. Mr. Chorley apparently was never quite so
happy as when discovering the fly in the ointment.

For a long time the cause of dispute between Reeves
and the Sacred Harmonic was unknown to the general
public, and not until September did it come out that
the difference was simply a matter of money. Reeves
had raised his fee, which he had a perfect right to do,
but the committee would not agree. The time came
when they repented their short-sightedness. After a
lapse of some six months they rearranged their terms,
and in September Reeves returned to the fold. Meanwhile he had received from Mr. G. W. Martin just
double what the Sacred Harmonic had given him.

During 1863 the absurdities which custom had imposed upon certain musical performances in regard to
applause and encores came in for considerable criticism.
Audiences at " popular " concerts, whether at St. James's
Hall or elsewhere, had long ago settled the matter after
their own fashion, but it was far different where oratorios
were concerned. The Sacred Harmonic Society Committee could never get the word " sacred " out of their
heads. Oratorios, they held, should be listened to with
silent reverence, and audiences were expected to subdue
their feelings, no matter how impassioned might be
the rendering of the music. The etiquette of the great
provincial festivals carried this curious notion to a ludicrous height. While the audience had to remain like
Charles Lamb's " party in a parlour, all silent and all
damned," the noble president was at liberty to let his
emotions run lose and " command " some piece, which
had taken his fancy, to be repeated.

This species of despotism was of course a relic of
German Court pedantry which came over to England
with the Hanoverians, but even in those prim days it
is doubtful whether anything more nonsensical was ever
perpetrated than the regulations laid down by the

magnates who organised the Norwich Festival in 1863. When *Judas Maccabæus* was given, the slightest sign of approval was interdicted—Reeves's soul-stirring " Sound an alarm " was received in solemn silence. For his equally rousing " Call forth your powers " not a hand was raised. Reeves must have had an absolutely unique experience, and how the audience managed to restrain themselves is hard to imagine. What made the childishness of the proceeding more apparent was that the performance did not take place in the Cathedral, but in St. Andrew's Hall ! Despite the patent absurdity and the protests of the Press, it was some years later before common sense asserted itself.

The festivals and the sticklers for solemnity and silence did not entirely monopolise the incongruous. Mr. Alfred Mellon, who ought to have known better, tried the experiment at his Covent Garden Promenade Concerts of sandwiching selections of *The Messiah* and *The Hymn of Praise* between operatic and dance music ! Those of to-day who remember what the " Proms " of the early sixties were like will hold up their hands in astonishment at this queer mixture. It is a slight satisfaction to be able to record that one night of the hodge-podge sufficed.

Meanwhile, Sims Reeves was without any opportunity of departing from his well-beaten track—almost *too* well beaten (one well-known critic plaintively suggesting that there might be too much even of " Adelaida ") until the middle of the season, when Mr. Mapleson commenced a short season of Italian opera at Her Majesty's with Tietjens and Sims Reeves as the stars. The series opened with Reeves's initial success in Italy, *Lucia*, and was followed by *Oberon*. Reeves had long been identified on the concert platform with " Oh, 'tis a glorious sight to see " (composed to " fit " Braham's love for display), and sung in its proper place in the opera it was naturally more effective. The cast was a strong one, as besides Reeves and Tietjens other parts were filled by Alboni, Trebelli, and Rose Hersee (italianised as Rose Ersini), but nothing could compensate for the shortcomings of the libretto and the inequalities of the music. Later on Reeves, singing in Italian, achieved a triumph in *Faust*, a triumph which he was destined to surpass in the beginning of the following year, when the first performance of the opera was given in English.

The translator of the French libretto was Mr. H. F. Chorley, who had furnished the Pyne and Harrison Company with his version some five years before, and although it was said that the opera had more than once been put into rehearsal it was never produced. Mr. Harrison doubtless had sense enough to know that *Faust* was quite out of his reach, but he could brook no rival who was likely to dethrone him, and so the work was shelved, Miss Louisa Pyne thereby missing the chance of being the first English Margaret. Perhaps had she foreseen the furore the opera was destined to create in 1864, she would have thought twice about the matter, despite Mr. Harrison's assumption of supremacy.

The production of the opera at Her Majesty's was not unattended by difficulties, as it was discovered that many of Mr. Chorley's lines were quite unsingable. Even before the first rehearsal complaints were made to Messrs. Chappell, by Mr. Sims Reeves, Mademoiselle Florence Lancia, and Mr. Santley, about the impossibility of singing Mr. Chorley's words. So strenuous and persistent were the complaints that Messrs. Chappell —much against their inclination, it was said—were compelled to have the greater part of the words of Faust, and one scene of Valentine, rewritten. Mademoiselle Lancia had all the verses of Siebel directly translated from the French, while Reeves had his own version written for him by Charles Lamb Kenney. All this was done unknown to Mr. Chorley—perhaps no one had the courage to tackle the autocrat—and the first intimation of the hacking and altering was conveyed to him as he sat listening to the first performance on January 23rd. It must have been a terrible shock, so much so that only a perfunctory notice of the first night appeared in the *Athenæum*, and all that the critic had to say of the singer whom he had been profusely eulogising for years past was : " Mr. Sims Reeves, who was in thorough voice, sang the music well—with great care."

No other mention of the opera was made for over a month, and only when in referring to the last perfor-

16

mance of *Faust*, announced for a week later, did Mr. Chorley take occasion to allude to his grievance. Apropos of Mr. Swift deputising for Reeves, the critic wrote that he " sung the hero's part well and in one respect much to the benefit of the opera, the effect of which has been seriously imperilled by a singular translation. Wherefore it pleased the former English Faust, without the slightest warning to or permission from the author, to have his part entirely rewritten, let the Sibyls declare. The result (whether the new words were better or worse it is not for us to decide) was inevitable confusion in loss of rhyme, loss of consonance of vowel sounds, always of importance in concerted music." On this the *Musical World* sarcastically commented that " Mr. Chorley, evidently wroth with Mr. Sims Reeves, would fain oppose to him Mr. Swift, who, in his opinion, ' sang the part well on Monday, much better in one respect, etc.', but as no performance came off on ' Monday ' we may fairly conclude that he drew on his imagination for the comparison. This proves that Mr. Chorley possesses at least one qualification for a poet."

The cold aloofness of Mr. Chorley in regard to Reeves, who in his eyes was evidently the chief offender, was more than counterbalanced by the enthusiastic praise by the Press generally. The *Times*, for instance, wrote : " The English performance of *Faust* is in few respects inferior and in some superior to the Italian at the Haymarket or Covent Garden. Although Sig. Giuglini and Tamberlik are Italians, the English representative of the hero is a far more practised musician than either ; and as M. Gounod would naturally prefer having his music, solo or concerted, sung as he wrote it without shirking or subterfuge, it is probable on hearing the most recent version of his opera, whether he understands our language or not, he would give the palm to the English Faust as the one who most perseveringly adheres to the text. Apart from this, however, Mr. Sims Reeves, who had already played Faust in Italian with eminent success, reveals a conception of the part in the highest degree poetical. . . . There is no surer test of real artistic worth than the ability to give to every passage its intrinsic value. . . . It is to the credit of Mr. Reeves that to him the physically prostrate and mentally abused philosopher appears in a light no less interesting than the Faust newly restored to youth and once more seemingly with a whole life in prospect." Coming to details, the critic, in referring to Reeves's rendering of " Salve dimora," says : " A more expressive and perfect reading of this truly exquisite soliloquy has not been heard."

Of Madame Lemmens Sherrington we read that " her execution of the music is as correct as it is charming. In the brilliant air where Margaret, finding the jewels of Faust, straightway neglects the modest flowers of devoted Siebel, the shake which introduces the quick movement is for the first time as intended. Madame Carvalho could never execute it in tune, while the imposing voice of Mademoiselle Tietjens could never accommodate itself to its light and glib delivery, but Madame Sherrington does it to perfection." Equally laudatory—as indeed it deserved to be—was the notice of Mr. Santley, that " a comparatively small part was never made so much of in our remembrance," while the new air or cavatina (" Loving smile of sister kind," written specially for the English baritone) " is given in such a manner that, notwithstanding its being an interpolation, we should be loth while Mr. Santley is the Valentine to dispense with it." It may not be generally known that it was Santley who suggested to Gounod that the theme in the overture could be made into an aria for Valentine, and the idea was heartily approved by the composer.

The opera ran from January 25th to March 5th, and the house was crowded at every performance. Towards the end of the run Santley played Mephistopheles, to the infinite advantage of the *tout ensemble*, his predecessor, Signor Marchesi, giving to the Tempter a suggestion of the buffoon quite out of keeping with the character. On the last night, as already mentioned, Mr. Swift deputised for Reeves.

One of Reeves's characteristics which endeared him to his friends was the readiness with which he responded to any appeal in furtherance of a good cause. On June 27th, 1863, Charles Kean wrote him thus : " MY DEAR MR. REEVES,—Your kind letter with its liberal enclosure reached me last night while in conversation with the

Hon. Secretary of the Shakespeare Fund. I immediately
handed him the cheque, but I find on referring to your
letter that the gift is intended as a subscription towards
a monument for Shakespeare. The object of the Fund
for which I read last evening in St. James's Hall is for the
purchase of the Garden of Shakespeare at New Place,
Stratford-on-Avon, and *of everything there* and in the
neighbourhood connected with the poet, to conclude
with the erection and endowment of a Shakespeare
Library and Museum. If therefore you did not intend
to subscribe to that particular Fund, perhaps you will
kindly let me know or put yourself in communication with
Mr. J. O. Halliwell, the Hon. Secretary, who resides at
No. 6 St. Mary's Place, West Brompton, S.W. I
thank you most sincerely for your good wishes and hope
to be back in England within a twelvemonth and tell you
' all my travels' history.' We sail to-morrow week or
else on the following morning, July 6th, from Liverpool
on the *Champion of the Seas.* Adieu, and believe me ever
truly yours, C. KEAN."

Later in the year the much-talked-of " Royal English
Opera Association," sometimes dubbed the " Limited
Liability Opera Company," made its initial effort. The
original venture formed some three years or so before had
been compelled to dissolve without achieving anything
practical, notwithstanding that the capital called for
had been subscribed. The company was reconstituted,
and the public, having complete faith in its pretensions,
rushed to buy shares and a prosperous future was
confidently hoped for. The scheme put forward in no
way differed from that of previous undertakings of a
similar character. " National English Opera "—whatever might be understood by that—was to be its strong
point. One would have thought that such ambition
would be best realised by the engagement of the finest
English artists available. Sims Reeves and Santley,
who were head and shoulders in their particular rôles
above everybody else, should have been included in the
prospective arrangements. But this was not so, and as
for " National English Opera," the management appeared
to have forgotten its promises and opened with—
Masaniello ! Shortly after, however, a new English

" grand " opera was produced in the shape of Macfarren's *Helvellyn*. It was rewarded by nothing better than a *succès d'estime*. The public expected much from the composer of *Robin Hood*, but they were disappointed and they refused to take any interest in either Macfarren's music or John Oxenford's libretto. *Helvellyn* was, after a brief and inglorious run, put upon the shelf, where it is likely to remain.

Meanwhile, the Pyne and Harrison combination, having come to an end of its resources and temporarily suspended its operations, buckled on its armour afresh. Mr. Harrison, apparently coming to the conclusion that there might be tenors in the world besides himself, awoke to the existence of Sims Reeves, and much speculation followed the rumour that the only English tenor who could be relied upon to draw the crowd had been engaged, and that—wonder of wonders !—he and Mr. Harrison might possibly sing together in *The Lily of Killarney*. Benedict indeed was eager to have Reeves as Myles na Coppeleen, and this would have come to pass but for Harrison insisting upon reserving the part for himself. Another unfulfilled expectation was that Meyerbeer's *Le Prophète* would be produced with Sims Reeves as John of Leyden. Meyerbeer had not long been dead, and it was no doubt thought that the public would be interested in his operas. It was otherwise with Sims Reeves. He knew the part of John of Leyden would do him no credit and he said so, greatly to the satisfaction of the *Athenæum*, which remarked, " In this we hold him wise. The music does not suit his voice, demanding falsetto notes which he is judicious in not giving, and the part being as little adapted to his powers as an actor." However, both Reeves and Santley were engaged, and the inevitable *Faust* was put on with Louisa Pyne as Margaret. She sang admirably, as she always did, but she did not efface the public's recollection of Madame Lemmens Sherrington.

Turning from opera to oratorio, the outstanding event of 1864 was the production of Costa's *Naaman* at the Birmingham Festival. The overpowering success of *Eli* was not forgotten, and *Naaman* was looked forward to with much eagerness. The soloists were of exceptional excellence—Patti, Rudersdorff, Dolby, Santley, and Sims Reeves. The band and chorus were of the best, and nothing was left undone to ensure success.

The President encored twelve of the numbers—the audience would never have dared to be so voracious—and thus added an extra hour to the length of the performance. The critics were unanimous in praise, almost as exuberant as they were over *Eli*, when Costa was hailed as occupying a place between Handel and Mendelssohn. As for the Birmingham audience, the critic of the leading musical journal, letting himself go, wrote: "The enthusiastic reception accorded to *Eli* nine years ago was beaten hollow by the demonstration of to-day [September 7th]. The man must be endowed with qualities apart from ordinary who under any combination of circumstances and at any period in his career could realise such a moment as that when after the last grand burst of the Hallelujah which brings *Naaman* to an imposingly harmonious close, Mr. Costa stood before 2,000 people —a host of singers and players towering up behind him from the orchestra platform to the roof and swelling the number to 500 more—to listen to thunders of acclamation pealing from every side and assuring him to his heart's content that his second oratorio was emphatically voted superior even to his first."

There is much in the music of *Naaman* that is of great excellence considered from the oratorio point of view. Costa thoroughly understood his business, and he took care of the artists who were to interpret the work. The quartette "Honour and Glory" and its opening phrase declaimed by Reeves in clarion-like tones, the trio "Haste to Samaria," the air "I dreamt I was in Heaven" —charming in its simplicity—and the "Hallelujah" chorus are all fine examples of effective writing, each in its different style, and it may be said that Costa did wonders with the depressing story of Naaman the leper, which Mr. Bartholomew twisted and "wrote in" what was necessary for lyrical purposes.

It may be asked why so uninspiring a subject was selected. The answer can be advanced that nearly all the dramatic narratives and passages in Jewish history had been monopolised by Handel. One was left for

Mendelssohn, and the rest were distributed among the minor composers. *Naaman*, if I am not mistaken, was the last of its race, at least of any importance. Henceforth the New Testament was drawn upon for cantatas, such as Sullivan's *Prodigal Son* and *The Light of the World*, and the search for a purely dramatic Biblical story was abandoned. This phase of musical art does not much trouble the concert-goer of to-day, since oratorios and Biblical cantatas are practically dead. But in 1864 the taste was very different and a new oratorio was an important event. Whether it would have been so regarded had not exceptionally gifted exponents been at work is a debatable question. It is hardly too much to say that the enthusiastic Birmingham audience were as anxious to hear Patti, Sainton Dolby, Santley, and Sims Reeves as Costa's music. All came in for laudatory notices, and it may not be deemed superfluous to quote the words of the *Musical World* as to Reeves's singing of the music given to *Naaman*. " It is doubtful," wrote the critic, " whether any other tenor than Mr. Sims Reeves, who in his reading imparts almost as much dramatic significance as if he were surrounded by all the accessories and appointments of stage representation, could be found to make Naaman the striking character he makes him. Never has this artist been more completely master of his resources than at this festival, and never did he exert his rare powers with more assiduity and success than on behalf of Mr. Costa's new work." But the desire to hear *Naaman* was never so keen as that which followed the first performance of *Eli*. There was in it no soul-stirring " Philistines, hark ! " which Sims Reeves's trumpet tones could alone do justice to, and the " groundlings " were not attracted.

CHAPTER XXI

1865–1868

Stagnation in English music. The Triennial Handel Festival. A German tenor at the Gloucester Festival. Reeves in great demand in the provinces. Influence of Gounod on English song-writing. Stupidity of the public in regard to Reeves's indisposition. Charles Hallé produces *Jephtha* at Manchester. Reeves's marvellous singing. The encore fiend again. Mr. Chorley protests against the high musical pitch. Reeves throws down the gauntlet and declares in favour of a lower standard. Refuses to sing for the Sacred Harmonic Society while the high pitch is maintained.

VERY little during 1865 calls for notice so far as Sims Reeves is concerned—indeed, music in England at this period was singularly uneventful. Huge choral gatherings were no longer novel; no great *cantatrice* other than Patti had made her advent and Patti had established her fame. Santley was unapproachable by any other baritone, and there was but one Sims Reeves. The furore excited by *Faust*, and Gounod's music generally, was subsiding, and the only operatic attraction talked about was Meyerbeer's *L'Africaine*. The position of English opera was as indefinite as ever, and its prospects seemed hopeless when Mr. Harrison (the Pyne and Harrison combination had dissolved) could only keep Her Majesty's going with the assistance of Donato, the one-legged dancer! In February Harrison himself gave up the task in despair. It was whispered that his operatic career was over and that he intended to take to the drama and would make his first essay in *The School for Scandal*. This, however, did not happen. The Royal English Opera Company, Limited, struggled in vain for success. Its efforts in the interests of native composers failed, and it scored only in one opera and that of French origin, *Le Médecin malgré lui* of Gounod. At the end of the season it could pay no dividend.

The triennial Handel Festival at the Crystal Palace was the chief choral fixture of the year, but beyond recording that the chief soloists were Patti, Sainton Dolby, Santley, and Reeves, there is nothing to single out. The performances were fully up to the standard already attained. Of the great provincial festivals, Gloucester distinguished itself by ignoring Sims Reeves—for what reason it did not appear—and engaging Dr. Gunz, a German tenor who had to master what he could of the English language a day or two before the Festival began! Why this extraordinary engagement was made was a puzzle to everybody. The *Athenæum* had nothing to say concerning the German tenor nor indeed about the Festival generally. The *Musical World* let him down gently; the *Orchestra*, after referring to his " bad English," sarcastically remarked of *Elijah*, that " not too much of the oratorio was confided to Dr. Gunz. Even Dr. Wesley (the conductor) could not trust him too far and Mr. Cummings had the real hard work. It was for this that Mr. Sims Reeves was sacrificed."

Climatic conditions dealt severely with Reeves at intervals during the greater part of the year. However, he was able to sing for the Sacred Harmonic Society in December. As indicating the depth to which English opera had sunk, the Royal English Opera Company, Limited, produced a pantomime, and made the intrusion still more ridiculous by issuing a pathetic appeal to its shareholders not to use their privilege of free seats " too much " and so lessen the room for the (presumably) clamorous public!

The placidity of 1865 extended to 1866. Reeves did not find much opportunity in London, but in the Midlands he was in great demand and received everywhere with great enthusiasm. At Leicester, Huddersfield, Sunderland, Liverpool, and other towns he sang to large audiences. Newcastle showed its delight by greeting him when he arrived with " a merry peal of bells " from the steeple of St. Nicholas'. Some of the provincial critics were hard put to it to express their feelings, and the representative of the *Huddersfield Chronicle*, overcome by " Thou shalt dash them," burst out with " The effect of giving the G sharp and A an octave higher and then dropping to the loco was just like the breaking of a potter's vessel and drew down the house." As a correspondent of the *Musical World* unkindly asked, where did he find the G sharp ?

It is interesting to note that a certain section of the musical public was becoming restive under the spell of Gounod. Music publishers and *entrepreneurs* were responsible for the surfeit of melodious sweetness. Everything that Gounod wrote, good, bad, and indifferent, was dragged to light. The opposing factions came face to face in connection with a concert in St. James's Hall on behalf of the University College Hospital, when selections from *Ulysses* and *Tobie*, early works of the French composer, were given. The *Musical World's* critic fiercely denounced the music, contending that " there was scarcely a tune of any sort to be heard from one end of the concert to the other." But the *Athenæum* found much in it to admire, and was of opinion that " the tenor song in *Tobie* was given by Mr. Sims Reeves as we never heard any song by any tenor before—just irresistible." Thus musical critics, like doctors, sometimes disagree.

It would seem that the influence of Gounod upon English song-writers was not altogether for the best. It did not tend to distinction and individuality. Overmuch of it was of the sort " made to sell." Reeves found the sentimentally passionate effusions of Blumenthal to his taste, but Blumenthal was not English. The vapid ballads of Claribel had caught on (Madame Sainton Dolby actually introduced " Maggie's Secret " at the Worcester Festival !) Frank Mori's songs found publishers, and the Glovers' " pretty " compositions were highly popular. Sullivan had not then come into his own, though he was advancing rapidly into public favour, and it may be noted in passing that at the Norwich Festival of 1865 was the first performance of his *In Memoriam* overture. Pinsuti was unknown as a composer, but he had ambitions which justified his relinquishing teaching as a profession for composition during the year, " to the great regret," as one reads, " of his many pupils."

Mr. Chorley, writing in the early part of 1866 of a " ballad concert " given by Madame Sainton Dolby, thus delivers himself : " The ballad style which this country possesses, artless and unscientific as it may have been, is no longer in existence. Our most popular composers display in their tunes and still more in their handling of the same not merely a curious disregard of the words to be said, but a sort of eclectic attempt to combine the humours of many countries. . . . Our melodies have come to be written in a *lingua franca* the use of which is, as all the world knows, no sign of increasing culture, but the reverse." It may be added that the Balfe and Wallace phase of musical taste was passing, and it was left for Sullivan to revive the straightforward melody of the Bishop school. But this did not come about for some few years.

The year 1866, like its predecessor, was marked by inclement weather and the prevalence of influenza. Reeves suffered severely and was compelled over and over again to disappoint expectant audiences. His monetary loss in consequence was very serious, but this point of view did not occur to those senseless persons who accused him of caprice. It might be thought that Exeter Hall would be the last place where one would expect such stupidity, but this was not the case. When at a Sacred Harmonic Society's concert in the beginning of the winter it was stated that he was so seriously ill that he was unable to sing, the announcement was received with " derisive cheers," and when it was further explained that " Mr. Reeves's malady was a severe cold, peals of uproarious laughter broke out in all directions," remarked the *Paris Times*, " as if one of the finest jokes in the world was the indisposition of a great singer whose vocal organs happened to be peculiarly sensitive to weather fluctuations."

Reeves was able to take part in the Christmas performance of *The Messiah* on December 28th and was enthusiastically cheered. He had by that time completely recovered, so much so that in January 1867 he was singing at his best the arduous tenor music in *Jephtha*, produced at Manchester under Charles Hallé.

" Out of all the intellectual flashes," wrote a correspondent of the *Musical World*, " I have enjoyed in oratorio music, and there is a many that are endeared

in my memory, Mr. Sims Reeves's singing of the tenor
recitative-airs in *Jephtha* surpasses them all. He never
was greater as an artist than on this occasion, and I
feel persuaded that I have heard the great Sims Reeves
at the greatest inspired moment of his artistic career."
This is high eulogium, but it is no more than the truth.
No more difficult solo than the air " Open thou thy
marble jaws, O tomb " can be found in all Handel's
oratorios, and I fancy that on this occasion it was sung
for the first time. All other tenors—even Braham—
have shirked it. *Jephtha* was repeated at Liverpool in
February by the Philharmonic Society, when Reeves
again triumphed.

There was little chance during 1867 of Reeves aspiring
to music of the highest character for which he was so
well fitted. Italian opera offered him no opening and
English opera simply did not exist. In a way he was
isolated, and he contented himself with repeating the
old English favourites with which he was identified. Nor
did he sing much in London. Manchester, Bath (where
the time-worn *Guy Mannering* was revived), Nottingham,
Birmingham, Hanley, and other provincial towns saw
him delighting thousands who must have known his
ballads by heart and yet were never tired of hearing them.
Needless to say, the encore fiend pursued him wherever
he went, and on a second visit to Manchester at the
end of the year a tumult arose because he declined to
repeat a verse of " My pretty Jane." An uncontrollable
confusion ensued, the concert broke up in disorder, and
the programme was left unfinished. Despite the dictum
of a writer in *All the Year Round* that English ballads
were dead, Reeves held undisputed sway whenever he
chose to sing them.

A letter from " Alfred Crowquill " (A. Forrester) is
worth quoting as one among many proofs of the affection
and admiration with which Reeves was regarded by those
who understood him best. It is dated August 12th, 1867,
from the City of Norwich Water Works Company,
Manager's Office, Surrey Street. " DEAR REEVES,—Thank
you for your very excellent photo. It is as fine as anything
I have ever seen. I was at a party when I received it.
The young ladies thereat made such exclamations about

SIMS REEVES IN 1868.

the ' dear thing ' that out of respect to your wife's feelings I omit them. The middle-aged ladies were equally enthusiastic and said something about ' charming,' but whether they meant you or your voice I did not ask as their husbands were present. One old lady who ought to have had her epitaph written years ago said ' Pooh ! pooh ! put it up. The fellow's very well.' One old gentleman said that he was told he should have had a voice exactly like yours if it hadn't been for something in his throat ! ! ! Rest satisfied with this and believe me, Yours sincerely, ALFRED CROWQUILL."

Things were equally uneventful in 1868, though the year was destined to be one of supreme importance both to Reeves and to musical history. During the first six months of the year, save for occasional appearances for the Sacred Harmonic Society and of course for the Handel Festival, he was in the provinces ; among other towns, singing at Birmingham, Wolverhampton, Shrewsbury, Dundee, Newcastle, and in the south at Exeter, Bristol, and Southampton.

Despite his numerous engagements he did not neglect his correspondence and never forgot his old friends. The following letter, dated March 14th, 1868, from Rowney Abbey, Ware, speaks for itself : "My DEAR REEVES,—Your kind letter came to hand all right and made me feel happy. A day after I fell ill and have been under the doctor's hands for the last twelve days for a fearful congestion of the coats of the stomach, intestines, etc. My sufferings have indeed been great. I am a little better, but no chance of being able to accept your jolly invitation for the 17th. I trust, dear fellow, that your concerts are filling your purse and that the beastly Chatterton affair will soon be forgotten by you. Give our kindest regards and love to Mrs. Reeves and believe me, ever affectionately yours, M. W. BALFE."

Of the triennial Crystal Palace Handelian celebration little need be said. No extended notice appeared in the *Athenæum*, Mr. Chorley contenting himself with the pronouncement that " no musical performances in any country have approached in excellence those of this year's Handel Festival," and this judgment will suffice.

The occasion, however, was notable, for it was the last function of the kind in which Reeves appeared. This was owing to circumstances which will presently be gone into. Apropos of the Festival, Miss Louisa Kellogg, an American soprano, one of the principal soloists, says of Reeves : " He was a real artist, and when he was not troubling about the temperature or his diet he was an artist with whom it was a privilege to sing. I remember singing with him and Madame Patey at a concert at Albert Hall. Madame Patey was an admirable contralto and gifted with a superb technique. We three sang a trio without a rehearsal, and when it was over Reeves declared that it was really wonderful the way in which we all three had ' taken breath ' at exactly the same points, showing that we were all well trained and could phrase a song in the only one correct way."

During the month of November, in criticising the singing of Miss Minnie Hauck in *Sonnambula*, Mr. Chorley threw a bombshell into the camp of the orchestral conductors. Miss Hauck's first appearance in the character was not satisfactory, but of her second the critic wrote : " The chief cause of her greater success was unquestionably the judicious lowering of her principal airs. On the first night she fairly broke down in the final rondo ; on the second, when it was transposed half a note lower, this outpouring of recovered joy became the most thrilling feature in her performance." Mr. Chorley followed this up by a characteristically vigorous attack upon the abnormally high pitch in England in comparison with that in use on the Continent.

Mr. Chorley's opinions coincided with those of Sims Reeves, and in the following issue of the *Athenæum* appeared the following :

" Grange Mount, Beulah Spa, Upper Norwood, November 10th, 1868.—" I read with great interest your comment upon Miss M. Hauck's Amina at Covent Garden, that it is high time the pitch of our orchestras should be adapted to the normal diapason used in France and Germany. Your complaint is one which I have strenuously, although in vain up to the present, insisted upon, and I can only trust now that so influential a paper as yours has taken up the subject that your complaint will meet with greater attention than my individual reiteration of it.

" Not only foreigners accustomed to foreign orchestras will be indebted to you for thus protesting against, as you most truly remark, the human voice, the most delicate of all instruments, being sacrificed to the false brilliancy attained by perpetually forcing up the pitch, but English artists generally. And as you truly remark, ' the pitch in this country is a half-tone higher than that of most foreign orchestras and a whole tone higher than it was in the time of Gluck.'

" So strong is my conviction upon this subject that some time back I intimated to the Committee of the Sacred Harmonic Society my final decision, notwithstanding grave reasons for my coming to a contrary determination, not to sing for that Society so long as the pitch of the orchestra was maintained at its present height and until it was, as you suggest, ' assimilated to the normal diapason of France.' "

CHAPTER XXII

1868–1869

No anthill disturbed by a stick could have been thrown into greater confusion than that produced on the musical public by Sims Reeves's letter. Consternation reigned. Sims Reeves singing no more for the Sacred Harmonic Society meant that his voice would never be heard again at the Handel Festivals, and possibly not at the Gloucester, Hereford, Norwich, and similar great oratorio fixtures, always looked forward to by the provincial public with the keenest interest. Those who regarded musical art as a matter of pounds, shillings, and pence could not understand how a singer could forgo such a comfortable source of income. It could not be true. Sims Reeves would alter his mind. But it *was* true and Reeves remained fixed in his determination. When at the end of November Mr. Costa at Exeter Hall revived *Naaman*, the tenor for whom certain music had been written and who only could sing it as it should be sung was absent, " in pursuance, we presume," said the *Athenæum*, " of the resolution expressed in his letter addressed to us a fortnight ago. . . . It is a reform which must come sooner or later, let the obstructives oppose it as much as they may. All credit to those who are first in forcing the way."

Reeves followed up the attack. In the *Athenæum* of June 2nd, 1869, he wrote : " Thanking you sincerely for what you have already done, I deem it my duty to inform you that a performance will take place during the ensuing spring with the pitch lowered according to the French standard. Mr. Hallé has given in his adhesion and will adopt the same standard next season. Mr. Martin, I have every reason to believe, will also adopt the same in the course of the season, and there can be no reason why others should not immediately follow the same good example."

The *Musical Times* joined the ranks of the reformers. "The letter of Mr. Sims Reeves," it stated, "addressed to the *Athenæum*, in which he positively refuses to sing at the Sacred Harmonic Society whilst the present high pitch is maintained, has decided the matter, and as most of the competent musicians of the country are, to our knowledge, ranged on his side, there can be little doubt that, whatever may be the difficulties to be overcome, the change must be made. During the ensuing season a series of six concerts will be given in which the Standard French pitch will be adopted. These concerts will consist exclusively of sacred music (and mostly of oratorios), and Mr. Sims Reeves has pledged himself to sing at each performance."

Then Mr. A. Manns put forward a practical suggestion, prefacing it with a luminous narrative as to how the pitch had in modern days gradually sharpened. He pointed out that "the rise in the pitch commenced in the desire to amalgamate the pitch of Chor- and Kammer-ton, which a couple of centuries ago differed in some countries more than a whole tone, the Chor-ton being the highest. When from the beginning of the seventeenth century the orchestra gradually became so important an accompanying instrument at musical performances in churches, its diapason had necessarily to be regulated according to the Chor-ton—that is, to the pitch of the church organs of the time. But the real mischief commenced when the orchestra emancipated itself from the church and went as an independent musical body into the concert-room, for after increasing its family by all sorts of wood and brass instruments, it also pressed closely to its heart the pianoforte. Concertos were composed for pianoforte solo and with orchestral

17

accompaniments. The piano, carefully tuned to the pitch of the wind instruments which had to accompany it, proved all right during the rehearsals in the empty saloon in the daytime, but was found much too flat during the evening performance when the heat created by an artificial light and a crowded audience had tuned the wind instruments up considerably. After that no doubt the piano was tuned up also; unfortunately, however, it was occasionally wanted for morning performances without artificial light and then found to be much too sharp. The wind instruments were harassed, and in order to meet the difficulty determined to sharpen the pitch for the next morning concert, and so things went on, increasing more rapidly still with the introduction of the brilliant gaslight into concert-rooms until they gradually reached their present unavoidable climax."

Mr. Manns's suggestion was that the pitch should be lowered a full half-tone. " By doing this the new wind instruments necessary for an orchestra would be confined to flutes, piccolos, oboes, clarinets in A and C, and bassoons. The present A clarinets would become B flat." Mr. Manns dealt with the technicalities of other instruments, showing how some could be adapted at a little expense. Others, he admitted, would have to be purchased. As thus put, the question resolved itself into one of money. How the money was to be found was a problem not easily solved.

The lowering of the pitch was no new thing. As a matter of fact a controversy had for years been raging intermittently. In February 1838 a correspondent of the *Musical World* pointed out that for a long time the French Conservatoire had been protesting against the concert pitch then in use and had succeeded in reducing it a whole tone, and the writer suggested that a standard should be based on the tuning fork used by Handel. Nothing came of the proposition until 1859, when the Society of Arts took up the matter. A committee was appointed and in the following May a report was issued. This report embodied five points for consideration : " (1) The pitch or varieties of pitch obtaining at foregoing periods of musical history. (2) The pitch or varieties of pitch obtaining in the most eminent and important English operas at the time. (3) Pitch in its relation (*a*) to voices, (*b*) to artificial instruments. (4) The difficulties likely to impede a change of the existing pitch were any change thought desirable. (5) What pitch it is advisable to recommend for general adoption." The report discussed these points at considerable length and from every requisite aspect, and came to the conclusion that the pitch should be that of Stuttgart fixed in 1834 and a quarter of a tone below the Philharmonic standard. But orchestral conductors took no notice, and matters went on as before until Sims Reeves, strengthened by Mr. Chorley's opinion, uttered his protest.

Following Mr. Manns, Mr. Joseph Barnby entered the lists and, commenting on the former's letter, pointed out that the suggestion " would prove a mere compromise between the necessity of altering and the anticipated expense of new instruments, inasmuch as one of the greatest disadvantages of the present pitch is that it is different from that of any other country, and were Mr. Manns's suggestion acted upon, it would still remain so. I further beg to state that, although it is called the French pitch on account of its origin, it may now be considered European by its adoption, and I for my part consider it as necessary to adopt the European standard as to change the pitch. Lest it should wound our *amour-propre* to have to follow the French lead, it might be as well to mention *le diapason normal* was fixed by the representatives of three of the most musical nations of the Continent : Rossini, Meyerbeer, and Auber. Under any circumstances I have determined to introduce the French pitch for the first time in England at our own oratorio concerts, and I believe Mr. Charles Hallé has signified his intention of also making use of the diapason normal."

Mr. Barnby was as good as his word. With his newly formed choir, an excellent body of voices, he produced *Jephtha* at St. James's Hall on February 5th, with Sims Reeves in the title-rôle. Eighteen years had passed since the oratorio had been performed in London, and the hall was packed. Reeves was at his best, and expert judges could detect no difference in the tone and effect, though the pitch had been lowered. I had the good fortune to be present (as already mentioned), and though I had heard him in oratorio many times I can recollect no occasion on which he sang more splendidly and with greater fervour. The additional accompaniments provided by Arthur Sullivan were praised on every side.

The battle raged furiously for some weeks. The *Times*, *Telegraph*, and *Saturday Review* joined in the fray. The abnormal pitch had no defenders. What Sterndale Bennett, Dr. Goss, Cipriani Potter, Macfarren, Henry Smart, Benedict, Arditi, and Sullivan thought about it no one could say : they held aloof. So also did Costa, but he was known to favour the utmost limit and his silence was not surprising. Besides, was he not the conductor of the Sacred Harmonic Society ? By the end of February all was chaos.

" The whole matter," wrote the *Musical World* mournfully, " shows that nothing is so easy as to unsettle what may be very difficult to arrange. . . . With more enthusiasm than prudence the reform was urged on, and the result is a precious muddle out of which a way by no means shows itself. Nobody ever contemplated the possibility of having three distinct pitches in use at one and the same time. Nevertheless to that we have come. At the Sacred Harmonic Society's concerts the A is the familiar 910. At those of Mr. Barnby's choir it drops to 870, and the National Choral Society quotes a still lower figure. In point of fact it is impossible to say off-hand what value A has." The trouble was that no one was disposed to defray the cost of providing the hundreds of instrumentalists with new instruments where necessary. The conductors of military bands were quite contented with high ringing tones and so also were pianoforte manufacturers. What singers thought or felt did not concern them. After all, it was only oratorios and operas that mattered. At concerts there was nothing to prevent a vocalist asking his or her accompanist to transpose a song half a note. As a matter of fact this was constantly done. Adelina Patti sometimes availed herself of this facility and so did Sims Reeves. As with the elaborate report prepared by the Society of Arts, so also with the agitation of 1869, the furore simmered down and things went on pretty much as before. Mr. Barnby, however, adhered to the normal diapason and Reeves sang at his oratorio concerts throughout the season.

Meanwhile the Sacred Harmonic Society—in other words Mr. Costa—refused to give way and commenced the season (1868–9) with *Judas Maccabæus*, Mr. Vernon Rigby taking the place of the rebellious Reeves. Mr. Rigby was greeted with " uproarious applause," but was reminded by the critics in more than one quarter that this applause was not so much in admiration of his efforts as in resentment against the absent one, as though to assure the latter that he could be done without. But it may be doubted whether the majority of the Society's patrons really thought so.

What may be taken as the final word on the subject, at all events for the moment, was said in March 1870, arising out of a performance of Beethoven's Mass in D by Mr. Barnby's choir. The *Pall Mall Gazette*, referring to the diapason normal, declared that in England it had proved a failure and that it was inferred Mr. Barnby had made up his mind to abandon it. The *Pall Mall* further observed that " although Mr. Barnby has spent a good deal of time, pains, and money (for new instruments from Paris) in vain, those who heard Beethoven's colossal Second Mass on Wednesday most probably heard it as Beethoven wrote and intended it, *for the last time*, and have therefore good cause to remember the occasion." Mr. Barnby protested that he had *not* abandoned the lower pitch, drawing from the *Musical World* the assertion that " several of the artists engaged on the occasion referred to were heard to declare positively that this concert was to be *the last* with the pitch of the diapason normal. Among other reasons stated were, first, that Mr. Sims Reeves himself would no longer sing with that pitch ; secondly, that Mr. Santley had refused under any conditions to sing with that pitch at the Oratorio Concerts ; and lastly, that the members of the orchestra were against it almost to a man." The *World* applied the closure to the discussion in the following fashion : " We, like Mr. Barnby, may think them all in the wrong : but if Mr. Barnby imagines that a ' Utopia ' in musical affairs can be reached by the magic of his name alone, he is likely to be as wrong as the rest of them."

As for Reeves, his pecuniary loss must have been very heavy. The cessation of his engagements with the Sacred Harmonic Society was not compensated in any other direction. English opera was moribund, and he had mainly to depend upon concerts. He had, however, warm-hearted and appreciative provincial patrons and he was heartily welcomed—indeed too much so in some instances—wherever he went. Of the Festivals, Worcester was the only one at which he sang, and the occasion was of some importance. Sullivan's *Prodigal Son*, the tenor part in which was written expressly for Reeves, was produced and met with instant success. The work set the seal on the composer's genius. In regard to Reeves's singing, it is only necessary to quote the *Athenæum*: " Probably few things in music—assuredly none outside the writings of the great masters—are more powerfully suggestive than the Prodigal's *scena*, ' How many hired servants of my father's.' As sung by Mr. Reeves this indeed commends itself as a rare effort." It is doubtful whether these are the words of Mr. Chorley, he having through ill-health resigned his post the year before. His trenchant criticisms, bitter and prejudiced as they were sometimes, were a distinct loss to musical progress.

It is not too much to say that at this period Reeves was not only the best-known man in the English musical profession, but in England itself. Naturally he paid the penalty. Any bit of gossip, no matter whether true or untrue, relevant or irrelevant, was eagerly accepted and circulated. A most glaring instance of perversion of facts occurred at Cheltenham in the spring of 1869, and unless the foundation was the utterance of a deliberate falsehood on the part of someone maliciously disposed, it is difficult to find an explanation for what resulted in gross injustice towards Mr. Sims Reeves. A paragraph appeared in the *Times* of February 22nd, 1869, embodying the report of an action in the Cheltenham County Court brought by the lessee of the Cheltenham Theatre against Mr. Harrison, agent to Mr. Sims Reeves, to recover £26 17s. for losses alleged to have been sustained by

the non-appearance of Mr. Reeves at a concert at Cheltenham in the previous October at which he had engaged
to sing with Madame Patey Whytock, Miss Banks, and
others. " Mr. Reeves," to quote from the report, " did
not sing at Cheltenham, the reason given being that he
was ill. However, he sang at Worcester next night. Mr.
Reeves had been subpœnaed on the trial but did not
appear, and a letter was read from Mr. Reeves enclosing
a certificate from Dr. Phillips dated February 18th
that Mr. Reeves was suffering from severe cold and ulcerated throat, that he was confined to his house, and that
it would be highly dangerous for him to leave it. Mr.
Gough, who appeared for the plaintiff, applied that Mr.
Reeves should be fined for non-attendance, stating that
the utmost difficulty had been experienced in serving
him with the subpœna, and that when served he tore it
up and said he would not appear. The judge thereupon
fined Mr. Reeves £10 for non-attendance, saying he
should disregard the medical certificate. The case then
went on, and it was proved, on it being announced that
Mr. Reeves would not sing, Sir Alexander Ramsay rose
in the theatre and called on the rest of the audience to
follow him and demand a return of their money, which
they did. The trial occupied four hours, and ended
in a verdict for the plaintiff for the sum claimed."

This report was very far from being accurate, so much
so that Reeves, writing to the *Musical World*, stated that
on inquiry the counsel for the plaintiff distinctly denied
the statement attributed to him or that " any such statement was made by any person in his hearing." Reeves
went on to say that no subpœna was ever served upon
him, nor did he tear up the subpœna which was served
upon his servant. " I could not," he added, " and never
for a moment would entertain the slightest disrespect
to the Court or any proper authority, and I would have
attended the trial, though in no way pecuniarily interested in the result, had I been physically capable of
doing so."

As to the rejection of the medical certificate, Mr.
Reeves explained that though it was read, the judge,
acting upon the rule of receiving no evidence except
viva voce, held the certificate to be no legal evidence

of the facts stated in it, and he felt there was no course open but to reject it.

The inner history of this attempt to injure Reeves in the estimation of the public was never brought to light. Mr. Reeves intimated in his letter that he was " given to understand it proceeded from an interested quarter," and this view appears to be confirmed by the *Leeds Express*, which in a sympathetic article defending the singer's anxiety to preserve his voice against all risks said, " A recent action against Mr. Sims Reeves has been gloated over by certain Goths who express their opinion that the result of that action ' will bring him to his senses.' A great deal of unnecessary feeling has been exhibited in this case ; and for an ill-concealed reason misstatements have been made to the injury of Mr. Sims Reeves as a citizen."

Mr. Harrison, the well-known Birmingham *entrepreneur*, under whose auspices the concert was given, intimated that the matter would not rest with the County Court, but that it would be taken further ; but it does not appear that he carried out his intention, nor is it recorded anywhere that the fine which was so unfairly inflicted was ever remitted. " The greatest artist of my recollection," once said Mr. Harrison, who had had a vast experience of singers, " was Mr. Sims Reeves."

CHAPTER XXIII

1870–1872

Reeves visits Italy. Sings in Benedict's *St. Peter* at the Birmingham Festival, 1870. His adherence to English ballads. English ballad opera revived at the Gaiety Theatre. Its renewed popularity. *The Beggar's Opera* and the opinion of the day. Santley plays Tom Tug in *The Waterman*. The taste for the old English ballad preserved by Reeves. An action at law against the Edinburgh Choral Union. Curious ruling by the Sheriff. Scottish thrift. An extended provincial tour. Reeves's continual ill-health. A vigorous defence of his "disappointments" by the *Liverpool Porcupine*. Reeves takes part in Barnby's oratorio concerts with the lowered pitch. A "Penny Concert" at the Albert Hall. The "Royal National Opera" fiasco.

WITH 1870 came a partial cessation of Reeves's activities. He had during the past two years suffered much with his throat, and after a short tour in Scotland he had a sort of farewell at one of Boosey's ballad concerts in March and set out for Italy. He did not return until the late summer, his first public appearance of any moment being at the Birmingham Festival in September, when he took part in the production of Benedict's *St. Peter*, singing with all his pristine vigour and freshness. A notable item at one of the Festival concerts was Costa's trio "Vanne e colei" for two tenors and a soprano, given by Sims Reeves, Vernon Rigby, "the two best tenors of the day," said the *Athenæum*, and Madame Tietjens. An irresistible encore followed, and it was remarked how very similar in tone were Reeves's and Rigby's voices. But when Vernon Rigby attempted any of the music with which Reeves was identified, the difference was at once apparent. No English tenor had a better chance of achieving celebrity than Vernon Rigby. He had taken Reeves's place in oratorio ; he had sung for the Sacred Harmonic Society throughout 1869–70, and yet had missed the highest mark. He was applauded and deservedly so, but he excited no enthusiasm. Unfortunately for him, he was wanting in individuality, in dramatic force, in poetic fervour. In all these qualities Reeves excelled.

It may be fairly claimed that Reeves's unrivalled power in appealing to the emotions impelled him to adhere to the English ballad of unpretentious melody and homely pathos. Considering how in 1870 he had been singing over and over again for nearly thirty years " The Death of Nelson," " The Bay of Biscay," " My pretty Jane," " The Pilgrim of Love," and other songs of the same school, it was nothing short of marvellous that he never showed the slightest sign of staleness, nor any tendency to exaggeration consequent upon repeated performances. Audiences were always sure of his best, and, like himself, were never tired. It is not too much to say that Reeves kept alive the taste for simple lyrics which belongs to the English character. For this the nation owes him a debt of gratitude, and 1870 showed very significantly how the attachment to simple, expressive melodies, though not apparent outside Reeves's sphere of action, was not dormant, in spite of the various phases of musical fashion.

It would almost seem at that time as if the public had had enough of the elegancies of Balfe and Wallace and their imitators. English opera for some years had subsisted on little else and was now a melancholy example of inanition. National opera had during the previous half-century been the subject of more controversy than any other branch of musical art, and in spite of innumerable attempts to establish a " school," all the fine talk and vague aspirations had led to nothing. Ridiculous though it appeared to many superior persons, *The Beggar's Opera* still remained the only model of an English opera which had stood the test of time. In the autumn of 1870 a revival of the English ballad opera came about, and for no reason that one can divine save a reaction against artificiality, combined with an assertion of human instincts. A series of the bygone operatic delights of the eighteenth century was started at the Gaiety Theatre and was seized upon with avidity. *The Quaker*, *The Waterman*, *The Beggar's Opera*, and others were hailed with delight. Some unexpected impersonations were witnessed. Nelly Farren played Lubin in *The Quaker*, Constance Loseby sang the songs of Polly in *The Beggar's Opera* with all the roulades fashionable in the days of Catalani, Kitty Stephens, and Miss Paton. The producer, of course, had his own ideas how things should be done. It did not to him seem incongruous that the rollicking, reckless Macheath should be played by a languishing, lovesick tenor, nor that Pepusch's quaint prelude should be banished in favour of Boieldieu's *La Dame Blanche* overture. We find an influential critic writing : " The satire of Gay is no longer applicable ; how can it be when nearly a century and a half has passed since its production, and roving highwaymen with their patrons the Peachums and the Lockits are extinct ? " The writer ignored the power of imagination. Nearly two hundred years have gone and yet thousands to-day find Gay's wit as fresh as in the days of Lavinia Fenton and Tom Walker, and find no difficulty in accepting the highwayman and thief-taker. But maybe in the seventies it was difficult to escape the influence of the Victorian " prunes, prisms, and potatoes."

Reeves was undoubtedly the outstanding figure when-ever he played in *The Beggar's Opera*. Macheath's songs, whether rollicking or amorous, emphatically demand a ringing tenor voice. Reeves could make his sonorous, sympathetic tones suit every gradation of human passion, and he revelled in the old English ballad. He had his own ideas of the part, the " business," and the costume. Mr. Herbert Reeves says his father never wore a wig ; he had his hair " clubbed," and the drawing of the late Alfred Bryan so represents him. This fashion, to my thinking, must have been far more effective than the expansive full-bottomed curled wig descending on the shoulders worn by the present-day Macheath, who is more suggestive of a fantastic dandy than of a bold and reckless highwayman. The portraits of Tom Walker, the original Macheath, show him with a short wig which does not touch the shoulders. Reeves's " clubbed " hair was nearer this than is the full-bottomed wig.

It must, however, be admitted that the costume adopted by Reeves was hardly in accordance with early eighteenth-century fashion. His coat was not unlike a soldier's tunic; it was buttoned closely from neck to waist, ornamented with "frog" bands and confined by a broad belt and big buckle. He did not wear knee-breeches and stockings, but high boots with spurs. Round his neck was a cravat with the ends hanging down. This dress does not correspond with Hogarth's Macheath, either in the group representing *The Beggar's Opera* Company or in Walker's " Benefit ticket." The dress was, however, picturesque, and perhaps this was all that mattered. By the same reasoning the retention of the characteristic moustache is to be pardoned; the audience wanted to see the real Sims Reeves and would not have put up with a disguise.

One of his best effects was his first entry on Polly releasing him from the place of concealment. He did not walk on the stage as if he had dropped in to tea. One felt that he had been in hiding and was overjoyed at his freedom. His singing of " Pretty Polly, say " was full of tenderness. A startling surprise was produced in " Women and Wine," the drinking chorus of his comrades of the road. When the last verse was commenced, his unmistakable voice was heard a distance behind the scenes. At the final chord he appeared, and his resonant upper G rang out with a brilliancy that brought down the house.

In the betrayal scene he was at first gaiety itself, and he greeted the various ladies of pleasure with infinite abandon, half-seated on the table, the pistols by his side. One of the women having secured his weapons, Peachum and his men entered and captured him. It was all very realistic. In the embarrassing situation between the rival importunities and upbraidings of Polly and Lucy, his affectation of indifference was perfect. An imaginary fly at which his hand made a snatch seemed to absorb his interest, and " How happy could I be with either " with its " Tol-de-rol " came with a light-hearted carelessness which completed the picture. Reeves's singing and acting throughout were most exhilarating.

From September nearly to Christmas English ballad opera held its sway, and the climax was reached when Santley essayed one of the characters which hitherto

Sims Reeves had made his own. Of the former's appearance as Tom Tug the *Athenæum* said : "The revival
of Charles Dibdin's ballad opera *The Waterman, or the
First of August*, at the Gaiety has terribly disturbed the
equanimity of the partisans or rather bigots of the
classical school, but it is really of little use to indulge in
diatribes against our national taste. There are ballads
and ballads. That the English drawing-room song of
the present period is in an awfully rotten state cannot
be denied. French, German, and Italian songs are
murdered by girls, and no one hears or cares for the poetry ;
but the case is different with old English ditties—the
words must be heard, distinct articulation is indispensable,
but for that reason young ladies will not sing them. . . .
The announcement that Mr. Santley was to sing Tom
Tug provoked many gibes and sneers, directed first against
the ballad opera itself and next against the assumed
presumption of the baritone-basso poaching on the tenor
parts, . . . but it appears from all records that this
ballad opera has always been regarded as of sufficient
interest and importance to include the leading tenors and
sopranos of the day. . . . What, then, is the secret of
this vitality ? It is to be found in the attachment of our
audiences to simplicity of tune, something ear-catching,
whilst the words touch some national or homely feeling.
. . . When the Gaiety orchestra struck up the symphony
of the air 'And did you not hear of the jolly young
Waterman ? ' there was a burst of applause before Mr.
Santley had sung a note, but when he did sing, 'the
cheering,' to quote William's words in ' Black-eyed
Susan,' ' might have been heard at Greenwich.' And
the hearers cared not a straw about transposition. . . .
Ballad opera is not dead. If modern composers are
not up to the mark, it is plain that audiences will be too
glad to fall back upon the ancient ditties."

At Edinburgh during November 1870 occurred a
memorable incident which led to an action at law which
became to some extent a " leading case " in differences
between concert promoters and artists, arising out of
alleged non-fulfilment of engagements. The Edinburgh
Choral Union produced Sullivan's *Prodigal Son* with Sims
Reeves in the principal part. Reeves was a great favourite

with the Edinburgh people, and eager were they to hear the solos which Sullivan had written for him. The directors of the Union made the most of their trump card, and on the day of the concert sandwich-men with boards bearing the announcement " Sims Reeves has arrived " paraded the principal streets. The hall was packed in consequence, a fact which the directors subsequently ignored, though it was tolerably clear that but for Reeves's name the receipts would not have been so satisfactory.

When Reeves sang his first solo, it was clear to many in the audience that he was not in his usual form. However, he went on to his fourth number (the rôle of the leading part comprises five), and at its conclusion, according to an eye-witness, Reeves nodded to Sullivan, the conductor, left the platform, and hurried out of the hall. The second half of the concert was of a miscellaneous character, and in the interval one of the directors announced that as Mr. Sims Reeves had left the hall, the Handelian music which had been allotted to him would be omitted. The apology, if apology it could be called, was not fair, as it was not explained that indisposition was the cause. From what was said in the law courts subsequently, Reeves told Sullivan he could not go on, and from his singing it was evident that he was unwell. The ridiculous idea that Sims Reeves should have the presumption to be ill prevailed. The usual clamour arose, and one sapient person bawled out that a doctor's certificate should be produced—as though Reeves were in the habit of carrying such a document in his pocket. While the second half of the programme was in progress, a letter arrived from Mrs. Reeves stating that her husband had been compelled to leave through indisposition, and on the following day Reeves offered to reduce his fee from ninety to eighty guineas. This, however, was not agreeable to Scottish thrift, and the directors would only pay sixty, though it was quite clear that Reeves's lowered terms put ten guineas into their pockets, as it does not appear that they returned a single penny to any disappointed person in the audience.

The result was an appeal to the law, and the knotty point seems to have led to much argument as the proceedings dragged on from April 17th to October 30th, 1871. At last the sheriff gave his judgment—a judgment which looked at the matter purely from a business point of view, and left out of account the art side and the reputation of the artist. The sheriff decided that as Mr. Reeves had done two-thirds of the work for which he had been engaged, he should receive two-thirds of the fee agreed upon, together with 5 per cent interest from the date of the summons. He further observed that " the pursuer [i.e. the plaintiff] cannot claim for services which he did not render. Supposing the pursuer had gone to the concert and had been suddenly seized with illness which prevented him from opening his mouth, it cannot be maintained that he would have had a claim for payment of the fee which he was to receive for singing at the concert. . . . The defenders led evidence to show that the pursuer was not really disabled, but might have continued. In this the sheriff thinks they were unsuccessful."

The sheriff's way of putting the question savoured of the Gilbertian method, and the *Athenæum's* comments reduced it to an absurdity. " The Edinburgh Law Court," it remarked, " which has laid down the principle that the remuneration of a singer must be calculated *pro rata*, that is according to the quantity of notes an artist may sing of the announced pieces in the programme, will find the assessment a difficult matter at times. Supposing that Mr. Sims Reeves—who has been awarded sixty guineas instead of ninety guineas, his fee for singing at the Edinburgh Choral Union (because he only sang two-thirds of the music set down for him, and then owing to a sudden affection of the throat, which he is unfortunately for himself and the public so often liable to, was unable to sing the other third)—had got through half an air, would his honorarium be reckoned bar by bar ? The Choral Union had all the advantage of Mr. Sims Reeves's name, his presence, and his singing, and it was rather sharp practice to mulct him of a third of his fee when he had given evidence of good faith. If he had not sung at all, he would have lost the entire amount, a fact which should be recollected by those who have attacked Mr. Reeves with such severity because he has been actuated by truly artistic feeling and does not sing in

public unless fully prepared and able to do his work."
It may have been a consolation to Reeves to think that
the directors would have found it cheaper to have paid
him the full fee.

In the following year (1871) the old English ballad
boom saw no cessation. At the London Ballad Concerts
nothing but purely English songs, ancient or at least
bygone, to which Reeves contributed, mingled with
modern ones—Molloy, Frederick Clay, and Virginie
Gabrielle were now the popular drawing-room composers
—filled the programme for many weeks. Indeed, the
promoters were urged by some critics to go farther back
than Bishop and Dibdin and draw upon the rich store
of old English ditties, so many of which had been un-
earthed by the industry of Mr. W. Chappell in his
History of Music in the Olden Times. But the suggestion
was not adopted.

The influence of the popular taste was seen in the
extraordinary enthusiasm with which Reeves was received at every town he visited in the course of a very
extended provincial tour during the spring of 1871.
So much travelling in cold railway-carriages, the risk of
insufficiently aired beds, the sudden change from heated
concert-halls to the chilly atmosphere of the Midland
and Northern counties, incapacitated him continually,
but the public made no allowance. If people thought
about it at all—which they did not—they must have
considered he had a cast-iron throat, and that when he
disappointed them it was because he wouldn't sing.
Gross misrepresentations were freely current, and the
Liverpool Porcupine, moved to indignation, protested in
the following terms : " Mr. Reeves is and always has
been a most temperate person ; the fact that he has
retained his wondrous vocal powers unimpaired will
confirm this assertion to the reflective. No other living
tenor has done so. His indispositions are sometimes
ascribed to caprice, but we have yet to learn that he can
afford to indulge in so expensive a hobby. When we
affirm that Mr. Reeves has been obliged through indispositions to forfeit engagements during the past week
of no trivial value, in the previous one of 300 guineas,
and in the anterior of 300 to 400 guineas, we have perhaps

written enough to convince the sceptical and to induce a more generous construction hereafter of his conduct. . . . Mr. Reeves is an artist who has attained for himself a niche in the temple of fame and of whom Englishmen have reason to be proud. All men who achieve eminence incur one penalty—that of misrepresentation, which is the offspring too often of malice, but more frequently of thoughtlessness, which like bad money passes without detection for a time."

Meanwhile, English ballad opera was proceeding merrily. Reeves in the provinces renewed his old triumphs, and at the end of May sang in *The Beggar's Opera* and *The Waterman* at the Gaiety, when the series of revivals (intermixed with Offenbach) was continued throughout the summer. Classical music to some degree was relegated into the background. The public was disposed to take its pleasure less seriously. Offenbach and Hervé were the rage. The Philharmonic at Islington with Emily Soldene in *Geneviève de Brabant* suddenly became one of the most popular theatres in London. The lighter Italian operas came into vogue, and a season of *buffa* opera was entered upon at the Lyceum which proved very successful.

The interest in oratorio appeared to be waning, with no Sims Reeves at the Sacred Harmonic Society's concerts. However, he sang at Mr. Barnby's oratorio concerts and, to everybody's relief, took his share in the Handel Festival, the high pitch notwithstanding. The vexed question had subsided apparently, but was revived early in 1872 by a meeting at the Albert Hall (opened in the previous year) chiefly composed of musical amateurs who clamoured for the diapason normal. Practically it was an attempt to fight the air. Mr. Barnby, the stalwart of the conflict, had succumbed, and though Patti induced the Italian operatic management to lower the pitch to suit her requirements, everywhere else the old state of things was unaltered. Apart from Sims Reeves, the most remarkable instance of recantation was that of Sontheim, the favourite tenor of the King of Würtemberg. Sontheim, like Tamberlik, had a high C of phenomenal power and quality. He represented to the King that the modern pitch imposed too great a strain

18

upon the production of his favourite note ; his Majesty consented to sacrifice the necessary number of sound vibrations and what was known as the Stuttgart pitch was substituted. But no sooner was the decree pronounced than the tenor found that his former electrical effect was wanting ; he begged for the restoration of the old diapason, and restored it was.

CHAPTER XXIV

1873–1877

Reeves returns to the Sacred Harmonic Society. At his annual concert sings " The Lord is a man of war " with Santley. Comic opera the rage in London. Reeves in first performance of Sullivan's *Light of the World*. Is ill and visits Wiesbaden. The " pitch " question reintroduced. Adelina Patti and Christine Nilsson insist upon the lowered standard. The *Athenæum's* bitter attack on Sims Reeves. Reeves replies and again severs his connection with the Sacred Harmonic Society. Universal regret at his absence from the Handel Festival of 1877. Is defended by the *Saturday Review* and *Observer*. His services to high-class music lost.

THE year 1873 was marked by the return of Reeves to the Sacred Harmonic Society after an estrangement lasting five years. The oratorio was *Israel*, and Reeves signalised his reappearance by singing his *tour de force*, " The enemy said," more brilliantly than ever. Little has to be recorded during the year which was at all out of the beaten track, save a curious experiment Reeves introduced at his annual concert. He sang with Santley the duet in *Israel in Egypt* for two basses, " The Lord is a man of war," transposed one note higher !—an exhibition of comparison, contrast, and resemblance which must have been worth hearing, though doubtless it would have shocked the purist Mr. Chorley. But Mr. Chorley was dead.

As for music generally, in a popular sense, it was nothing but English ballad opera and *opéra bouffe*. During the summer Offenbach, Hervé, and Lecocq drew crowds to four London places of amusement at the same time—the Surrey Gardens, the Islington Philharmonic, the Opéra Comique, and the Alhambra. At the St. James's Theatre *Madame Angot* was performed by a French company. The Gaiety was still finding English opera of the old school attractive and did not disdain a revival of Bishop. During the year Reeves sang several times in the Albert Hall, then newly opened, and he took part in the first performance of Sullivan's *The Light of the World* at the Birmingham Festival. The oratorio was hardly a great success, and subsequently the composer saw reason to make considerable alterations.

The year 1874 began badly. Reeves suffered considerably from an attack of suppressed gout, and his appearances were so few a rumour got abroad that he contemplated retiring from the concert-room. He had, however, gone to Wiesbaden, and at the end of May he wrote as follows to a friend in London: " I am deriving very great benefit from the use of the waters at this charming place. I found that I could not get well in England, so I threw up everything and started, and I have every reason to be thankful I did so. We are up to our necks in gaiety, the Kaiser being here. I have been to the theatre to hear Herr Walter, the Viennese tenor who has been giving some representations and songs, for a German very well—his least best character was Lohengrin. I like the opera ; the orchestration is enchanting ; but the ' Music of the Future ' will ruin all the voices—more so than the execrable high pitch of England. Herr Wagner does drown the singers' voices ! What a contrast to Schumann's *Genoveva* ! How lovely is the opera ! I am enchanted with it. The singers did extremely well and the orchestra was excellent ; the music is poetical in the extreme, and the story most interestingly told in the music. It certainly was a great treat. The band in the Kursaal is excellent. The pitch here is not the diapason normal of Paris, but as nearly as possible that of the Society of Arts, which is the best, I think. How I should like to sing for you [the Newspaper Press Fund] on the 30th ! I will, too, if I can get my course of baths over. I must be in London for the 1st of June for my own concert."

He returned to London in the early summer, and the current of his engagements flowed much in the same channel as heretofore. On June 11th Balfe's last opera, *Il Talismano*, was produced at Drury Lane—an event which would not call for mention in the present connection but for the interest it must have had for Reeves. Balfe, it is said, wrote the opera in 1870 in the hope of seeing in it Reeves, Santley, and Madame Tietjens. So fixed was he with the idea that he declined an offer urged upon him by Napoleon III to have it produced in Paris. The opera was not brought out until four years after the composer's death, and not with the cast which Balfe had in his mind, but with Madame Nilsson and Campanini as the leading characters. Whether the opera would have given Reeves an opportunity of adding to his laurels may be doubted, as Balfe's attempt to write in a style which was foreign to his genius was not deemed successful.

Reeves took part in the Handel Festival of 1874, his last appearance as it proved to be at these great choral gatherings. During the second half of the year he paid his usual visits to the provinces, he sang the familiar songs and received the usual encores, sometimes followed by the usual uproar when he resisted unreasonable exactions.

The question of musical pitch, as is evident from Reeves's letter, was still vexing the souls of singers, especially tenor and soprano singers. Unknown to the outside public, quite a confusion of sounds was going on in the various operatic undertakings. It was now whispered that Patti had made it a *sine qua non* that the pitch should be lowered, and it was said she had agreed to pay £100 towards the outlay for new wood and brass instruments. The result turned out to be disastrous, and the pitch became a source of confusion, sometimes higher, sometimes lower, according to the demands of the soloists. For one prima donna to be outdone by another was not to be thought of, and so Christine Nilsson followed Adelina Patti, and in her contract with Mr. Mapleson at Drury Lane had an article inserted that the diapason normal should be the pitch. New instruments were ordered, and on the first night the consequences were painful. The opera was *Faust*, and throughout, says the *Athenæum*, " Principals and choralists were alike singing sharp or flat, and as regards the newly imported brass and wood from Paris, the clanging tone of the former and the flatness of the latter served to diminish the effect ordinarily produced by the splendid orchestra." One further learns that at this time the pitch at Covent Garden was a quarter of a tone and at Drury Lane half a tone lower than the pitch of Exeter Hall, the Crystal Palace, the Royal Albert Hall, and other concert-halls. One consequence of the lowering of the pitch at the operas was certainly not foreseen by either singers or impresarios. The new instruments were the property of the latter and not of the former, and were put by when not required. It was forgotten that when instruments are out of use the tone becomes affected and the pitch varies in consequence. " The vocalists," remarked the *Athenæum*, " at whose instiga-tion the old pitch has been lowered have been as much punished as those singers who never wished for the alteration."

Reeves was ever at the disposal of his dramatic friends. He sang in 1875 for Buckstone, whose letter of request dated from Bell Green Lodge, Sydenham, runs : " My dear Sims Reeves,—I really have not the ' cheek ' to ask you the favour, but can only say my benefit and the last night of the present season is fix'd for Saturday the 26th June, six weeks hence. If it is again in your power to honour and serve me once more on the occasion, I am sure you will do so. Mr. Sothern rents the theatre of me for the vacation commencing the 12th July until the commencement of my new lease of the Haymarket Theatre on the 1st October, during which time I intend to take a holiday and shall go either to Australia, Singa-pore—or Herne Bay. I am delighted to hear you are at work again, and I hope this glorious weather will do you a world of good. Faithfully yours, Jno. B. Buck-stone."

In the spring of 1876 a performance of Bach's Mass in B minor was given under the direction of Otto Gold-schmidt, the husband of Jenny Lind. In reference to this Goldschmidt wrote : " My dear Reeves,—It is long since we met—long since I have heard you—but not long since I have watched your movements, of the varying state of your health. This is a private personal note which may result though—if it pleases you—in my meeting you and hearing you again ere long. The performances of Bach's Mass which will be sent to you with this note have been fixed for the evenings of Wednesday, April 26th, and

Thursday, May 8th, at St. James's Hall. The enclosed circular explains the chief points of the undertaking, and my first note in reference to soloists goes to you. There are *two* numbers only for tenor in the work—one a duet with soprano (and solo flute), No. 7, which I fancy you would not dislike (with lovely six bars at the end), and the Benedictus, No. 22, with a violin obbligato. Whether you would think it worth while to help crowning the performances as you did crown the Passion Music at St. James's Hall I cannot say, but come to ask you. If you do, will you kindly say on what terms, and I will get a decision from the Committee at once. But pray bear in mind that we are morally bound to ask you to attend *one* of the two rehearsals, either Saturday afternoon, 22nd April, or Monday evening, 24th, in consequence of having promised admission to the choir for their friends to these rehearsals. Kind regards to Mrs. Reeves and your children. Ever truly, OTTO GOLDSCHMIDT." Apparently Reeves was unable to comply with these requirements, and the tenor music was sung by Mr. W. H. Cummings.

Meanwhile the pitch controversy was by no means settled, and in 1876 it was renewed with a very offensive personal reference to Reeves. The *Athenæum* critic (Mr. Gruneisen), who, unlike his predecessor, had pinned himself to the high-pitch party, was instrumental in reopening the dispute. In his notice of the Birmingham Festival in August 1876, he complained of the flatness of the organ consequent upon lowering the pitch. Reeves did not sing at the Festival, nor was he able to do so at the Hereford Festival a fortnight later, but writing of the Hereford function the *Athenæum* returned to the charge with a direct attack upon Reeves. " What happened at Birmingham," it declared, " was repeated at Hereford—the result of tuning an organ to a tenor's tuning fork,' " the tuning fork being that of Reeves. Furthermore it asserted that " the organ was tuned to meet the whim of Mr. Sims Reeves and the organ was nearly a full tone below the orchestral pitch." Not contented with this, the critic allowed his indignation to get the better of his good taste and wound up by remarking that " singers who fancy that their voices will

be destroyed by the high pitch had better retire or . . .
accommodate themselves to it." [1]

Reeves was not the man to take an unjust accusation
lying down, especially one accompanied by so much dic-
tatorial heat. He wrote an emphatic remonstrance.
" Why not," he asked, " be honest and lay the blame (if
blame there be) where most deserved ? The fault lies
with Sir Michael. Who raised the pitch of the Birmingham organ for the Festival of 1873, and when too late
found that the instruments could not tune up to it ?
Who caused the organ to be lowered again for the
accommodation of the orchestra of 1876 ? Sir Michael.
. . . The organ at Hereford was tuned to the fork
adopted by the Society of Arts, not the normal diapason.
Why then single me out and call it a whim of mine?
Why not attack Madame Patti, Madame Nilsson, and
others ? "

The reply of the critic was that he did not ascribe
the responsibility of the lowering of the pitch of the
Birmingham Festival because he believed " that Mr.
Sims Reeves has been the main cause of an agitation that
has led only to confusion and discord." He pointed out
that in 1870 the pitch of the organ at the Festival fell
below that of the instruments and therefore in 1873 the
standard was raised, on which Mr. Sims Reeves wrote
to the *Birmingham Daily Post* (August 22nd, 1873) " that
the organ has been tuned to the pitch of the only orchestra in the world that has so high a pitch, that of the
Drury Lane Italian Opera." When the Birmingham
Committee referred the complaint of Mr. Sims Reeves
to Sir Michael Costa, the latter concurring at once with
their suggestions to reduce the pitch to the lowered
Drury Lane diapason the critic repeated his assertion
that the resultant confusion was due to " the whim of

[1] Shortly after this exhibition of ill-manners Reeves and Gruneisen
met in the artists' room at a Crystal Palace concert. Reeves would not have
noticed him, but the critic advanced with outstretched hand and in his
stuttering, guarded way lest his false teeth should fall out, which they were
in the habit of doing, said, " Don't you know me, Mr. Reeves ? " " Oh,
you're Mr. Greenteahyson," remarked Reeves contemptuously, and
held out two fingers. Then he turned his back upon the crestfallen
critic and walked away, to the silent amusement of those who witnessed
the scene and heard the words.—HERBERT REEVES.

the tenor." *Inter alia*, he remarked that he had known almost every singer of note in Europe for many years and had never heard any of the great tenors, Rubini, Donzelli, David, Duprez, Nourrit, complain of the pitch of that period.[1] " As for the Hereford organ, we were assured by the officials that it was lowered according to a fork sent by Mr. Sims Reeves."

Reeves's contradiction was direct enough. He repudiated any responsibility regarding the Birmingham organ, letters from the managers which he possessed proving that the lowering of the pitch was an absolute necessity. He asserted that he could prove by forks in his possession that the pitch in Italy and Germany had never been so high as that of Sir Michael Costa. As for the pitch of Donzelli, David, Duprez, and Nourrit, that was all that he asked for. The pitch at Hereford was tuned to that accepted now both at Covent Garden and Drury Lane. In conclusion, Reeves wrote : " I have no delusion on the subject of pitch. Uniformity is doubtless most desirable, but it must be uniformity in that which is normal and natural, not in that which is abnormal and extraordinary. The pertinacity of my old friend Sir Michael Costa has alone so long retarded this essential reform, which, however, may be said to have carried the day finally." The critic, of course, used the position which gave him the advantage of the last word, and with this the controversy ceased.

It is pleasant to turn for a moment from this somewhat painful controversy to a letter from the Baroness Burdett-Coutts, who was one of Reeves's warmest admirers. She writes (Stratton Street, December 23rd, 1876) : " MY DEAR SIR,—Will you accept the engraving which accompanies this note with my best wishes of this season to Mrs. Sims Reeves and yourself. I hope you may think that the likeness is a good one, for many do, and if it reminds you of some past years I shall be the better pleased, for you will remember with it dear Tom Bowling and the numerous enjoyments you have given the original —delightful whilst listening to you at the time and still and ever remembered, and recalling to me so many and

---

[1] Why should they, when the pitch of the period was that of the diapason normal ?

varied exquisite renderings of your art. I could, as you know, never resist prolonging the pleasure, and I have to thank you for so often and so kindly acceding to my requests. With my compliments to Mrs. Sims Reeves, I remain, my dear Sir, Yours sincerely, BURDETT-COUTTS."

After his bout with the *Athenæum* critic Reeves never sang again for the Sacred Harmonic Society, and when the 1877 Handel Festival came round his familiar face was not seen nor his glorious voice heard, to the intense regret and disappointment of thousands. Reading between the lines, it is easy to see that the words which appeared in the *Daily News* were intended as a valedictory notice and that the writer knew full well the blank which was so apparent at the Handel Festival of 1877 was one which would never be filled. " No singer," wrote the critic regretfully, " has so especially identified himself with the tenor solo music of Handel, which heretofore was probably never—and perhaps hereafter may never again be—so finely rendered as by him. His transcending merits as an exponent of the pathos, dignity, and declamatory grandeur intended by the composer (but so rarely realised by the interpreter) will long live in the memory of the appreciative section (now a large majority) of the musical public."

The sacrifice must have cost Reeves many hundreds of pounds, but he never flinched. It may be imagined that by this time the unthinking portion of the public realised that this conscientious and high-minded singer was not actuated by caprice or " whim." That it had not begun to do so in 1876 was very evident, and the stupidity of the attacks made upon him roused first the *Saturday Review* and afterwards the *Observer* to come to his defence. What the *Observer* said was so pertinent and put the case so well from Reeves's point of view that no apology is needed for quotation : " It is deeply to be regretted," said the writer, " that owing to the extreme delicacy and susceptibility of this incomparable artist's vocal organ the public hear less of him than they could wish. No one can have more cause to regret that fact than himself, seeing that he has been the loser of many thousands of pounds from his occasional inability to sing in public. But thanks to his conscientious and resolute determination not to sing unless able to do himself justice, he is never heard without awaking delight. No one has heard him sing out of tune, no one ever heard him phrase badly from physical weakness. His vocalisation is always masterly in the highest sense of the word ; and while the beauty of his vocal timbre, his clearness of articulation, and command of expression render his singing a delight to musical amateurs, his vocal method, his management of the breath, his matchless phrasing, render his performances an invaluable source of instruction to real students." When it is remembered that the opportunities of hearing the highest form of music interpreted by the greatest singer of that or any other time were virtually about to cease or at least to become fewer through the personalities introduced into a discussion which could as well have been conducted calmly, one can only say with Othello, " Oh, the pity of it ! "

CHAPTER XXV

1878–1882

THE year 1878 marked the approaching end of Reeves's association with oratorio, save in regard to the isolated solos with which his name will be for ever connected. Henceforth there were to be few opportunities for the full exhibition of his powers. Though he was now sixty years of age, these powers, despite his frequent throat and nerve troubles, showed little sign of deterioration when he was in good general health. But he very wisely refused to take any risks. His répertoire of ballads was extensive, and in addition to the old favourites Sullivan provided him with songs which became enormously popular, and on which he stamped his individuality as he had stamped it on every ballad he had ever sung. The St. James's Hall Ballad Concerts gave him facilities for the display of his lyrical gifts, and his appearances here during the summer were fairly regular. But he had done with oratorio, and the subjoined letter from the secretary of the Sacred Harmonic Society is probably an answer to some kind of intimation to that effect : " Sacred Harmonic Society, 18th August, 1879 : " DEAR MR. REEVES,—I am in receipt of your note, for which I thank you very much. I will not forget your connection with the S.H.S.—nor the Norwich Festival of 1848, where I first heard ' The enemy said ' *really sung*—nor of course the Handel Festivals, for who that heard that

same tone there ever *can* forget it ?   It is fixed as indelibly in *my* memory as old John Braham's delivery of
' For the horse of Pharaoh ' at the Westminster Abbey
Festival of 1834.   With best regards, believe me, yours
very truly, WM. HY. HUSK."

Then followed provincial tours and a return to London
in the early winter.   Nothing new was undertaken,
neither did his audiences want anything new.   At Covent
Garden they were quite contented with *The Beggar's
Opera, The Waterman, Guy Mannering*, and *Rob Roy.
Punch* waxed eloquent over the revival of the musical
delights of bygone generations.   The writer's opinion,
however, of Gay's masterpiece reads very curiously at
the present day, when the wit and satire of *The Beggar's
Opera* are being appreciated with keen enjoyment by
thousands.   " But what a stupid play ! " wrote this
critic.   " What a set of sordid, squalid, ruffianly characters, all except Polly Peachum ! . . . I should like to
see *The Beggar's Opera* with a well-remodelled plot, an
efficient cast, of course Mr. Sims Reeves (it would be
nothing at all without his Captain Macheath), and produced under . . . careful stage management."   This
extraordinary yearning for an " improved " version may
be accounted for either by the supposition that the performers, save Macheath and Polly, must have allowed
the spirit of burlesque to escape, or that the critic was
himself amazingly dull.   Tradition, it may be added,
was carefully preserved in the presentment of *The
Waterman*.   Songs, as in the days of Braham, other than
those written by Dibdin, had to be dragged in.   It was
Reeves whom the audience wanted to see and hear.   They
did not care a fig for Tom Tug and the unities.   Of
course a link of some kind was necessary to bring in the
" extra turns " and the incongruous had to be condoned.
The *Punch* writer overlooked the exigency (as indeed did
the late Genevieve Ward, who, in her *Both Sides of the
Curtain*, ascribed the introduction of the incongruity
to Sims Reeves, whereas the responsibility rested on
Braham), and wrote thus :   " Mr. Reeves being all alone
soliloquises about his stupid rival Robin the Gardener
and observes, ' Ah, I should like to have seen what sort
of figure he would have cut on board ship in such a gale

as I was in when last I crossed the Bay of Biscay.' Cue
for band and ' Bay of Biscay' and delight of audience—
but Thomas Tug the jolly young Waterman has never
been to sea in his life, bless him ! and knew nothing about
the Bay of Biscay from personal experience." What did
it matter ? The public's favourite tenor brought down
the house with " The Bay of Biscay " and everybody was
pleased. This kind of thing intermingled with concerts
was Reeves's staple occupation for the next year or so,
touring as he did about the country with an operatic
company comprising Miss Howson, Miss Lucy Franklein,
Mr. G. Fox, with Mr. Sidney Naylor as conductor.

Reeves's relations with the musical critics were always
very friendly—Mr. Gruneisen notwithstanding—and they
entertained for him the highest respect and admiration.
A letter from Mr. Ebenezer Prout dated June 22nd, 1880,
is a pleasing instance : " MY DEAR SIR,—I must write a
few lines to thank you for your very kind letter just
received. We unfortunate critics get much more abuse
than thanks as a general rule, in the discharge of our
duties ; and a few words of recognition like yours are
therefore doubly welcome. I can only say that in the
notice of your son's appearance which I wrote for the
Athenæum I endeavoured, as I always do, to give a perfectly candid and unbiassed opinion. Had I been unfavourably impressed I should have ' let him down gently,'
so far as I honestly could ; but it is the simple truth to
say that I do not know when I have been more pleased
with a debut. I don't feel that I deserve your thanks,
because I have simply written what I believed to be
the truth ; but I am none the less obliged to you for
your kind letter. With best wishes for your son's future
success and the hope that the mantle of his father may
fall upon him, I am, my dear Sir, Yours very sincerely,
EBENEZER PROUT."

In the meantime music in England was in a transition
state. English opera showed no signs of life ; the attraction of oratorio was dwindling, choral societies were no
longer the rage. The existence of Exeter Hall, the
Handelian centre, was threatened, and though the Sacred
Harmonic Society secured an extension of its life for
two years, the stronghold of choral singing was doomed.

The hall which had played so important a part in musical progress, which had seen Sims Reeves rise to the height of his genius, was to be sold and there was no other accommodation for the huge forces which Costa had controlled for so many years. South Kensington was now acclaimed the coming Utopia of science and art, and music was not forgotten in its far-reaching schemes. The National Training School of music which was to have followed the opening of the Albert Hall had had but a languid reception, especially after the Royal Academy of Music had rejected a proposal to amalgamate the two schools ; but in 1880 interest was revived by the initiation of the movement to develop the National Training School into the Royal College of Music, and a petition, headed by the Prince of Wales, was sent to Queen Victoria in September 1880 asking for the grant of a charter of incorporation for the proposed college. The scheme had the warm sympathy of Sims Reeves, and a few days after an article on the subject appeared in the *Times* he wrote a letter, in the course of which he said :

" As the time draws nearer of my retirement from public life as an artist, which is to take place in 1882, I feel more and more desirous of being of some service to the rising generation of my countrymen as some little testimony of gratitude for the unfailing kindness of the public in the past and as a humble token of my wish to promote the true interests of British Art. . . . My idea is that, in the case of my services being thought desirable, I should be able to devote three or four hours daily to the work with the exception of Saturdays and Sundays. . . . The country of Purcell, Boyce, Sterndale Bennett, Macfarren, Sullivan, not to speak of Bishop, Balfe, Wallace, Loder, Barnett, and many other highly meritorious native composers, cannot be considered barren as the birthplace of music ; and I believe it may be affirmed with safety that in no country save perhaps Italy are children gifted with sweeter voices or a better ear. We have the raw material in plenty, thanks to our damp climate, which gives a certain mellowness both in speaking and singing to the *timbre* of the English voice ; and in addition to this we have a large stock of native energy and quickness of perception. But our very facility is apt to be overdone. Hard work and the aim after perfection are too often lacking among us, and herein our musical artists too often fail to attain the highest results. I hail, therefore, the foundation of the Royal College of Music with a lively hope, . . . and I venture to express my very strong desire to co-operate if possible in so good and practical a work."

This letter drew from Sir G. Macfarren, President of the Royal Academy, the following cordial response: "117 Hamilton Terrace, N.W. November 8th, 1880. MY DEAR REEVES,—I am indeed glad to learn from your printed letter that you are willing to give young vocalists the inestimable advantage of your tuition. Most earnestly I wish that this benefit to English music may be conveyed to the Institution in which you have more than once expressed an interest, and I shall be particularly gratified if you will allow me to propose you as a professor to the Committee of Management of the Royal Academy of Music. I do not suppose that while you are still before the public you can afford the amount of time named in your letter, but if it is possible for you to make an early announcement with however small a number of pupils, this may be extended when compatible with your own convenience. Your proffered service to Art warrants the hope that the principles which have made your own performances an universal model may be bequeathed to your successors through your own exposition. Ever yours with friendly regards, G. A. MACFARREN."

At that moment, however, no plans had been formulated for the proposed College, and the institution did not come into being until two years later. By this time Reeves was fully occupied with farewell concerts in London and the country, and apparently he was unable to renew his offer, and so the inestimable advantages of his great experience, of his mastery of correct vocalisation, and of his dramatic gifts were lost. Meanwhile engagements (one was at Belfast on September 27th, 1880, where Dr. Grattan Flood was his accompanist) were still open to him, and a notable one came from Charles Hallé, who wrote from Manchester on November 4th, 1880: "MY DEAR SIMS REEVES,—At last I am getting

GRANGE MOUNT, UPPER NORWOOD.

(From left to right) Mrs. Sims Reeves, Herbert Reeves, Sims Reeves, Constance and Maud Reeves, Ernest Reeves.

my concert into shape and come now to ask if you will sing for me on the 20th January *The Hymn of Praise*, and accept 100 guineas for doing so ? I shall in that case do in the first part Cherubini's *Requiem*, in which there are no solos, and so make your work as light as possible. I need not say how happy I should be to see you here once more, and hope you will give me an early and favourable answer. Always truly yours, CHARLES HALLÉ."

Reeves's letter was probably the first intimation the general public had that their favourite vocalist was contemplating retirement, and the announcement was received with profound regret, although, of course, it was inevitable such a step at some time must come about. What caused surprise, however, was that in 1881 and 1882 there was little sign of deterioration in his voice. But he rarely over-exerted it. He sang the music which did not make great demands upon his powers, and only now and again did he repeat his Handelian solos, sung as he only could sing them. In the spring of 1881, at a farewell oratorio concert at the Albert Hall with Barnby's choir, he gave " Call forth thy powers " (transposed to the key of C) with all his old vigour—" a wonderful performance for one full of years as well as honours," declared the *Athenæum*. *Elijah* and *The Messiah* formed part of the series, but he was too indisposed to sing in either. At the concluding miscellaneous concert he was, however, able to delight his audience with " Deeper and deeper " and " The enemy said," showing that his mastery of contrast was as consummate as ever. If any proof of this were wanting, it would be furnished by Mr. Barnby, who wrote to Reeves out of the fullness of his heart : " MY DEAR REEVES, I will come to you on Monday afternoon between two and three o'clock. Forgive me if this letter should be short—it is one of a large number I have to write, in a very short time—but if I had not another minute to live I must take the opportunity of saying that I never was more astonished in my life than I was by your magnificent effort in ' The enemy said.' And let me add—in perfectly cold blood—that I have never been so moved by another artist whatever—instrumental or vocal—along the whole gamut of emotions as

19

I have by you, and my admiration and gratitude are proportionate. Sincerely yours, J. BARNBY."

It is worthy of mention that Reeves's singing of " The enemy said " on this occasion was more than usually remarkable. He was suffering from an inflammation of the cheek and his face on one side was swollen. Despite this drawback and the pain he was enduring he never rendered the arduous solo more magnificently.

A series of operatic concerts was also undertaken in connection with these performances, but these were somewhat marred by his unavoidable absences. On October 12th, 1882, he gave with Christine Nilsson a joint benefit concert at the Albert Hall. The selections were of a popular character and do not demand any special comment. It would appear that a repetition of this combined benefit concert was contemplated by Reeves, but from the annexed letter there seems to have been some misunderstanding with Nilsson and the concert did not come off. The letter runs : " Hôtel Continental, 3 Rue Castiglione, Paris. August 25th, 1883. MY DEAR FRIEND,—It is perfectly true that I have promised to sing for Mr. Watts on my return from America. It is also true that I told you we could give a concert together next season—*not* on my first appearance—that I never mentioned, as I already had a conversation with Mr. Watts about this very first appearance before you ever mentioned to me your intention of giving a concert in conjunction with me before my leaving England this autumn when we sang together. At the last Watts concert you never said a word to me about any concert, so I of course came to the conclusion that you had given up the idea about next summer. I am always willing to join in a concert with you whenever you should like it, next season or even before I start for America, which I cannot possibly do before the 22nd of September. In this case we have no time to lose, and if you think it worth while telegraph *yes* or *no*, and perhaps Austin could arrange something. With affectionate regards to you both, believe me, dear friend, Sincerely yours, CHRISTINE."

CHAPTER XXVI

1883–1900

Reeves's last years. Benedict's pathetic appeal. Letters from Fred
Leslie, Sir Arthur Sullivan, Blumenthal, Charles Hallé, Sir Francis
Burnand, Sir Edward Lawson, Adelina Patti. Farewell concert in May
1891. Unprecedented scene. Henry Irving recites a poetical tribute
to Reeves's genius. Reeves's parting words. Press references to Reeves's
unparalleled career. A sad period of anxiety. Irving's touching letter.
Death.

DURING the next nine years Reeves undertook nothing that
was arduous. He had repeated attacks of ill-health and
sang only at concerts of a miscellaneous character, which
were really in the nature of farewell performances—at
least, so the public came to regard them—and whenever
he appeared he was received by an enthusiastic audience
eager to hear, possibly for the last time, those velvety,
resonant tones before they were veiled by age and
infirmity.

On May 18th Benedict sent him a pathetic entreaty
in these words : " MY DEAR MR. SIMS REEVES,—You have
perhaps heard that during three days I was at the brink
of the grave almost given up by the doctors, but that
thanks to Providence I am now after more than two
months quite convalescent and—but for the persistent
east winds—should have been permitted to venture out
of doors. Mrs. Kendal came quite unsolicited to see
Lady Benedict and told her that she and several other
distinguished dramatic artistes, *on her suggestion*, had
resolved to arrange some short bright pieces for my Benefit
to come off on Tuesday morning, June 23rd, at Drury
Lane Theatre. The Kendals will perform *Uncle's Will*,
Mrs. John Wood and Arthur Blunt *The Milliner's Bill*,
Mr. and Mrs. Beerbohm Tree *The First Night*, on which
occasion my dear wife Lady Benedict will attempt a little

part. These are to be interspersed with a few vocal
pieces of the first order. I hope Marie Roze, Trebelli,
Santley, Foli, and . . .

" It is now a good many years that you have sung for
me ' Tis sad thus to fall in the springtime of life,' but I
predicted then—what has come to pass—that in you we
beheld the future Idol of England, the real High Priest
of Art and the only interpreter of the loftiest of music—
Handel, Haydn, Mendelssohn—in the world. I had a
happy dream last night. At my Benefit—and the *only
time* I shall appear in public this year—I had the honour of
accompanying ' It is a charming girl I love,' appearing
then under the auspices of the greatest Artist of the day !
Can this illusion become a reality ? I know that to ask
such a favour after what you did for me last year is
rather too presumptuous, but anyhow and at nearly
eighty-one years I cannot trouble you many times more.
The Queen gives me her patronage, the Prince of Wales may
be induced to attend the performance, and other members
of the Royal Family. Why should the King of Vocal
Music not take the rank due to him among other crowned
heads ? Anyhow, let me thank you once more for all I
owe you, and with the most heartfelt wishes for your
health and happiness believe me ever most sincerely and
gratefully, Yours, JULIUS BENEDICT."

His services indeed were rarely denied to his friends.
Fred Leslie, writing from the Gaiety Theatre, June 5th,
1887, says : " MY DEAR SIR,—Accept my sincerest thanks
for the invaluable attraction of your name as well as the
generous assistance of your talent, which I am not un-
mindful contributed in no slight degree to the gratifying
success of my matinée. I am indeed sorry to say it is
not in my power to send you Planquette's address ; I
know it not. Yours truly grateful, FREDERICK LESLIE."

Reeves was ever ready to give advice. The following
letter, in answer to a request from a teacher of music,
is a case in point, and his counsel based on experience
given therein is of as much value now as it was then.
" Preston Park, Preston. November 4th, 1884. DEAR
SIR,—My advice is, weed your classes of the pupils with
defective ears. Five pupils with this defect will drag
fifty voices down. Let a small class of ten be allowed to

sing together. You will soon find out the good from the bad. Should you find the ten *all* good, place them with another ten, still with the intention of weeding out.

"Unless you carry out this system, you will always be liable to false intonation.

"A low ceiling has *always* a depressing influence upon the voices. The pupils should be placed in front of you at a distance of ten yards at least. Watch them well. The mouths of the pupils should be carefully scrutinised —teeth well open—tongue flat in the mouth—and to make the tone on the Italian A (ah !). Be careful not to make a mezzo-soprano sing that which should be sung by a soprano, as many modern professors do, ruining the voice in many instances. The teacher should have the instrument—whether it be harmonium or pianoforte— close to his hands, so that he can assist the pupils when they need assistance. I am, Yours faithfully, J. SIMS REEVES."

As a proof of his readiness to help others even at his own inconvenience, it is worthy of note that the above letter was written while on the way to Glasgow and at the end are the words " in great haste."

The affectionate relations which existed between Reeves and Sullivan are sufficiently indicated in the follow- ing, dated January 15th, 1887: "MY DEAR OLD BOY,— I was delighted to see your handwriting again, and such a handwriting. It would put to shame many a bank clerk at the age of twenty-four. I would have come and conducted the song for you on February 19th with the greatest pleasure, but please God I shall be abroad then— somewhere in the south, getting sunshine and rest, the latter of which I am sadly in need—so that I cannot come and help you. Ever yours, ARTHUR SULLIVAN."

The footing on which he stood with the composers Balfe, Blumenthal, Berger, Sullivan, and others who wrote songs for him was of the most friendly and cordial character. Nothing could be more appreciative than this testimony from Blumenthal, who, writing from Cannes on December 26th, 1887, said: "MY DEAR REEVES,—It seems an eternity since I have had news from you, and so I profit by the season of the year to send you and yours my best wishes and first of all good health, which to you more than anyone else must be the most precious gift. I hope you keep fairly well and that you have not suffered too much from the dreadful fogs which I hear have prevailed during November in England. . . . I want to know how you are getting on with your singing. Do you sing much and have you still to travel about in all weathers ? I thought you had an idea of going to Australia. Has that been given up ? . . . Oh, Reeves, I cannot tell how sad it is to me that when I write songs now to think that *you* won't sing them. I can't help having you always in my mind when I write, but I shall not hear your lovely voice giving utterance to my thought, making intelligent criticism, refining my dross and giving it value. I have written a lot of songs, but I keep most of them in MS. Some day I must show you a few if you care—just to show you I have not been idle. I have been writing a lot here, but what's the good ? Nobody but you cares for songs that are out of the common, and I verily believe that if you had not existed none of my big songs would have seen the light. But enough of the Jeremiad. Give my kindest regards to Mrs. Reeves and all the children. I hope Herbert is getting on well. I remain here till the 8th January, if you care to write. Then I go to Paris, and towards the end of January I hope to be in London. Always yours, most sincerely, JACQUES BLUMENTHAL."

On March 22nd, 1888, we have Charles Hallé writing : " MY DEAR SIMS REEVES,—H.R.H. Princess Mary is giving a concert on the 31st of May in the afternoon at the St. James's Hall in aid of the extension of the church at Kew, at which concert the Prince and Princess of Wales and most of the other members of the Royal Family will be present. I am desired by her to ask you if you would be so extremely kind as to sing *one* song on that occasion, and to tell you how very grateful she would be to you for doing so ; and as I have undertaken to manage the whole concert, I should feel not less obliged. Will you be so very good as to write me an answer which I may show to H.R. Highness, and believe me always most sincerely, Yours, CHARLES HALLÉ."

Here is a letter of a different kind. It is evidence, if evidence were necessary, that Reeves's purse as well as his services could be relied upon when the cause was a fitting

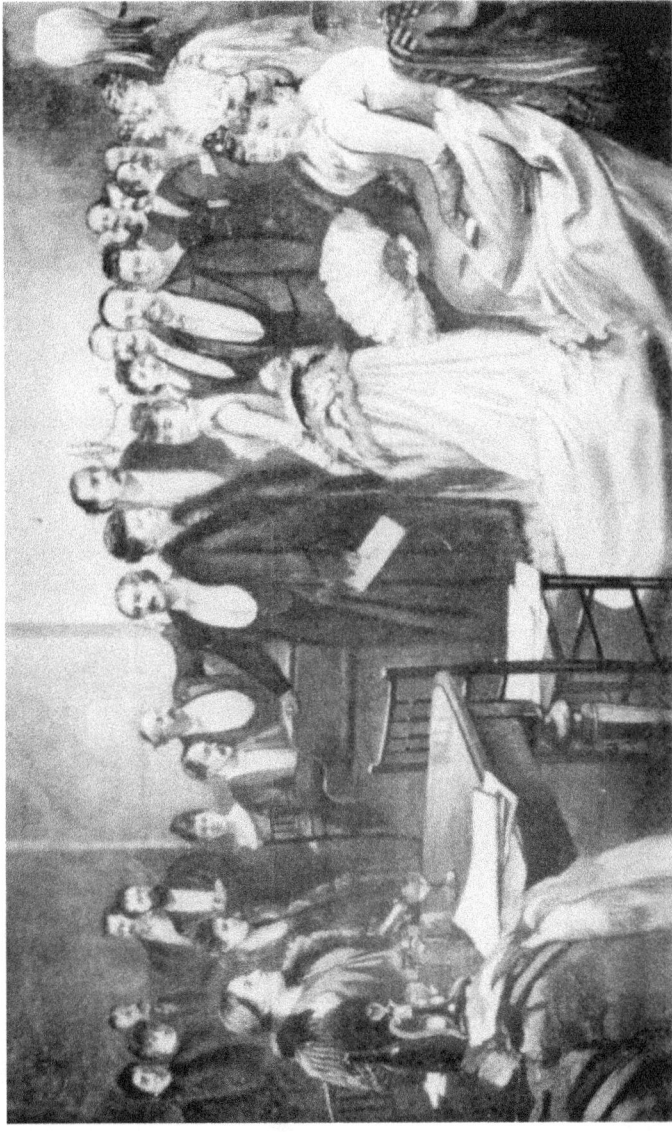

Miss A. Gomez.   Mrs. Henschel.   Mme. Nordica.   Mr. Sims Reeves.   Mme. Patti.   Sir C. Santley.   M. J. de Reszké.   Mr. Ben Davies.
Mme. Grieg.   Mr. Henschel.   Mr. Maybrick.   Mme. Albani.   Mme. M. Roze.   Miss M. Davies.   Sig. Ravelli.   Miss Fanny Moody.
M. Maurel.   M. Lassalle.   Mr. E. Lloyd.   Sig. Foli.   Mr. McGuckin.   M. E. de Reszké.   Mr. A. Oswald.   Miss McIntyre.

Mme. Antoinette Stirling.   Mme. Patey.   Mme. Belle Cole.

SIMS REEVES AND HIS MUSICAL COMPANIONS (1892).

From a drawing by Lance Calkin.   (By permission of the Proprietors of the *Sphere.*)

294]

one. "MY DEAR MR. REEVES,—I have been already
assisting as a committee-man on the Leech Sisters Fund
with purse and pen, and so have our Proprietors and the
whole of the *Punch* staff. The amount taken was
considerable, but I cannot at the moment recall the
figures : something like £2,000, I believe, and this was
not the first occasion only. I shall be happy to assist
in giving whatever publicity I can to your benevolent
design, and regret that your letter arrived too late for me
to avail myself of the next week's number. With best
wishes, I remain, Yours very truly, F. C. BURNAND. Is
it true that you intend taking a farewell—one last long
farewell ? If this be so, I must assist on such an occasion
and beforehand send all over the world to announce the
fact as a fact from your own lips. You'll have to make
the *one* farewell concert last a week in London only and
the same in every principal town."

A letter from Sir Edward Lawson (afterwards Lord
Burnham), written from The Fishery, Denham, Uxbridge,
dated November 13th, 1889, probably refers to one of
Reeves's farewell concerts, but this is unimportant.
What matters is the kindly feeling of the writer. Sir
Edward writes : "MY DEAR SIMS REEVES,—I will do with
pleasure all I can to serve an old and valued friend. In a
day or two I shall be in Fleet Street again after a short
holiday, and I will see what can be done consistently with
the ordinary rules to make your undertaking prosperous
and successful. I sincerely hope and feel assured your
retirement will be peace with honour. Most truly
yours, EDWARD LAWSON."

The last letter that need be quoted, brief though it is, is
not the least interesting. The date is November 23rd, 1890,
and is addressed from Craig-y-nos, Castle Ystradcynlais,
Swansea Valley, South Wales. It runs : "MY DEAR MR.
REEVES,—Thank you so much for your kind letter. I was
so glad to know that you were pleased with my voice and
that you found me looking so well. Both my husband
and myself are delighted to find that you are in such
excellent voice yourself—while your phrasing remains
*the best possible example and study for younger aspirants
to fame*. Believe me, Most sincerely yours, ADELINA
PATTI NICOLINI."

The time came for the fulfilment of what Reeves had foreshadowed two years before—his retirement. This did not mean that he would give up the concert-room entirely, but that he was no longer to be considered as a public singer open to accept engagements. On the night of May 11th, 1891, the Albert Hall was packed with an audience which though essentially democratic—for Reeves had ever been a singer for the people rather than for fashion—was yet representative of all classes from Royalty in the person of the late King Edward (then Prince of Wales) downwards. A distinctive feature was that a large portion of the huge crowd were elderly people. In this fact, as the *Daily Telegraph* pointed out, there was nothing surprising. "The present generation," said the writer, "knows little of Sims Reeves by comparison with the folk who were contemporary with him during his best days. . . . It seems that Mr. Reeves's admirers in the past, or such as are left of them, came out with one mind to see the close of a career whose prime they witnessed, and there was something in this peculiarly harmonising with the known faithfulness of the English public." His friends in the profession rallied round him, notably Madame Christine Nilsson, who came from her retirement in pursuance of a promise given to her old friend some time before. Madame Nordica, Miss Alice Gomez, Madame Antoinette Sterling, Madame Janotha, Mrs. Eaton (a pupil of Reeves's), Foli, Barrington Foote, Herbert Sims Reeves, Percy Sharman, the Westminster Glee Singers, and last, but not least, Henry Irving, contributed to the programme, while the orchestra was conducted by Mr. A. Manns. The versatility of the tenor (he was now seventy-three) was well shown in his selections. Oratorio was represented by "Total eclipse," Italian opera by the duet from Verdi's *Ernani*, "Ah morir," and "Da qual di" (*Linda da Chamouni*) sung with Madame Nilsson, the old English ballad school by "The Bay of Biscay," the Balfeian style by "Come into the garden, Maud," and by a drawing-room song of the period of the day, "I know a sweet old garden." Then there were the encores, which he could not find it in his heart to refuse. Altogether he must have sung seven times that evening. The culmination of hearty and affectionate admiration came when Irving recited Mr. Walter Herries Pollock's valedictory ode, which was couched in these words :

> " Oft have these walls beheld rapt crowds rejoice,
> Hushed by the wonder of a matchless voice,
> Yes, matched in this that 'twas its owner's part
> To wed its glory to a glorious art.
> Recall the past of platform and of scene,
> And learn how vast the artist's range has been.
> No depth of passion that he could not plumb,
> No pitch of gaiety that found him dumb.
> A master he of lightest interlude,
> Now thrilling us with Edgar's wild despair,
> Now brilliant in Macheath's contempt of care.
> He dealt alike with Jephtha's misery
> And Nelson's splendid death and victory.
> He knew the heart of Faust, and he could show
> How bright and brave was Fra Diavolo.
> In all the follower of a perfect plan
> To keep the perfect name of gentleman.
> How many times we, missing him, shall long
> To hear him sing Beethoven's noblest song,
> How many times remember with delight
> The lesson that we celebrate to-night.
> His ' Message ' in our hearts will ever live,
> Another message now 'tis mine to give.
> Not mine to sing—but mine it is to say,
> In his great name farewell to you to-day,
> Farewell—a word whose joy with grief contends,
> Farewell—a word of hope from friends to friends."

With what mingled grace and emphasis Irving delivered these lines need not be said. The actor keenly appreciated the genius of the singer. Once at a Lyceum Supper Irving put the question, " Who is the greatest artist in England ? " and answering the question himself he replied, " Sims Reeves." Irving was not alone in this opinion, for of all Reeves's admirers the most enthusiastic were his brother and sister artists. Difficulties which seemed so easy to the average audience they knew perfectly well had not been overcome without much study and thought.

An indescribable scene followed the reading of the ode. The audience rose *en masse*, every eye fixed on Reeves, who, overcome with emotion, was standing in the centre of the platform, while at the side of the orchestra were grouped the artists and organisers of the concert. It was some seconds before Reeves could sufficiently control himself to speak, then, in a voice the tones of which were as touching as any ever uttered by him in association with his art, he said, " For your great goodness to me through so many years I feel that I am poor in thanks—poor indeed. The brilliant scene before me to-night will ever be treasured in my memory. From my heart, charged with the deepest emotion, I wish you, ladies and gentlemen, a respectful, grateful, and affectionate farewell."

" The singer's retirement from the platform," said the *Times*, " was the signal of a display of enthusiasm such as is seldom witnessed in this country. The whole audience rose from their seats and remained standing for some minutes cheering and waving their handkerchiefs, and it was not until Mr. Sims Reeves had repeatedly bowed his thanks that with three hearty cheers led by the gallery and taken up by the whole house the vast audience began to disperse." The critic of the *Daily Telegraph* summed up the scene truly enough. " There is," he wrote, " a strong element of pathos in the situation. The artist must feel it as the last applause dies away and he knows that the book of his active life is shut. . . . In a lesser though still approachable degree the public feel it likewise, conscious that a source of interest and pleasure has ceased to act." This note was echoed everywhere, but only a few of the sentiments expressed need be quoted. " No singer," said the *Morning Post*, " has in his time effected a greater influence upon vocal art than Mr. Sims Reeves, and though many rivals have appeared, he has surpassed them all ; and while he takes his farewell of public life the memory of his unequalled efforts will serve as a model for artists yet to come." The *Athenæum*, which when Mr. Chorley was won over had always been unstinting in its praise (save and excepting Mr. Gruneisen's carpings), was not less whole-hearted. Its words were : " At length the long career of Mr. Sims Reeves as a vocalist has come to a close. In every sense it has been remarkable, but in regard to length it is probably unique. . . . No public performer has been a more familiar figure to all classes of music-lovers than Mr. Reeves during the past fifty years. How he has managed to preserve even a portion of his vocal powers to the present time is sufficiently clear. His method was perfect, and proper voice production entails little or no tax upon the vocal organs, decay only setting in with advancing age, and further, though greatly to the disappointment of the public and at serious loss to himself, Mr. Sims Reeves always declined to sing except when in perfect health."

Reeves without doubt looked forward to a well-earned rest. No singer had won more laurels and he might well have had dreams of wearing these laurels without disturbance. But fate ordained otherwise. As years went on circumstances compelled him to take up the lyre which he believed he had permanently laid aside. His last days were clouded with worries, to the great concern of his many friends. A letter from Sir Henry Irving during this troublous time shows the depth of the great actor's friendship for the greatest of singers. It is dated December 14th, 1898, and runs : " DEAR OLD FRIEND,— Believe me, I never forget you. You are often in my thoughts and I have deeply sympathised with all your anxieties. I have had a rough time, but am now nearly recovered and only need sunshine and rest. I saw Santley in Glasgow and we talked much of you. He's a good and true friend. I hope we may meet soon and ' talk our battles o'er.' God bless you. Believe me, ever yours, H. IRVING."

It is not necessary to follow Reeves's career further. One can only regret that necessity forced him to appear before the public when his powers were enfeebled and little remained but his masterly method. The new generation which heard him in his decadence could not possibly realise what his wondrous singing was like in the days of his prime.

The hour-glass may be rapidly turned. Death was merciful, for after a brief illness he passed away in his sleep on the night of October 25th, 1900, at Worthing, where he had gone to reside. His age was given in many journals as seventy-eight, but, as shown in these pages, he had reached his eighty-second year.

CHAPTER XXVII

REMINISCENT AND ANECDOTAL

WHILE Reeves numbered among his many devoted admirers the highest musical judges, his principal "following" was of the people, and these were attached to him with an affection of which no other singer could boast. And it is to be observed that this attachment never wavered. The multitude are said to be fickle. It was not so in the case of Sims Reeves. They were never weary of welcoming him, and to the very last days of his long career they remained faithful to their early love. From the mass of correspondence which has accumulated during the writing of these memoirs a few extracts may be made illustrative of this. Reeves's matchless tones heard in his prime fixed themselves upon the memory, and confirmation of this is to be found in nearly every letter which has reached me.

"I heard Sims Reeves sing in the Albert Hall in 1886," writes Mr. D. Williamson, "and shall never forget his thrilling voice soaring above the sounds of a great thunderstorm which burst over London that afternoon." Mr. Williamson adds: "Charles Dickens, as chairman of a charitable society's banquet, had to announce that a telegram had been received from Sims Reeves regretting that a cold prevented him singing. The company expressed their feelings in a scornful laugh, upon which Dickens remarked with an irony that silenced the sneers, 'Mr. Reeves regrets he cannot sing because he has a *highly amusing cold.*'"

Sims Reeves once attended one of Moody and Sankey's services, and after listening to the singing of Sankey observed, "He takes all sorts of liberties with the time, but he gets a wonderful effect in spite of everything, and therefore he is a great soloist."

Another correspondent writes: "I was at the Surrey

Gardens Music Hall when Jullien's concerts were held there. Sims Reeves sang 'My pretty Jane,' and although I was a lad at the time I have not forgotten how impressed I was by his splendid voice. There was something ethereal, celestial, something that you can scarcely define in the tones of that voice. Over sixty years have passed since then, but even now it is scarcely an exaggeration to write that some catches of his matchless voice still haunt my ears."

Mr. Charles Holdsworth, who was a member of the Sacred Harmonic Society, Henry Leslie's choir, and of the Handel Festival chorus (for thirty years), recalls the delight with which he heard the first performance in London of Rossini's *Messe Solennelle* in 1871. The singers included Madame Alboni, Foli, and Reeves. " In the great trio," says Mr. Holdsworth, " Alboni's wonderful voice seemed to pervade the middle and lower registers, while Mr. Reeves, with exquisite quality of voice, appeared to be singing an octave higher. The effect was thrilling and emotional in the extreme. In the orchestra we were all entranced, and I remember Mr. Leslie saying it was 'the moment of his life.' At a performance of *The Messiah* at Exeter Hall I was an honorary steward. The area was much overcrowded, and I undertook to get about 100 persons up to the western gallery. We got as far as the stairs when Mr. Reeves commenced to sing 'Thy rebuke.' I begged the people to sit down and not move during the recitative and aria. We could see nothing, but the acoustic properties of the position were astonishing. We could hear and feel every intonation —could spell the words! When he concluded with a broken sob on ' Like unto his sorrow,' I thought it the finest Lenten sermon I had ever heard. There was hardly a dry eye in the immense audience."

Apropos of encores Mr. Manfred Fisher writes : " I happened on one occasion to be on the stairs leading from the artists' room to the platform and he said to me during the clamouring of the audience for more, ' I can't shout that again,' a way of putting the matter which not only showed his modesty but indicated his sense of the persecution which it was too often his lot to endure." Of the extraordinary height to which the feelings of

an audience could be wrought the Rev. A. Metcalfe
gives a forcible example. Mr. Metcalfe was at a concert
in the Newcastle Town Hall somewhere about the year
1878, and Sims Reeves appeared fairly early in the evening
and he received a rousing encore to which he did not
respond, contenting himself with bowing. Still the
applause continued, and the singer following Mr. Reeves
could not obtain a hearing. The uproar was kept up
persistently, and the manager endeavoured to remonstrate
with the unruly shouters, but all in vain, and at last the
concert broke up in confusion and the greater portion of
the programme was abandoned through the stupidity of
an unreasonable crowd.

A letter from Mr. Percy A. Bull, who writes : " As
a youth I adored his singing and I shall never forget
on one occasion at St. James's Hall the number of people
round me who were crying during his singing of " Waft
her, angels," is representative of many others. Mr. B.
Morris, a nonagenarian and one of Reeves's oldest and
most valued friends, speaks with enthusiasm of his
singing. Mr. Morris heard him as far back as 1850.

Of the many tributes which have appeared in print,
not the least striking is that contained in an obituary
notice published in the *Daily Telegraph*. The writer
recalls how " during the evening preceding the day fixed
for the first performance of Arthur Sullivan's sacred
cantata *The Prodigal Son* at the Worcester Festival of
1869, the principal part in which admirable work was to
be rendered by Sims Reeves, the illustrious tenor received
a dispatch informing him that he had lost £11,000
by the sudden failure of a bank in which he had invested
a considerable part of his professional earnings. The
following passage may without indiscretion be here
textually reproduced from a letter addressed by Mr.
Reeves to the writer of this memoir a few months ago.
' The news of this terrible catastrophe prostrated me
completely at first. I sent for Sullivan and explained
what had happened. He was very much cut up about it,
and so was I, for I had taken the music to my heart.
Sullivan came in the next morning, begging me to sing
the part. He looked green, and I looked both green and
grey. After drinking some very strong coffee, and having

a chat over the work, I determined to put on my armour and fight the fight. I did so, and succeeded. It was a great effort, but it really did me good.' Skilled and trustworthy musicians who were present at the performance that ensued have since warmly testified to the super-excellence of his interpretation of the rôle assigned to him, that of the Prodigal Son, and are unanimous in asseverating that his singing of the principal solo, ' I will arise, and go to my father '—a veritable wail of heart-broken, remorseful agony—drew tears from a large majority of the audience. It cannot be doubted that such touching words and music, sung by a man who had just seen the savings of a lifetime ruthlessly swept away by an unmerciful blast of cruel calamity, must have thrilled the souls of well-nigh all present on that memorable occasion, though the vocalist's hearers were necessarily ignorant of the dread disaster that lent exceptional pathos to his masterly deliverance."

The late Rev. Arthur Mursell, in one of his discourses, spoke in eloquent terms of the genius of Reeves (and his words are all the more notable because Mr. Mursell confessed that he was, to use his own expression, about as technically musical as an oyster) and of the singer's character as a man. " This nightingale of the nineteenth century " (I quote from a newspaper report of the discourse) " had not escaped innuendoes which charged him with indulgence physically impossible, for it would have destroyed such an organ of song long before fourscore years. He would give one fact out of his own knowledge to dispose of the charge that Sims Reeves was an untender husband or luxurious as a man. He recollected a day in the late fifties when a crowded concert was in progress at the Free Trade Hall, Manchester. The lion of the evening was Sims Reeves, who had a short time previously disappointed an audience in the same building. The people were in an unforgiving temper and determined to be revenged upon their idol, who had a hostile reception. Afterwards some friends went to his room and found his wife—herself an artist of great charm—in tears. ' I don't mind their hissing him,' she said ; ' he can very soon put that right. But it is cruel to malign him. A simpler living man or a more tender husband than Sims

Reeves is not to be found.' It was right," added Mr. Mursell, " that these things should be known. He could tell facts of the great and boundless generosity of this man, and it seemed to him that the world owed a deep debt to one who had brought a thrill of joy into so many dull lives."

Reeves's method of practice has more than once been the subject of discussion. He may be allowed to speak for himself. A writer in the *Gentleman's Magazine* (March 1896) says that when asked on one occasion how he was able to put such pathos and feeling into a song and make a great success of it when other singers failed, the great tenor replied, " It is because I have always studied my words. I have read them and phrased them in every possible way, asked myself what they meant and interpreted them according to my own feeling. I walk up and down trying this line and trying that until I feel that I have struck the right idea. But I am never satisfied. Nowadays singers do not study elocution sufficiently, if at all. In a recitative, for instance, the words are sacrificed to the music. In my method they are of equal importance. I worry and fidget lest my voice should not be at its best when the evening comes. I go to the piano over and over again and run over a few notes. I always rehearse the songs I propose to sing—yes, even ' Tom Bowling ' or ' The Death of Nelson '—not, of course, at concert pitch, but singing them over, trying a phrase or a run, and always endeavouring to get a fresh effect."

The late Sir August Manns, in the course of an interview with a Press representative, related the following : " A curious scene occurred at one Good Friday concert. The orchestra and the choir were small, and I placed the singers on a little platform near the organ, thinking that they would be better heard, but owing to this position being assigned to them those of the audience who were not seated in the centre transept could not see them. The artists took the first piece with us all right, and then there was the ' Quis est homo ' from the *Stabat Mater*. Madame Patey, then Miss Whytock, and Miss Westbrook were young people at that time. Miss Westbrook's voice was not large and Madame Patey did not use hers.

The people grew restless, not being able to see the singers, and at the next piece they cried out ' Come to the front.'

" The band began several times, but the uproar was great. Then Sims Reeves walked right down amongst the people, twenty yards away from me, and there he stood signing to me, and we began ' Comfort ye' from *The Messiah*, and with that distance between us I tried to catch what he was singing. However, it was successful, for the audience could see him well. The next item was the ' Inflammatus ' from the *Stabat Mater* and Madame Rudersdorff had to sing the air. She took her place near the orchestra and began. The audience roared for her to come down, but she shook her head and would not.

" I had to stop a second time, but she said to me very angrily, ' It is impossible. A woman cannot walk on people's heads. Go on.' I gave the sign to my trombones, and they did blow as though they were about to blow the walls of Jericho down. There was an immense uproar, but then Madame Rudersdorff showed what was in her, and at the first note she sang—the high G—the audience was suddenly silenced. They were as still as though they had been in a church. The change was simply marvellous. The artist had conquered ; but having done so, in the next piece she went down to the front."

Sir Michael Costa's appreciation of Sims Reeves has been alluded to more than once in these pages, and he once showed his admiration in a very pretty compliment. On the morning following an oratorio performance in the provinces Costa called at Reeves's hotel and left his visiting card, having written on the back, " *In paradiso non si canto meglio.*"

Mention has been made more than once in the fore-going pages of Reeves's extreme nervousness. Sir Charles Santley, whose close friendship with Reeves reached little short of half a century, gives several instances of this peculiarity in his *Reminiscences of my Life*.

" Reeves," writes Sir Charles, " like the major part of the human race, had his little idiosyncrasies, failings, if you like the name better. He was full of nerves, and like all nervous people at times very irritable. I had literally to push him on to the platform at St. James's Hall on a

20

Burns night, when he was going to sing in Howard Glover's cantata, *Tam o' Shanter*, a very trying part."

Among these idiosyncrasies may be mentioned his dislike of the aroma of certain flowers. It is related that on the occasion of a Scottish festival at which he had arranged to sing, a lady called at the hotel where he and his wife were staying, with a big bunch of flowers. She was about to hand the flowers to Reeves, when Mrs. Reeves cried excitedly, " Don't, Jack, don't," and explained to the visitor that the perfume of flowers so affected her husband that he was sure to be off his singing form that night. Whether this was so or not, it receives confirmation in this caution, which he gives in his *Art of Singing* : " Flowers with strong scents are said to have the mysterious power of affecting the singing voice deleteriously. Ladies who love to appear on the platform with bouquets should remember this fact."

Nothing in recent years has been heard of " musical pitch," in the lowering of which Reeves was so deeply interested. In the *Windsor Magazine* of March 1896, then under the editorship of Mr. David Williamson, a letter from whom is given earlier in this chapter, the question was, however, discussed. In the course of a conversation with Mr. Williamson, Reeves said, " Don't forget when you are writing about music to continue working for the Continental pitch. I've worked all my life in that direction, I've preached and I've practised, and those who have the interests of English music at heart must do the same. I've been abused over and over again, but I keep on. The English pitch is absolutely bad for the voice ; it is only a question of money to alter it, and the money will be forthcoming as soon as the convictions are aroused." It is to be feared that " convictions " on this matter, as on many others, are as lethargic as ever. So far as Reeves is concerned, there are few cases on record—certainly not one in relation to musical art— where convictions have involved such heavy pecuniary sacrifices. His severance from the Sacred Harmonic Society, by reason of the " pitch," must have meant a large loss of income. As for his rigid determination, from which he never flinched, never to sing when he felt he might be unable to do justice to himself and his art, the surrender of his fees amounted during his career to no less than £90,000.

The largest audience he ever sang to was at the Alexandra Palace on the opening day, the vast concourse consisting of no fewer than 102,000 people. One of the most noteworthy events in connection with large audiences occurred when he was singing at one of Jullien's concerts in the Surrey Gardens Music Hall. Upwards of 13,000 people filled the place, and the crush was so great that a woman carrying a child nearly fainted under the pressure. She was not far from the platform, and Reeves, seeing her distressed condition, stopped in the middle of his song and called to her to come to him. The audience made way for her, and said the singer : " Give me the child and I'll take care of it until you get round " —a touch of kindly human nature which brought down thunderous applause.

Another touch of kindliness, combined with glory in his art, not as applied to himself but to a brother-singer, ought not to be passed over. " Santley is a true artist," he exclaimed during a conversation with the representative of the *Worthing Gazette*, " a true artist," he added, this time with increased emphasis, " and I should like that recorded. The proof is that whenever he sings at the Handel Festival and elsewhere he is recognised as the only artist before the public who knows what he is doing." This tribute had in it the elements of pathos, for it was probably his last allusion to the great world of music of which for so many years he had been the most prominent figure. He died the following day. It was in keeping with the modesty and unselfishness of Reeves's nature that his final utterances should not be of his own incomparable attainments, but of those of a comrade with whom times out of number he had been so closely associated in mutual triumphs.

Mr. Herbert Reeves writes : " My earliest recollection of hearing my father sing in public is of one of the Handel Festivals, when I was six years old. Adelina Patti on that occasion sang for the first time in oratorio, and there was some doubt as to whether her operatic training and her light if wonderfully brilliant and flexible voice would enable her to do justice to Handelian music.

I well remember when she began 'Let the bright seraphim' noticing my father and Santley following her singing and wondering if she possessed the sustaining power necessary to give full effect to the trying air. She passed through the ordeal triumphantly, and after receiving the congratulations of her brother and sister artists she caught sight of me, and exclaiming 'You pretty little boy !' took me on her knee and gave me a kiss.

"I was still a boy when I heard my father in one of the performances of *Faust* at Her Majesty's Theatre. Young as I was, his extraordinary breadth of tone in the first act impressed me so much that even now I can in imagination recollect it. His declamation was beautiful and his voice had a magnetic quality in it such as no other tenor possessed. It is perhaps not generally known how the wonderfully rapid change from old age to youth was contrived. The patriarchal garb, wig, beard, etc., were fitted on to a series of laces or strings so manipulated that the entire costume and facial disguises could be pulled off with one movement. At the critical moment when Faust was standing in front of the vision of Marguerite with Mephistopheles a little to the left, a little bell was rung as the signal to the operator below, a slit opened in the stage, and with one tug at the cord attached to the laces the outer semblance of the aged Faust vanished through the slit and the new Faust in a dress appropriate to his youth burst into the joyous strains symbolical of the vigour of early manhood and the joy of life. My father would trust no one for this duty but a valet who had been in his service for years and who was greatly attached to him. The whole operation was so quickly and adroitly performed that the transformation had all the effect of magic. In connection with *Faust*, I may also mention that my father had a strong aversion to descending into the infernal regions as designed by the author of the libretto and composer. At Her Majesty's the opera terminated with Faust kneeling at the couch of Marguerite as the angels were bearing her aloft.

"I may, I hope, be pardoned if I say that my father's solicitude concerning my musical studies was unceasing. He was never wanting in encouragement. I went with him to Italy and was introduced to Mazzucato, under whom I studied for a time, the death of the great maestro depriving me all too soon of the benefit of his instruction. It has always been to me a pleasurable memory that I was permitted—short though the period was—to have the advantage of the experience of this unequalled master of singing, from whom thirty-eight years before my father had learned so much. With Mazzucato you felt you had to sing and that all that was best in you was being developed.

"My father was not present at my first appearance in England at a concert given by Ganz. He was extremely anxious as to the result and was unable to do anything but pace the garden of Grange Mount, Norwood, until a telegram arrived announcing my success. Subsequently I deputised for him several times and played Mat o' the Mint in *The Beggar's Opera* to his Captain Macheath.

"These personal reminiscences might be extended, but I refrain. I refer to them simply because I wish to express my deep affection for and sincere admiration of my father, and my satisfaction at being able after too long a lapse of time to assist in placing on record a faithful chronicle, so far as the materials would permit, of his long and distinguished artistic career. It perhaps may not be inappropriate if I say that his domestic life was one of great happiness. Long absences from home were inevitable, but he always returned to us with a sense of pleasure at being once more among those who loved and revered him. His joy was to be surrounded by his family and his circle of many friends whom he delighted to entertain.

"Finally, I ought not to leave without mention the companion of his struggles and partner in many of his successes—my mother. To her devotion he owed much, and if she was always anxious concerning his health, she had ample reason for anxiety. But for her incessant care and watchfulness my father would not have preserved his wondrous organ unimpaired for so many years, and thousands would have been deprived of the pleasure and privilege of hearing one of the greatest singers who ever lived."

Thus Mr. Herbert Reeves, and I agree with every

word. I will only add that the work of digging up the records of fifty years, arduous as it was, has been constantly stimulated by the remembrance of a matchless voice and a perfection of dramatic vocalisation in oratorio, opera, and ballad. Schoelcher's tribute to Reeves has often been quoted. Nothing finer or more appropriate to his genius has ever been written, and I make no apology for repeating the critic's words. He spoke of him as :

"One who has written his name beneath that of Handel in the golden book of musical renown, to be read a hundred years hence when new singers and new celebrities are projected."

THE END

INDEX

Alboni, Madame, 128, 240
Allcroft, 115, 175, 176, 179
Allen, G., 43, 44, 45, 47, 48, 53, 59, 67
Anderson, J. H., 24, 72
Anderson, James, 52, 53, 58
Angri, Mlle, 156
Arditi, 131
Arne, 41, 89
Auber, 129, 234

B

Bach, 130, 189
Balfe, 41, 92, 98, 100, 118, 236, 253, 276
Banks, Miss, 263
Barker, George, 28, 29, 32, 154
Barnby, 115, 195, 259, 261, 273, 288
Barnett, John, 41, 42
Barrett, W. A., 100, 119
Bartholomew, 187, 246
Bartleman, 85, 234
Bass, 67
Bassano, Miss, 196
Bauer, Miss Jenny, 184
Baynham, 47, 69
Beale, F., 172
Beale, Willert, 37, 78, 140, 142, 143, 149, 150, 180, 181
Beethoven, 90, 91, 96, 126, 127, 142, 163, 168, 183
Beletti, 61, 196
Bellini, 62, 81, 217
Belton, F., 32, 54
Benedict, 58, 92, 144, 172, 175, 220, 245, 291
Bennett, Sterndale, 181, 208, 234, 235
Berger, F., 158
Berlioz, 92, 93, 96, 101, 105, 153, 168
Bexfield, Dr., 170
Birch, Miss, 71, 89, 93, 100, 101, 104, 157
Bishop, Sir H. R., 30, 42, 68, 92, 93, 113, 159, 174
Blumenthal, 250, 293
Bochsa, 40
Bodda, F., 159, 168
Bordogni, 37, 60, 63, 66, 70, 71, 75

Bowley, R., 172, 194
Braham, John, 21, 30, 61, 67, 74, 82, 83, 87, 108, 109, 112, 135, 136, 137
Bunn, Alfred, 99, 129, 130, 165, 166, 167
Burghesh, Lord, 84, 87
Burnand, F. C., 295
Byrne, Pitt, Mrs., 122, 123

C

Calcraft, 73, 143, 144, 145, 146, 159
Calkin, 115
Callcott, 24, 65, 174
Calzolari, 161, 164
Campanini, 277
Carvalho, Madame, 243
Case, G., 175, 191
Castelan, Madame, 125, 182
Catalani, Madame, 114, 125
Chorley, H. F., 80, 112, 117, 140, 141, 151, 152, 156, 165, 170, 198, 204, 205, 212, 217, 241, 242, 250, 254
Coleman, John, 24, 30, 71, 72, 73
Coletti, 165
Cooke, T., 36, 37, 38, 42, 48, 53, 58, 87, 96
Cooper, Wilbye, 210
Costa, 40, 130, 131, 168, 181, 182, 193, 235, 246, 305
Coutts, Miss Burdett, 39, 40, 281
Cowell, Sam, 64, 65, 129
Cox, J. E., 71, 79, 80, 81, 109, 113, 114, 162, 234, 237
Cramer, John, 24, 80
Croft, Alban, 75
Croger, T. R., 93, 173
Crowquill, A., 93, 252
Cruvelli, Mlle, 160, 163, 164, 165
Cummings, W. H., 128, 249, 279
Cunningham, 145, 146
Cusins, W. G., 187

D

Damcke, 143, 144
David, Félicien, 155, 156
Davies, Ben, 24

314 INDEX

Reeves—*Continued.*

Drury Lane concert, 85; sings at the Antient Concerts, 88; appears at Drury Lane in *Lucia di Lammermoor* under Jullien and electrifies the house, 94; Balfe's opera *The Maid of Honour*, 99; his generosity towards Jullien, 104; first appearance in oratorio in London, 106; is criticised by Mr. Chorley, 112; his debut in Italian opera, 117; Mr. Lumley fails to keep faith with him and he abruptly terminates his engagement, 117; the Gardoni controversy, 122; at the Provincial Festival Concerts, 124; in Italian opera at Manchester, 128; at Covent Garden under Alfred Bunn, 129; is engaged by the Sacred Harmonic Society, 132; the "Wednesday Concerts," 133; his duet with Braham, 137; pursued by the "encore" fiend, 139; his debut in *Sonnambula* at Covent Garden, 141; an operatic breakdown in Dublin, 143; Reeves comes to the rescue, 144; sings at the opening of St. Martin's Hall, 150; in Italian opera under Lumley, 151; at the first performance of the *Messiah* in Wales, 154; his marriage to Miss Emma Lucombe, 158; appears with great success in Italian opera in Paris, 161; sings in *Fidelio* at Her Majesty's, 163; in Thalberg's opera *Florinda*, 165; in *Fra Diavolo*, 167; in Beethoven's Ninth Symphony at the New Philharmonic, 168; at Provincial Festivals, 170; in Italian opera at Drury Lane under Jarrett, 176; concert engagements, and in English opera at the Haymarket, 180; his stupendous success in Costa's *Eli*, 182; sings at Windsor Castle, 187; in oratorio under Jullien at the Surrey Gardens Music Hall, 190; "Come into the garden, Maud," 196; at the First Handel Concert at the Crystal Palace, 197; his "The enemy said" at Exeter Hall creates a sensation, 206; in English opera at the Standard, 209; at the Monday "Pops," 210; the Handel commemoration Festival, 211; championed by Madame Clara Novello, 214;

Reeves—*Continued.*

sings in *Iphigénie in Tauride* at Manchester, 217; Macfarren's *Robin Hood*, 225; at the first performance of the *Messiah* in St. Paul's Cathedral—his impassioned singing of "But thou didst not leave," 230; the first Handel Triennial Festival at the Crystal Palace, 236; his estrangement from the Sacred Harmonic Society, 238; sings for the National Choral Society, 239; in Italian opera under Mapleson at Her Majesty's, 240; *Faust* in English, 241; in Costa's *Naaman* at Birmingham, 246; frequent disappointments through illness, 251; the high pitch controversy—Reeves's letter and refusal to sing for the Sacred Harmonic Society, 257; Mr. Barnby produces *Jephtha* with the lowered pitch—Reeves's magnificent singing, 259; is treated with great injustice at Cheltenham, 263; in Benedict's *St. Peter*, 265; *The Beggar's Opera*, 267; curious law suit over Sullivan's *Prodigal Son* at Edinburgh, 271; returns to the Sacred Harmonic Society, 275; the "pitch" controversy renewed, 277; is attacked by the *Athenæum*, 279; refuses to sing again at the Handel Festival, 282; his popularity in English opera, 285; formation of the Royal College of Music—Reeves's generous offer, 287; his retirement foreshadowed, 289; his Farewell at the Albert Hall, 297; death at Worthing, 299; tributes to his genius, 300–310

Reeves, Mrs. Sims (see Miss Lucombe)
Reeves, Rosina, 17, 18
Reeves, W. H., 23, 24, 30
Reichardt, 168
Reszké, J. de, 27
Richards, Brinley, 124, 196
Rigby, Vernon, 261, 265
Rodwell, G. H., 41
Roger, 128
Romer, Miss, 44, 45, 129
Ronconi, 39, 141
Rossini, 21, 101, 138, 140, 142, 217
Roxby, R., 69
Rudersdorff, Madame, 176, 190, 305
Russell, Henry, 61
Russell, Scott, 181
Rutherford, 205
Ryder, J., 55

*Printed in Great Britain by Hazell, Watson & Viney, Ld.,
London and Aylesbury.*

Music and Books published by Travis & Emery Music Bookshop:

Anon.: Hymnarium Sarisburiense, cum Rubricis et Notis Musicis.
Agricola, Johann Friedrich from Tosi: Anleitung zur Singkunst.
Bach, C.P.E.: edited W. Emery: Nekrolog or Obituary Notice of J.S. Bach.
Bateson, Naomi Judith: Alcock of Salisbury
Bathe, William: A Briefe Introduction to the Skill of Song
Bax, Arnold: Symphony #5, Arranged for Piano Four Hands by Walter Emery
Burney, Charles: The Present State of Music in France and Italy
Burney, Charles: The Present State of Music in Germany, The Netherlands ...
Burney, Charles: An Account of the Musical Performances ... Handel
Burney, Karl: Nachricht von Georg Friedrich Handel's Lebensumstanden.
Cobbett, W.W.: Cobbett's Cyclopedic Survey of Chamber Music. (2 vols.)
Corrette, Michel: Le Maitre de Clavecin
Crimp, Bryan: Dear Mr. Rosenthal ... Dear Mr. Gaisberg ...
Crimp, Bryan: Solo: The Biography of Solomon
d'Indy, Vincent: Beethoven: Biographie Critique
d'Indy, Vincent: Beethoven: A Critical Biography
d'Indy, Vincent: César Franck (in French)
Frescobaldi, Girolamo: D'Arie Musicali per Cantarsi. Primo & Secondo Libro.
Geminiani, Francesco: The Art of Playing the Violin.
Handel; Purcell; Boyce; Geene et al: Calliope or English Harmony: Volume First.
Hawkins, John: A General History of the Science and Practice of Music (5 vols.)
Herbert-Caesari, Edgar: The Science and Sensations of Vocal Tone
Herbert-Caesari, Edgar: Vocal Truth
Hopkins and Rimboult: The Organ. Its History and Construction.
Hunt, John: Adam to Webern: the recordings of von Karajan
Isaacs, Lewis: Hänsel and Gretel. A Guide to Humperdinck's Opera.
Isaacs, Lewis: Königskinder (Royal Children) A Guide to Humperdinck's Opera.
Lacassagne, M. l'Abbé Joseph : Traité Général des élémens du Chant.
Lascelles (née Catley), Anne: The Life of Miss Anne Catley.
Mainwaring, John: Memoirs of the Life of the Late George Frederic Handel
Malcolm, Alexander: A Treaty of Music: Speculative, Practical and Historical
Marx, Adolph Bernhard: Die Kunst des Gesanges, Theoretisch-Practisch
May, Florence: The Life of Brahms
Mellers, Wilfrid: Angels of the Night: Popular Female Singers of Our Time
Mellers, Wilfrid: Bach and the Dance of God
Mellers, Wilfrid: Beethoven and the Voice of God

Travis & Emery Music Bookshop
17 Cecil Court, London, WC2N 4EZ, United Kingdom.
Tel. (+44) 20 7240 2129

Music and Books published by Travis & Emery Music Bookshop:

Mellers, Wilfrid: Caliban Reborn - Renewal in Twentieth Century Music
Mellers, Wilfrid: François Couperin and the French Classical Tradition
Mellers, Wilfrid: Harmonious Meeting
Mellers, Wilfrid: Le Jardin Retrouvé, The Music of Frederic Mompou
Mellers, Wilfrid: Music and Society, England and the European Tradition
Mellers, Wilfrid: Music in a New Found Land: ... ... American Music
Mellers, Wilfrid: Romanticism and the Twentieth Century (from 1800)
Mellers, Wilfrid: The Masks of Orpheus: ...... the Story of European Music.
Mellers, Wilfrid: The Sonata Principle (from c. 1750)
Mellers, Wilfrid: Vaughan Williams and the Vision of Albion
Panchianio, Cattuffio: Rutzvanscad Il Giovine
Pearce, Charles: Sims Reeves, Fifty Years of Music in England.
Playford, John: An Introduction to the Skill of Musick.
Purcell, Henry et al: Harmonia Sacra ... The First Book, (1726)
Purcell, Henry et al: Harmonia Sacra ... Book II (1726)
Quantz, Johann: Versuch einer Anweisung die Flöte traversiere zu spielen.
Rameau, Jean-Philippe: Code de Musique Pratique, ou Methodes.
Rastall, Richard: The Notation of Western Music.
Rimbault, Edward: The Pianoforte, Its Origins, Progress, and Construction.
Rousseau, Jean Jacques: Dictionnaire de Musique
Rubinstein, Anton : Guide to the proper use of the Pianoforte Pedals.
Sainsbury, John S.: Dictionary of Musicians. Vol. 1. (1825). 2 vols.
Simpson, Christopher: A Compendium of Practical Musick in Five Parts
Spohr, Louis: Autobiography
Spohr, Louis: Grand Violin School
Tans'ur, William: A New Musical Grammar; or The Harmonical Spectator
Terry, Charles Sanford: Four-Part Chorals of J.S. Bach. (German & English)
Terry, Charles Sanford: Joh. Seb. Bach, Cantata Texts, Sacred and Secular.
Terry, Charles Sanford: The Origins of the Family of Bach Musicians.
Tosi, Pierfrancesco: Opinioni de' Cantori Antichi, e Moderni
Van der Straeten, Edmund: History of the Violoncello, The Viol da Gamba ...
Van der Straeten, Edmund: History of the Violin, Its Ancestors... (2 vols.)
Walther, J. G.: Musicalisches Lexikon ober Musicalische Bibliothec

Travis & Emery Music Bookshop
17 Cecil Court, London, WC2N 4EZ, United Kingdom.
Tel. (+44) 20 7240 2129
© Travis & Emery 2009

Discographies by Travis & Emery:

Discographies by John Hunt.

1987: 978-1-906857-14-1: From Adam to Webern: the Recordings of von Karajan.

1991: 978-0-951026-83-0: 3 Italian Conductors and 7 Viennese Sopranos: 10 Discographies: Arturo Toscanini, Guido Cantelli, Carlo Maria Giulini, Elisabeth Schwarzkopf, Irmgard Seefried, Elisabeth Gruemmer, Sena Jurinac, Hilde Gueden, Lisa Della Casa, Rita Streich.

1992: 978-0-951026-85-4: Mid-Century Conductors and More Viennese Singers: 10 Discographies: Karl Boehm, Victor De Sabata, Hans Knappertsbusch, Tullio Serafin, Clemens Krauss, Anton Dermota, Leonie Rysanek, Eberhard Waechter, Maria Reining, Erich Kunz.

1993: 978-0-951026-87-8: More 20th Century Conductors: 7 Discographies: Eugen Jochum, Ferenc Fricsay, Carl Schuricht, Felix Weingartner, Josef Krips, Otto Klemperer, Erich Kleiber.

1994: 978-0-951026-88-5: Giants of the Keyboard: 6 Discographies: Wilhelm Kempff, Walter Gieseking, Edwin Fischer, Clara Haskil, Wilhelm Backhaus, Artur Schnabel.

1994: 978-0-951026-89-2: Six Wagnerian Sopranos: 6 Discographies: Frieda Leider, Kirsten Flagstad, Astrid Varnay, Martha Moedl, Birgit Nilsson, Gwyneth Jones.

1995: 978-0-952582-70-0: Musical Knights: 6 Discographies: Henry Wood, Thomas Beecham, Adrian Boult, John Barbirolli, Reginald Goodall, Malcolm Sargent.

1995: 978-0-952582-71-7: A Notable Quartet: 4 Discographies: Gundula Janowitz, Christa Ludwig, Nicolai Gedda, Dietrich Fischer-Dieskau.

1996: 978-0-952582-72-4: The Post-War German Tradition: 5 Discographies: Rudolf Kempe, Joseph Keilberth, Wolfgang Sawallisch, Rafael Kubelik, Andre Cluytens.

1996: 978-0-952582-73-1: Teachers and Pupils: 7 Discographies: Elisabeth Schwarzkopf, Maria Ivoguen, Maria Cebotari, Meta Seinemeyer, Ljuba Welitsch, Rita Streich, Erna Berger.

1996: 978-0-952582-77-9: Tenors in a Lyric Tradition: 3 Discographies: Peter anders, Walther Ludwig, Fritz Wunderlich.

1997: 978-0-952582-78-6: The Lyric Baritone: 5 Discographies: Hans Reinmar, Gerhard Huesch, Josef Metternich, Hermann Uhde, Eberhard Waechter.

1997: 978-0-952582-79-3: Hungarians in Exile: 3 Discographies: Fritz Reiner, Antal Dorati, George Szell.

1997: 978-1-901395-00-6: The Art of the Diva: 3 Discographies: Claudia Muzio, Maria Callas, Magda Olivero.

1997: 978-1-901395-01-3: Metropolitan Sopranos: 4 Discographies: Rosa Ponselle, Eleanor Steber, Zinka Milanov, Leontyne Price.

1997: 978-1-901395-02-0: Back From The Shadows: 4 Discographies: Willem Mengelberg, Dimitri Mitropoulos, Hermann Abendroth, Eduard Van Beinum.

1997: 978-1-901395-03-7: More Musical Knights: 4 Discographies: Hamilton Harty, Charles Mackerras, Simon Rattle, John Pritchard.

1998: 978-1-901395-94-5: Conductors On The Yellow Label: 8 Discographies: Fritz Lehmann, Ferdinand Leitner, Ferenc Fricsay, Eugen Jochum, Leopold Ludwig, Artur Rother, Franz Konwitschny, Igor Markevitch.

1998: 978-1-901395-95-2: More Giants of the Keyboard: 5 Discographies: Claudio Arrau, Gyorgy Cziffra, Vladimir Horowitz, Dinu Lipatti, Artur Rubinstein.

1998: 978-1-901395-96-9: Mezzo and Contraltos: 5 Discographies: Janet Baker, Margarete Klose, Kathleen Ferrier, Giulietta Simionato, Elisabeth Hoengen.

1999: 978-1-901395-97-6: The Furtwaengler Sound Sixth Edition: Discography and Concert Listing.

1999: 978-1-901395-98-3: The Great Dictators: 3 Discographies: Evgeny Mravinsky, Artur Rodzinski, Sergiu Celibidache.

1999: 978-1-901395-99-0: Sviatoslav Richter: Pianist of the Century: Discography.

2000: 978-1-901395-04-4: Philharmonic Autocrat 1: Discography of: Herbert Von Karajan [Third Edition].

2000: 978-1-901395-05-1: Wiener Philharmoniker 1 - Vienna Philharmonic and Vienna State Opera Orchestras: Discography Part 1 1905-1954.

2000: 978-1-901395-06-8: Wiener Philharmoniker 2 - Vienna Philharmonic and Vienna State Opera Orchestras: Discography Part 2 1954-1989.

2001: 978-1-901395-07-5: Gramophone Stalwarts: 3 Separate Discographies: Bruno Walter, Erich Leinsdorf, Georg Solti.

2001: 978-1-901395-08-2: Singers of the Third Reich: 5 Discographies: Helge Roswaenge, Tiana Lemnitz, Franz Voelker, Maria Mueller, Max Lorenz.

2001: 978-1-901395-09-9: Philharmonic Autocrat 2: Concert Register of Herbert Von Karajan Second Edition.

2002: 978-1-901395-10-5: Sächsische Staatskapelle Dresden: Complete Discography.

2002: 978-1-901395-11-2: Carlo Maria Giulini: Discography and Concert Register.

2002: 978-1-901395-12-9: Pianists For The Connoisseur: 6 Discographies: Arturo Benedetti Michelangeli, Alfred Cortot, Alexis Weissenberg, Clifford Curzon, Solomon, Elly Ney.

2003: 978-1-901395-14-3: Singers on the Yellow Label: 7 Discographies: Maria Stader, Elfriede Troetschel, Annelies Kupper, Wolfgang Windgassen, Ernst Haefliger, Josef Greindl, Kim Borg.

2003: 978-1-901395-15-0: A Gallic Trio: 3 Discographies: Charles Muench, Paul Paray, Pierre Monteux.

2004: 978-1-901395-16-7: Antal Dorati 1906-1988: Discography and Concert Register.

2004: 978-1-901395-17-4: Columbia 33CX Label Discography.

2004: 978-1-901395-18-1: Great Violinists: 3 Discographies: David Oistrakh, Wolfgang Schneiderhan, Arthur Grumiaux.

2006: 978-1-901395-19-8: Leopold Stokowski: Second Edition of the Discography.

2006: 978-1-901395-20-4: Wagner im Festspielhaus: Discography of the Bayreuth Festival.

2006: 978-1-901395-21-1: Her Master's Voice: Concert Register and Discography of Dame Elisabeth Schwarzkopf [Third Edition].

2007: 978-1-901395-22-8: Hans Knappertsbusch: Kna: Concert Register and Discography of Hans Knappertsbusch, 1888-1965. Second Edition.

2008: 978-1-901395-23-5: Philips Minigroove: Second Extended Version of the European Discography.

2009: 978-1-901395--24-2: American Classics: The Discographies of Leonard Bernstein and Eugene Ormandy.

Discography by Stephen J. Pettitt, edited by John Hunt:

1987: 978-1-906857-16-5: Philharmonia Orchestra: Complete Discography 1945-1987

Available from: Travis & Emery at 17 Cecil Court, London, UK. (+44) 20 7 240 2129. email on sales@travis-and-emery.com .